THE STILL PERFORMANCE

Writing, Self, and Interconnection in

Five Postmodern American Poets

The Still Performance

Writing, Self, and Interconnection in Five Postmodern American Poets

JAMES MCCORKLE

UNIVERSITY PRESS OF VIRGINIA
CHARLOTTESVILLE

THE UNIVERSITY PRESS OF VIRGINIA
Copyright © 1989 by the Rector and Visitors
of the University of Virginia

First published 1989

Since this page cannot legibly accommodate all the copyright notices,
pages x–xii of the Acknowledgments constitute an extension of
the copyright page.

Library of Congress Cataloging-in-Publication Data

McCorkle, James.
    The still performance : writing, self, and interconnection in
five postmodern American poets / James McCorkle.
        p.   cm.
    Includes index.
    ISBN 0-8139-1196-6
    1. American poetry—20th century—History and criticism.
    2. Postmodernism—United States.   3. Reader-response criticism.
    4. Self in literature.   I. Title.
    PS325.M4   1989
    811'.54'09—dc19   88-35305
                                                                CIP

Printed in the United States of America

for my parents

CONTENTS

Acknowledgments   ix

Introduction   1

1. Concordances and Travels: The Poetry of Elizabeth Bishop   7

2. John Ashbery's *Artes Poeticae* of Self and Text   46

3. "Fiery Iconography": Language and Interconnection in the Poetry of Adrienne Rich   87

4. W. S. Merwin's Poetics of Memory   130

5. "Things that Lock Our Wrists to the Past": Self-Portraiture and Autobiography in Charles Wright's Poetry   171

Notes   213

Index   227

ACKNOWLEDGMENTS

Though many friends and colleagues offered advice and support during the writing of this book, I would especially like to thank Fran Bartkowski, Ed Folsom, Kate Kazin, Adalaide Morris, and Oliver Steele for their initial readings of the text. I should also like to thank my editor at the University Press of Virginia, Cynthia Foote, for her thoroughness and kind attention to details. My deepest thanks go to Donald G. Marshall and Laura Mumford; their advice, encouragement, and, most importantly, friendship enabled me to complete this project.

THE STILL PERFORMANCE

Writing, Self, and Interconnection in

Five Postmodern American Poets

INTRODUCTION

What kind of beast would turn its life into words?
What atonement is this all about?
—and yet, writing words like these, I'm also living.
    (Adrienne Rich, "Twenty-One Love Poems," no. 7)

The light that was shadowed then
Was seen to be our lives,
Everything about us that love might wish to examine,
Then put away for a certain length of time, until
The whole is to be reviewed, and we turned
Toward each other, to each other.
The way we had come was all we could see
And it crept up on us, embarrassed
That there is so much to tell now, really now.
    (John Ashbery, "As We Know")

In a period that seems to be another fin-de-siècle collapse, language risks formulaic indulgences. The enormity of the cultural and social fragmentation in the late twentieth-century has reduced—or inflated[1]—language to the hollow counters found in self-help books and political sloganeering well-practiced in the sensational. Implicit in the diminishment and abstraction of the personal and the public is the erosion of language and its power of interconnection. The demands for the poet—to be a voice that names, remembers history, praises and admonishes, and provides a voice for the voiceless—remain the same. But, the task of purifying the language of the tribe has undergone a necessary reenvisioning: rather than recovering the old language and tradition, aesthetic and political realignment is sought through a radical examination of language and the self.

In a distinct fashion, the condition of poetry mirrors that of the culture—whatever criticisms are leveled at the practice of poetry or the direction that poetry seems to take must correspondingly be leveled at the culture. Though recent poetry is by turns hermetic, discursive, and expressive, its role is never severed from culture, and, in fact, to seek merely a descriptive criticism of recent poetry fails to address either the endeavor of the poetry itself or the culture inscribed by and inscribed in that poetry. Critics such as Charles Altieri and Mary Kinzie argue that a self-indulgent expressive mode generated from the romantics typifies much recent poetry;[2] the expressive mode, however, indicates not mere self-indulgence but an extreme anxiety and ambivalence toward the world. In addition, the most important of recent poetry concentrates on developing its capacity for speculation; the poet is a traveler whose maps are never complete and whose travels are not concluded. Poetry proposes an investigation and criticism of itself and of culture, with the hope that the process of transformation will be initiated. To initiate any form of transformation, however, language must be recognized as a gift offering the possibility of discourse among readers, authors, texts, and histories.

I see in the works of the poets I admire most—and among those are included the five poets discussed in the essays that follow—the insistence on the writing, the recovery, and the revision of interconnection in a poem or book, throughout their oeuvres, and among the participants engaged with or sharing a poem. Interconnection is described in the following essays as the process of writing and how we move through the written text. By moving into the space of writing (in contrast to the tradition of writing being a mere shadow of speech and reality), relations are reinvented and redefined. Whether personal, political, or spiritual, these relations are material and insist on the possibility of presence and immanence. Insofar as Jacques Derrida's writings illuminate my concerns with language, this poetry could be called grammatological, if we understand this term as describing the inclusion of the function of critical reflection within a poem so as to interrogate the relation of knowledge to metaphor.[3]

The poetry of Elizabeth Bishop, John Ashbery, Adrienne Rich, W. S. Merwin, and Charles Wright is examined because I find their writing to be an investigation of the ethical and ontological significance of the art of writing, the place of writing in culture, and the mirroring or composition of the self through writing. Though each poet's work differs in form and temperament, each poet is a speculative writer sharing a focus on the self-reflexivity of language. Self-reflexivity functions both as self-criticism and as a means for interconnection. More than a self-conscious turn remarking on the craft of poetry, self-reflexivity is language's demand for the possibility of presence and the personal. Far from being narcissistic, self-reflexive language creates a harbor shared by a variety of travelers. Language, and writing in particular, is the place where self and others converge.

The relationship of these five poets to their culture and to the dominant society has shifted from that of the poets of modernism, particularly Pound and Eliot. Modernism's sublime—impersonal and elite—has failed us, these poets argue. Interconnection, predicated on self-definition, informs any social or political domain for these five poets. Yet, as will be seen, interconnection in its reflexive and ironic capacity does not validate overtly or implicitly the preexisting domains of culture, politics, and society. Rather than participating in a poetry of solipsism and autotelic formalism, these five poets share a regard for the necessity of self-definition. Their demand for ethos, or character, extends far beyond the notion of an aesthetic of self-sensitivity. In fact, self-definition can be considered a prescription against a solipsistic aesthetic and the impersonality of modernism.

Though often portrayed in the static terms of unity and continuity, the self is always provisional, splintered, impoverished, but also copious. The poetry examined in the following essays forms a critique of any theory adhering to a vision of unity and objectivity. In response to the destruction of the personal through bureaucratic and technocratic definitions, these poets express deconstructed visions of the self. This vision of the self allows full play of irony, ambiguity, and collage through which a textual plenitude is created. These essays propose that such play inscribes the recognition of the provisionality of the self. By re-visioning the self, language and all forms of interconnection are explicitly and fundamentally questioned and reenvisioned.

The position of writing needs to be emphasized because it is the trace and record of interactions. Writing proposes presence, intention, and meaning. Yet the possibility of repetition and the activity of interpretation erode and enrich writing. Writing's capacity for generation, self-definition, and memory is an ambivalent potential in the poetry of Bishop, Ashbery, Rich, Merwin, and Wright. Writing's provisionality and plenitude—an essentially ironic or doubled position—is expressed in the textual surface as well as in thematic weavings of the poetry: the textual surface mirrors the thematic density.

Textual density, plenitude, or materiality is, then, the place of interconnection. While arguing for interconnection, I am not also arguing for a neoromantic or high-modernist vision of unity. Interconnection is the means of engaging the phenomenal world and implies a reinvention of the self that can engage a variety of voices, fragments, and inadvertent glimpses. Interconnection also implies a community; though I perceive this community as the dialogic relations M. M. Bakhtin describes ("language is not an abstract system of normative forms but rather a concrete heteroglot conception of the world"[4]), the dialogic community is also a political vision. Essential to this vision of interconnection is the potential for discourse or exchanges among author, poem, and reader;

the pursuit of relations thus undermines the demand or necessity for authority. Interconnecton also inscribes both an incorporation within a tradition and an exclusion from participation. This paradox or double bind is central to describing the work of these five poets; though they are lyric poets in their general pronominal forms and addresses,[5] they also recognize the possibility of recasting (not reestablishing or renewing) the self through the insistence that the lyric is breached and traversed by writing.

In contrast to these thematics of interconnection and writing, recent works on contemporary American poetry have stressed such issues as autobiography, influence, and cultural history.[6] Of these works, Charles Altieri's *Self and Sensibility in Contemporary American Poetry* is the most provocative—both for poets and for critics.[7] The importance of Altieri's book lies not only with its questioning of recent poetry's cultural role but also with his argument's failure to address issues that compel us to read these contemporaries. Altieri suggests, in what he terms a phenomenological rather than an explanatory criticism,[8] that the scenic mode's inherent passivity and timidity results in vaguely emotive images and a nostalgia for immanence and reveals a lack of conjectural thought and philosophical inquiry.[9] The argument that contemporary poetry lacks or refuses to engage in a speculative discourse is an argument with which I strongly disagree. The demand in recent American poetry to make present, however provisionally, a personal voice clearly risks (as Altieri has noted) becoming a nostalgic and limited poetry. But the personal voice, including all its ironic and self-conscious moments, is in fact subversive, for it refutes a commodities-based culture and importantly asks for our participation and intimate connection.

Of the five poets, Rich assumes the role of actively envisioning a new language that is no longer oppressive, but is lucid and passionate. Bishop and Ashbery share in an ironic vision of a language that is highly figurative yet deeply ambivalent and interminable. Silenced and nearly extinguished, language must be remembered and retraced in Merwin's most powerful work. Finally, language in Wright's poetry is envisioned as a process of spiritual energy, subject to growth and decay. The strength of the poetry of these five poets is twofold. First, their meditations are confrontations with the provisionality of language, and, in particular, of writing. Any confrontation with language is also one with the world, in that language mediates between ourselves and the world—or more radically, constitutes both in language's fabrics. Second, these five poets reconsider language as a transcendent event, where the transcendent is the process and contact of writing. Their poetry revalues the possibility of transcendence by inscribing it within the interconnective dynamics of self-definition and the generation and figuration of writing.

In postmodern poetry, affirmation is ironic at best. Postmodern poetics, which these five poets develop and illuminate, reveal differences and the uncertainty of definition, synthesis, unicity, or affirmation. The centrality of writing, explored by all five, develops beyond referring solely to the making of the poem. They explore writing as the gesture, or body, of and the interpretation of observation, memory, materiality, presence, and energy. Writing extends seeing, remembering, and presence while paradoxically casting all under the shadow of change and mortality. What is of greatest concern is what the poets can tell us of our time and of ourselves. The truth of poetry resides in the offering of a common and empowering language. In particular, writing forms an ecology of our spirit as well as of our body—it reveals our condition as individuals and as a culture. At its best, writing extends and gives sustenance to our seeing, remembering, and presence. At its worst, language is empty and corrosively mirrors the impoverishment of the self and culture. The extreme provisionality of language is central to the vision of these five postmodern poets and reflects the deepening crises of self, culture, and society.

CHAPTER ONE

Concordances and Travels: The Poetry of Elizabeth Bishop

Elizabeth Bishop instructs us at the end of the poem "The Monument" to "Watch it closely."[1] Bishop insists on the importance of observation; indeed, of all the poets in recent American poetry, she is considered the most observant and precise in her descriptions.[2] Bishop explores the minute details of objects, offers descriptions of place and voice, and records acute changes of perception and interrelation. Each of her poems engages the phenomenal world. Though, for Bishop, engagement provides a detailed description of the world, depending on facts gathered from sensory experience, it also offers us new sensations—leading to new knowledge—of life and breaks our automatic responses to experience arising from force of habit.

Through the acts of speculation, transcendentalism or modernist synthesis is undermined. Speculation offers neither unity nor necessarily celebration, but, as in Bishop's "Florida," creates a concordance of possibilities, impressions, and glimpses that unsettle the given order. Naming, describing, and looking are forms of interconnection. Hans-Georg Gadamer writes, "The word has a mysterious connection with what it represents, a quality of belonging to its being." Bishop's language mirrors the very traveling of the eye; the desire to belong—word to object, seer to the seen. Gadamer continues, "We seek for the right word, i.e., the word that really belongs to the object, so that the object comes into language."[3] The poetry of Bishop works by drawing in or figuring the object in the traveler's language, and self-reflexively, the traveler goes toward the other, becoming another. As one of Bishop's figures and, indeed, an emblem of her own character and that of the poet, the traveler is used to describe the self in a state of flux, provisionally present, liminal, and, like the very medium of the poetic line, existing in durations and gestures of time.

No representation is final, nor is representation the goal; what Bishop explores is the process of seeing that draws us, momentarily, into contact with others. Despite the often profound absence of a narrating "I," the self or personal voice is never lost. Indeed, the self seeks its own provisional identity or ethos. In every poem Bishop has a sustained and individual voice: weary travelers, a Robinson Crusoe longing for his island, a girl recognizing her bonds with other women, a child recognizing death, a picky elderly woman at a dirty filling station. Like a seventeenth-century Dutch painter, Bishop records what may pass as a domestic or even an aphoristic moment; like the Dutch painters, however, this certainty of depiction belies a deeper uncertainty and skepticism.

Locality sustains as important a tension in Bishop's poetry as it does in that of her contemporary and friend Robert Lowell. However, Lowell developed, especially in *Life Studies*, a historical and personalist self reacting against the landscape of culture and society. This self foundered in the desire to escape the very name *Lowell*, and yet also struggled in a furious celebration of that past. Bishop endeavors to enter a place, a new geography; hence the titles of collections emphasize and inscribe metaphors of maps and traveling—*North and South*, *Questions of Travel* ("Brazil" and "Elsewhere" being the titles of the two sections of this collection), and *Geography III*. The eye metaphorically travels and crosses boundaries that mark differences and change. The subtle and ongoing process of seeing penetrates not only subjects ("The Fish") but names ("Florida") and symbols ("The Roosters"). Through her gaze, the self enters the field of others—Bishop privileges the other and the activity of perceiving the other, not in order to create further distinction, but to reaffirm the possibility of interconnection. The eye becomes explorer and mapmaker of a terra incognita that can never be fully mapped or known.

"Over 2,000 Illustrations and a Complete Concordance" exemplifies what Svetlana Alpers describes as taxonomic qualities in seventeenth-century Dutch painting. Alpers offers this formulation, derived in part from Bacon's philosophical enterprise: "To know is to name is to describe, but it is also to make."[4] Though Bishop's poetry shares with seventeenth-century Dutch painting a highly descriptive surface quality, the rhetorical quality of evocative description and *ekphrasis* is only part of the achievement of Bishop's work. Ekphrastic poetry, as exemplified by Keats' "Ode on a Grecian Urn," creates a tension between stasis and process within an illusion of literary space, where the poem desires to form a pictorial rather than descriptive figure.[5] Dutch painting developed a form of seeing distinct from the modes of representation described by Alberti or by Kepler—that is, "the picture tak[es] the place of the eye with the frame and our location thus left undefined."[6] Ambiguity, the play of observations and probings, and *ekphrasis,* rather than the authority of the observed and the observer's place, are as central to Bishop as they were to seventeenth-century Dutch painters. The refusal to locate the position from which the landscape is seen frees the viewer from being a conscript of the artist or author. The eye is free to wander across the expanse of the landscape, which seems limitless and unpunctuated by the props of set perspectives. Bishop instructs us in the art of observation, but through her art she also teaches us of the ambiguity inherent in possibilities of choice.

In "2,000 Illustrations and a Complete Concordance," Bishop glances through an illustrated Baedeker; her glance never rests, because the pictures themelves deny any completion, but instead form a metonymical procession. Likewise, the vistas of the cities that form the border of the resplendent map in Jan Vermeer's *The Art of Painting* are brief, partial, and linked to the central and abstract map. Furthermore, each of these vistas is blurred, unlike the map's crisp focus. Yet the map is not complete either in what it depicts or as the center of observation in the painting. The depicted woman or her partially painted representation within the painting is no more privileged than the self-portrait of the painter. Vermeer refuses to allow the painting to be of himself— the painter has literally turned his back on us. Bishop's poetry parallels this ambiguity of presence and place (while at the same time seeming to evoke presence with all the certainty of description), for her poetry unsettles any strict autobiographic portrayal while also refusing the confessional use of *I*. The voice or gesture of a particular self is there, but as a gesture or showing of the process of seeing and poem-making. Bishop, like Vermeer, insists on the inadvertency of seeing and hence the provisionality of presence.

To look is to form a concordance where "Everything [is] only connected by 'and' and 'and'" (58). Connection exists here through the frailty of language's conjunctions. Similarly, in the Vermeer painting, relationships only arise through the probings of our glances, and their sum is never the complete pictorial truth. Nor is such a closure desired—or deemed possible—by Bishop or Vermeer, for closure would deny the ambiguity central to their visions. The poem, like the painting, is self-reflexive, revealing its own composition:

> The eye drops, weighted, through the lines
> the burin made, the lines that move apart
> like ripples above sand,
> dispersing storms, God's spreading fingerprint,
> and painfully, finally, that ignite
> in watery prismatic white-and-blue. (57)

The eye probes the marks of the printmaker—where creator and Creator converge—transforming their fact into fictions. The "watery prismatic white-and-blue" burns our eyes and all of our senses like the acid used by printmakers. The verbal harmony of elements of fire and water, though beautiful and prismatic like the rainbow at the end of "The Fish," is achieved not only through the painstaking attention to language but also through the personal experiences of pain. Beauty is not opposed to pain, nor does beauty transcend pain. In Bishop's poetry the two are inseparable. Likewise, the reader or seer, as much as the writer or artist, must take the responsibility for creation.

These scenes or travels should have been "serious, engravable" (57), but they form an uncertain and incomplete taxonomy. They are the records or maps of the probing glances of the poet. As such, they are also memories or representations, and thus removed from the originary scene:

> Open the heavy book. Why couldn't we have seen
> this old Nativity while we were at it?
> —the dark ajar, the rocks breaking with light,
> an undisturbed, unbreathing flame,
> colorless, sparkless, freely fed on straw,
> and lulled within, a family with pets,
> —and looked and looked our infant sight away.   (58–59)

Bishop moves from the uncertainty and incompleteness of any system or myth of order to confront history and knowledge as founded on loss. Childhood gives way to adulthood, or Blake's world of experience, because of the awareness of the conjunction of time and loss. The originary, "our infant sight," doubles as the object lost and the process of losing. Loss is never final or complete; rather, it is metonymical and ongoing. Thus, representation always reinscribes and furthers loss, since representation works through displacement and replacement. The process of gaining experience—and losing one's childhood—is linked, nonetheless, with the insistence of a child's longing found in the eye's far-reaching and interconnecting travels.

The provisionality of interconnectedness suggests not simply a question of perceptual psychology but a spiritual necessity, as she describes in "The Imaginary Iceberg":

> Icebergs behoove the soul
> (both being self-made from elements least visible)
> to see them so: fleshed, fair, erected indivisible.   (4)

Bishop examines the liminal moment: the convergence of sea and shore, or of air and water. Distrustful of her art and techne, Bishop seeks the natural world with its possibility of concordance and self-definition. Though there is a basic connection between things—each is "self-made" from common "elements least visible"—the natural world does not accommodate us; its mysteries remain undisclosed:

> This iceberg cuts its facets from within.
> Like jewelry from a grave
> it saves itself perpetually and adorns
> only itself, perhaps the snows
> which so surprise us lying on the sea.
> Good-bye, we say, good-bye, the ship steers off
> where waves give in to one another's waves
> and clouds run in a warmer sky.   (4)

Though language is a place of meditation and departure, it also "saves itself perpetually and adorns / only itself."

These "least visible" elements combine to form a provisional whole, where even the "crudest scroll-work says 'commemorate'" (24). If one's look is directed to and by an object, then one will inevitably enter into a process of definition of the self and the other— each will be "fleshed, fair, erected indivisible." By reflexively and provisionally entering a relationship with the other, Bishop's self-reflexive look ultimately diminishes the subject-object dichotomy and implicitly attempts to locate a provisional moment of communion during the travels of the eye.

Perhaps nowhere else in Bishop's poetry is the eye's journey so celebrated as in her much anthologized poem "The Fish." The journey begins with the external, in the realm of the unseeing self, with the prosaic opening lines:

> I caught a tremendous fish
> and held him beside the boat
> half out of water, with my hook
> fast in a corner of his mouth.   (42)

The first word, "I," a pun on the self and the self that sees, preludes the opening—and flowering—of our eyes and our language. The direct and graphic description of a situation remains a moment when we look but are not yet actively and imaginatively engaged. We are external and separate since we have no connection with the other.

While Bishop examines the fish, she also begins to enter the body of figurative language:

> his brown skin hung in strips
> like ancient wallpaper,
> and its pattern of darker brown
> was like wallpaper:
> shapes like full-blown roses
> stained and lost through age.   (42)

The simile creates depth: we enter the house of language, where things stand behind things and each is dependent on the others—for they are linked by the trope's marker "like." By repeating the wallpaper simile, the apparent domesticity of the narrator is revealed and there is a convergence of two distinctly different worlds. Implicit in this convergence is a revelation of decay and mutability through the lucidity of her observation of the fish's patterned and peeling skin.

After continuing the examination of the exterior of the fish with an increasing degree of metaphor and precision—barnacles are "fine rosettes of lime," the fish is clothed with "rags"—the poet is rhetorically self-defined and imaginatively penetrates the fish:

> I thought of the coarse white flesh
> packed in like feathers,
> the big bones and the little bones,
> the dramatic reds and blacks
> of his shiny entrails,
> and the pink swim-bladder
> like a big peony.   (42)

The power of observation and looking resides in and rises with the power of imagining. We move closer to the certainty we believe lies in the tactility of physical presence—be it fish or rhetoric. At each of these liminal moments transformation takes place, since we cross the abyss between the two halves of a metaphor or simile.

The movement into the fish also initiates self-interrogation. Through the use of self-reflexive tropes, the narrator crosses the threshold of exteriority—where objects remain either marginalized or idealized discretes—into a realm where objects are interrelated not only among themselves but with us. The narrator stares into the fish's eyes, only to have the fish "not / . . . return my stare" (43) and deny any anthropomorphic pathos and sympathy. Self-reflexivity at this moment becomes transparent: the narrator acknowledges her own regard, seeing herself in relation with the other as two beings, rather than a subject distanced from (and desiring appropriation of) an object. The aside that qualifies the event—"It was more like the tipping / of an object toward the light" (43)—qualifies the perception and makes presence more provisional. The fish mediates between the narrator and a language with which she can picture herself. The description of the wallpaper, the flower imagery, and the metaphors of ornament and clothing comprise a taxonomy that composes the speaker and creates the mystery of the speaker's presence. She is both present in these details and absent, in that the details are metaphors whose other term is left unstated. Figurative language becomes the common and defining ground that both the fish and the speaker, in their mutual mysteriousness, share.

The narrator implicitly acknowledges the limitations of language through the use of such asides as "if you could call it a lip" (43). In using language, we impose it upon the world either to bring the world and ourselves into renewed relation or to subject the world to discipline, thus imprisoning the world and refiguring language as disciplinary. Yet figurative language also subverts the subjective and repressive qualities of language. To realize this double bind becomes a form of transcendence, though not the hierarchical transcendence of unicity. Transcendence here is the process of the dialectical movement of figurative language. The sharpening of observation, exemplified by the correction of "five old pieces of fish-line" to "or four and a wire leader / with the swivel still attached," reflects the process of reifying the self, the other, and language. Speculation is transformative and interminable, as exemplified when the fishing equipment becomes medals of valor "with their ribbons / frayed and wavering," before they are transformed again into "a five-haired beard of wisdom / trailing from his aching jaw" (43). The fish can never be defined or gazed upon as a totality—any definition of any particular is exchanged for another. The generation of metaphors, one displacing another, grants language its continuation and life; thus, the narrator is caught in an interminable process of focusing her vision—but at some point the vision can no longer be sustained; instead it must be relinquished.

Bishop's imperative in "The Monument" ("Watch it closely") echoes "The Fish" ("I stared and stared") and describes this potentially interminable movement of perception, which is tantamount to the poem. During the process of increasing attentiveness, the speaker glimpses a provisional fullness:

> I stared and stared
> and victory filled up
> the little rented boat,
> from the pool of bilge
> where oil had spread a rainbow
> around the rusted engine

> to the bailer rusted orange,
> the sun-cracked thwarts,
> the oarlocks on their strings,
> the gunnels—until everything
> was rainbow, rainbow, rainbow!
> And I let the fish go.   (43–44)

The fish fills with language until it can hold no more. It is at this moment that the generation of language can go no farther. The fish must be discarded and replaced. The self has also reached its own limits of creation and definition. Artifice, if it is to remain coherent, finds itself limited. Still unanswered is whether nature is equally limited, or if it is that which remains limiting and un-apprehendable. The rainbow of oil leaking onto the water's surface replaces the fish and allows discursive connections to continue. This dispensation, however, is ironic: it takes place in a grubby rented boat, where the language wears out, indicated by the repetition of "rusted" in two successive lines. The "victory" is the rainbow of a thin film of oil spreading across the bilge waters, overrunning the "pool of bilge," to spread over everything. Similarly, the rainbow draws together the multitude of colors found throughout the poem, which parallels a rainbow's concordance of the undistorted visible colors of the spectrum. The rainbow spreads over the boat and over language "until everything / was rainbow, rainbow, rainbow!" Though it is tempting to read the final lines as an ecstatic moment that marks the narrator's full recognition of the fish and interconnectedness, such a reading remains naive, for the poem has come to describe the generative and metonymical functions of language. Jerome Mazzaro considers these final lines a parody of "God's restoration of dominion to Noah" in which Bishop's wry evolutionist stance suggests that humans' dominion is only by accident and technology.[7] Although the rainbow reflects a new dispensation, it is one that inscribes, as Mazzaro argues, departure and uncertainty. The simple rhyme of "rainbow" and "go" underscores the provisionality of any interconnection, since it recalls the passage and loss of childhood. We must let go any notion of totality or synthesis, either rhetorical or existential. Instead, the materiality of language and time comes to be emphasized; the poem lets go of the symbolic, and reinvents the relational. The poem moves toward transcendent closure with "rainbow, rainbow, rainbow," but opens up and initiates a new, though unfigured, process that subverts closure and death: "And I let the fish go."

"The Fish," though an early poem, is important because it traces one moment of perception leading to another and parallels this with the generation of language through metaphors. This process follows the practice of Ignatian meditation—a means of moving from "composition of place, setting the spot," to analysis, and finally to the colloquy.[8] The idea of place, distinct from the process of placing, constitutes a poetry of fixity and definition, not one of seeing and speculation. As in the poetry of Robert Lowell, the self and the culture is already placed, and is no longer a reflective process. Lowell's poem "Inauguration Day: January 1953"—the title imposing a fixed time—illustrates Lowell's sense of a defined place:

> Ice, ice. Our wheels no longer move.
> Look, the fixed stars, all just alike
> as lack-land atoms, split apart,
> and the Republic summons Ike,
> the mausoleum in her heart.

Lowell, in the autobiographical essay "92 Revere Street"—its title a definition of a place—states that "the vast number of remembered *things* remains rocklike. Each is in its place, each has its function, its history, its drama. . . . they are endurable and perfect."[9] According to Lowell, one can only rage against or submit to these givens: that is our fate, our place, and our function.

Bishop explores and questions the activity of placing oneself in a scene, landscape, or field of depth in such poems as "The Map," "Questions of Travel," and "Crusoe in England." Unlike Lowell, Bishop never discloses the place; it is part of traveling and the provisionality of travel. "The Map" opens her first collection, *North and South,* and is a poem that is as much a thematic opening to her poetry as the better-known poem from the same collection, "The Fish." As the title implies, "The Map" is a meditation on the act of perceiving an object. The map, like a poem or a painting, re-presents (makes present again) a place and considers the presentness and certainty of any representation. The map compels us to look at it in such a way that we enter into the field of the object:

> We can stroke these lovely bays,
> under a glass as if they were expected to blossom,
> or as if to provide a clean cage for invisible fish.   (3)

The look becomes sensual as it examines the map through a magnifying glass; the translation of geography into cartographical marks is ethically refigured. Are such marks blossoms or cages, beauty or painful entrapment, and how then are we to read them?

The poem questions the autonomy of the other in its re-presentation: "Are they assigned, or can the countries pick their colors?" (3). The response, "What suits the character or the native waters best," suggests the imposition of interpretation on any representation or through representation. Though "Topography displays no favorites" and the mapmaker's colors are "More delicate than the historians,'" the poem questions expectations, assertions, truth statements, and any of the colors of rhetoric. But it is by rhetoric that the poem, of course, poses its questions. *Descriptio,* the method of the mapmaker and naturalist, depends entirely on the provisionality of interpretation.

The first stanza initiates the subversion of certainty by countering the initial proposition with a series of questions. The qualification of "Shadows, or are they shallows," further questions the insistence on language as an objective medium and interposes the mutability and diachrony of language as analogous to the mutability of presence. The gradation of colors on the map overlaps and overruns gradations of sound, and thus describes the energies of erosion and the impossibility of any definition. The relation of the seer and the other becomes analogous to the relation of land and sea: "Mapped waters are more quiet than the land is, / lending the land their waves' own conformation" (3). Profiles, like "Norway's hare" drawn from the outlines of a coast on a map (like a child finding figures in clouds or in cracks on a ceiling), "investigate the sea, where land is." To investigate place is to investigate one's own locus within that place and to enter into relationship with others, breaking the constraints of division, isolation, and silence.

"The Map" works as a conceit of self-definition, tracing the movement out of childhood "when emotion too far exceeds its cause" (3). Experiences are transferred from one sphere to another; thus, the transfer creates a metaphoric texture and an identity for the voice. Refigured in the transference is the transformation (and loss) of childhood play and free association into the world of work and commodities. Mazzaro notes that the "emotive adjectives are deliberately feminine," as are the occupational metaphors the poem employs.[10] By constructing such a metaphorical frame, Bishop invokes the world common to women—though founded on loss—and can be seen as positing a new discourse containing new symbolism. The comparison of the map's depiction of peninsulas to women feeling yard goods suggests for both "The feel of . . . the unfinished or what can be worked on."[11] In this self-reflexive *ars poetica,* Bishop expresses the connections between the mundane occupational world and the woof and warp of language. For Bishop, language's mystery, potential, or uncertainty exists within its material and tactile presence, which provides the backing and place of interconnection.

Each topological feature of the map blossoms into a metaphor. Such a movement maintains the diachronic aspects of language, for movement portends, not closure, but the ever-accumulating process of language. Through such accumulation the self or voice assembles itself, never as a whole or totality, but as a collection, map, or concordance. The narrator's eye glances across the map, unable to take in the whole, indeed, not wishing to, but briefly lighting upon and transforming, figuratively, its features. The poem is then a mapping of the eye-I's travels or gestured movement through time and space. As a mapping of self-definition, the poem selects the metaphors of the mapmaker, rather than the gardener, weaver, or historian, as the conceit of the self. The mapmaker, like the poet, creates interpretations, places of transference, or thresholds; and in these brief moments of transference interconnection occurs.

In "Questions of Travel," a tourist complains "Think of the long trip home. / Should we have stayed at home and thought of here?" (93). The complaint reveals the risk of any traveling—literal or figurative—and the dangers and anxiety of self-definition. The extreme process of self-definition, for Bishop, is the provisional and momentary act of writing and self-revelation. The poem becomes an interiorized debate—the two voices are less separate characterizations than they are a compound self that interrogates itself and reveals, not affirmation, but doubt. The complaining, unimaginative tourist in "Questions of Travel" echoes the complaining voice in "The Monument":

> "Why did you bring me here to see it?
> A temple of crates in cramped and crated scenery,
> What can it prove?
> I am tired of breathing this eroded air,
> this dryness in which the monument is cracking."   (24)

The voices in both poems cannot share what their companions experience. The companions mirror the poet's role: to be a guide, teacher, or mapmaker. In "The Monument," the companion's voice reveals to the complaining onlooker the potential of active or attentive looking: "It is the beginning of a painting, / a piece of sculpture, or poem, or monument" (25).

Unlike "The Monument," which describes the process of placing oneself in relationship to an object, "Questions of Travel" describes the process of placing oneself in a landscape. Furthermore, the poem questions the creative activity described by the metaphor of traveling:

Is it right to be watching strangers in a play
in this strangest of theatres?
What childishness is it that while there's a breath of life
in our bodies, we are determined to rush
to see the sun the other way around?
The tiniest green hummingbird in the world?
To stare at some inexplicable old stonework,
inexplicable and impenetrable,
at any view,
instantly seen and always, always delightful?   (93)

The complaining voice wants to restrain looking by morally questioning the motives for such looking and traveling. This is more than a reinvocation of the Puritan rejection of the "delightful." The complaining voice asks, "Is it right to be watching . . . ?" and denies the possibility of self-definition and personal delight, implicitly demanding a positivist and impersonal ethos, one that rejects childhood and *jouissance*. The repetition of "inexplicable" suggests difficulty and the limitations inherent in language, as well as an implicit demand for the explicable, habitual, and defined. To underscore the distinction between the voices, the complaining voice uses a drab language enlivened by few moments of figuration—the language is that of an isolated self entirely distanced from the landscape and thus antithetical to the traveler, poet, and eye-I.

The last seven lines of the first stanza counter the first, limiting lines of the complaining tourist. To this second voice the waterfalls are "streaks, those mile-long, shiny, tearstains" and "the mountains look like the hulls of capsized ships, / slime-hung and barnacled" (93). The mountains are not depicted in terms of an idealized sublime but as an ironic and transformational sublime: to idealize would be to gaze and impose the self on the landscape rather than to place oneself, however ironically or self-reflexively, into the landscape. Nevertheless, Bishop's simile renews our view of the mountain. Figurative language could indeed be said to figure the viewer as much as the viewed.

The modernist credo to "make it new" or to defamiliarize increases "the difficulty and length of perception." In so doing, Viktor Shklovsky suggests that the importance of art is to "recover the sensation of life; it [art] exists to make one feel things, to make the stone *stony*." In creating "a special perception of the object [the image] creates a 'vision' of the object instead of serving as a means for knowing it." [12] Any naive demand for defamiliarization, Bishop demonstrates, is limiting and would relegate her own poetry to the realm of extraordinary but mere description. Second, and more important, the denial of knowing—and Shklovsky does not elaborate on the possibilities and kinds of knowing—denies connection, community, and the interlinking function of seeing. Defamiliarization asserts a realm of discretes in a solitude of the most negative form: the silenced.

The second voice of "Questions of Travel" suggests the plenitude of perceptions and the plenitude achieved through the sharing of these perceptions. The sensual, found in the most mundane sights, is made full through sharing. The complaining voice sought the grand and exotic, while the second voice, celebrating the mundane, enters into the splendid field of others. In this world—the truly otherworldly—perception is not limited simply to the visual:

> —Not to have had to stop for gas and heard
> the sad, two-noted, wooden tune
> of disparate wooden clogs
> carelessly clacking over
> a grease-stained filling-station floor.   (94)

Experience is arbitrary and of the moment. There is no itinerary or agenda.

In "Questions of Travel" we move toward a moment of fuller perceptions as well as a moment of writing contained within another text. The growth of perceptions and the movement toward

the landscape are preconditions for writing and for the meditation that essentially recommences the poem. The self-reflexive
enfolding of another text swerves the poem from closure:

> —And never to have had to listen to rain
> so much like politicians' speeches:
> two hours of unrelenting oratory
> and then a sudden golden silence
> in which the traveller takes a notebook, writes:
>
> *"Is it lack of imagination that makes us come*
> *to imagined places, not just stay at home?*
> *Or could Pascal have been not entirely right*
> *about just sitting quietly in one's room?*
>
> *Continent, city, country, society:*
> *the choice is never wide and never free.*
> *And here, or there . . . No. Should we have stayed at home,*
> *wherever that may be?"*   (94; Bishop's italics)

The inclusion of the italicized transcriptions from a notebook emphasizes the durational quality of writing. Despite the seemingly
multitudinous range of experience and possibility, Bishop asserts
"the choice is never wide and never free," because we are governed by experience and language. The concordance of experience
is not a Linnaean process of ordering chaos and intellectual control but a converse process where ordering and interrogation lead
to further uncertainty. The moment of "golden silence" recalls the
adage leveled at children, "silence is golden." The transcendent
silences the two voices while returning us to writing and uncertainty. The adage, paradoxically, returns us also to childhood and
the subversive play of children. We thus return to the beginnings
of the poem, the journal's entries and questions, which break the
imposed silence of that Victorian adage and admonishment authorized by the discourse of fathers.

The power of the sensual world becomes overwhelming. The
poem moves, like "The Fish," from the realm of the self to a realm

of perceptions that place the self in a field of depth; and then to an ecstatic moment, a "golden silence," in which the second voice ponders the very nature of travel and imagination without coming to a final, hence limited, conclusion. Temporality does not disappear, nor can it be disclosed, for to do so requires the knowledge of the present, a sensual self-definition. Yet presence is ambiguous and knowledge of it is always of its passage and pastness. In turn, Bishop suggests that art, what inspires and holds us outside of time, is provisional and thus an artifact of presence, "the weak calligraphy of songbirds' cages" (94).

The two companion poems to "Questions of Travel" provide necessary placings prior to the moment of self-reflexive writing in "Questions of Travel." "Arrival at Santos," no doubt an autobiographical version, provides an entry into contemporary Brazil. The title marks a liminal moment that defines our temporality: one passage has been completed, and new travels are about to commence, for "we are driving to the interior" (90). The unconscious and oceanic are left behind; when we make landfall, we begin to see. In "Brazil, January 1, 1502," Bishop probes the historical landscape:

> Januaries, Nature greets our eyes
> exactly as she must have greeted theirs:
> every square inch filling in with foliage—
> big leaves, little leaves, and giant leaves,
> blue, blue-green, and olive,
> with occasional lighter veins and edges,
> or a satin underleaf turned over.   (91)

"Calling to each other (or had the birds waked up?) / and retreating, always retreating" (92), the Native American women disappear, hoping to hide from the Portuguese colonists. The colonists usurp the landscape and impose a blind hierarchy

> corresponding, nevertheless,
> to an old dream of wealth and luxury

already out of style when they left home—
wealth, plus a brand-new pleasure.   (92)

The narrator weaves a moral response into the very nature of perception and placing. Not to see is ultimately to colonize or impose
one's own self on a place rather than to be among others within
that landscape.

The poem threads the narrator's identity with the landscape of
history, language, and place. Images of embroidery run throughout the poem—"frame," "web," "detail," "backing," and "hanging fabric"—and reveal the personality of the narrator, a desire
for interconnection, as well as what Helen Vendler calls the element of "domestication."[13] Here the strange and the domestic are
coupled; to apprehend the strange we must apply what is known;
in turn, the domestic is made strange. Thus, in "Brazil, January 1,
1502," the landscape cannot remain mere description, for other
surfaces arise. The poem weaves together the narrator's identity,
marked by the embroidery images, and images of temptation:
"Still in the foreground there is Sin: / five sooty dragons near
some massy rocks" (91). The lizards repose in their precise detail,
but so too does the moral vision in which the actions of humans
correspond to those of the birds and lizards, which in turn symbol-
ize the abstraction "Sin."

The poet enters the language and a dialogue with history.
Through *ekphrasis,* or the art of description, Bishop suggests the
continuity of primal conflicts outside the constraints of human
measure or perspective. Her dependence on *ekphrasis* points to
the rhetorical aspect of power—the control of representations and
interpretations. The implicit vision is pessimistic and dismissive
of any humanistic impulse, for the poem suggests a fatal and deterministic naturalism at work. The poem welds danger and temptation together with such descriptions as "hell-green flames" and
"red as a red-hot wire." Sexuality and generation, vivid in the
first stanza's explosion of foliage and blossoms, become increasingly violent. The seminal "monster ferns" turn into male birds
puffing out their breasts during courting displays, while lizards

foreground the rape of the Native American women and the land by the colonists who "ripped away into the hanging fabric" (92). The violence depicted by the speaker turns against her when her personal imagery is subjected to the violence of the colonists and the institutionalized discourses of men. The violence of the male tears apart the world common to women and life. The various forms of the occupational metaphor of embroidery, an activity traditionally associated with women, serve to link the poet symbolically with other women. The image of weaving or embroidery arguably knits a space and time that locates women; thus Bishop in this poem has passionately woven her own identity into the site—historical and geographical—that she portrays. Vendler's notion of domestication, though helpful, misses the central vision of Bishop's work: the interconnectedness of actions and being through the fabric of language. Bishop, like Adrienne Rich, nominally links nature with the world common to women, in that both are subjected to the powers of men. However, the more closely Bishop watches, the more difficult any easy identifications become, for nature is revealed as sexually violent and inescapable—a contrast to the artifice of a forest's hanging fabrics. Left unstated is Bishop's vision of women: Does their condition mirror the contrastive and mutually subversive discourses describing nature?

Poems such as "Brazil, January 1, 1502," "The Weed," "Roosters," and "The Armadillo" transform a landscape into a moral topos. In these poems we are still "driving to the interior," but the movement is into the interior of a deterministic world and into the mind meditating on such issues as sexuality and history. Bishop's definition of history—personal, natural, and cultural—is one where "loss is gain" and her art "aims not to resist but to facilitate loss."[14] Yet this gain through loss is ironic, as seen in "The Fish." The moral topos must then be redefined; beyond the poet's beliefs in the human perspective or moral rule is the world of blind conflict. The human measure is the unrecoverable origin—often that of child's play. Bishop's narrators attempt, nevertheless, to retrieve what has been irrevocably lost. "The Prodigal," "The Burgler of Babylon," "In the Waiting Room," and "Crusoe in

England" share the prodigal's "shuddering insights, beyond his control, / touching him" (71). Knowledge is gained in these poems only through the ironic distinctions and contrasts of experience, not through judgment:

> The brown enormous odor he lived by
> was too close, with its breathing and thick hair,
> for him to judge. The floor was rotten; the sty
> was plastered halfway up with glass-smooth dung. (71)

Though meaning to return and often desiring to, we are all prodigals doomed to the sty.

"Driving to the interior," as a dynamic poetic process, creates relations between things while penetrating the landscape and moving deeper into the sensibility of the observer. Unmarked by an "I," the self becomes transparent while relating the experience of a particular bus ride in the poem "The Moose." In this poem, the communal and witnessing pronoun "we" replaces the self-locating narrative pronoun "I." Nevertheless, there still is the undeniable presence of the individuated activity of observation—the process that makes the self an identity and a voice through the selection of details. The westward journey moves away from the edge of the continent and toward the interior. The journey emphasizes the crossing of new thresholds that become less defined as we move away from the primal shore or originary locus. The emphasis is less on the lines of demarcation than on entering each successive field:

> Goodbye to the elms,
> to the farm, to the dog.
> The bus starts. The light
> grows richer; the fog,
> shifting, salty, thin,
> comes closing in. (170)

The more attentive we are, the more borders we become aware of and cross. With the mapmaker, the poet shares the desires of traveling and translating those travels into concordances. Both create denotative gestures or the naming of things and engage in acts of pointing rather than of stating. Neither engages in definition; rather, both their interests lie in transference, the making of languages. The poet explores the nature of edges and what is within them, as in the first four stanzas of "The Moose," where the bus and the lines of sight (and poem) travel from seaside, to bay, to river, and then "on red, gravelly roads, / down rows of sugar maples" (169).

The process of traveling in "The Moose" also entails penetrating the various spaces of human activity. These spaces are the preconditions for deictic observations—observation is the activity under observation. The space or depth of observation holds the relation between things:

> In the creakings and noises,
> an old conversation
> —not concerning us,
> but recognizable, somewhere,
> back in the bus:
> Grandparents' voices
>
> uninterruptedly
> talking, in Eternity:
> names being mentioned,
> things cleared up finally;
> what he said, what she said,
> who got pensioned;
>
> deaths, deaths and sicknesses;
> the year he remarried;
> the year (something) happened.
> She died in childbirth.
> That was the son lost
> when the schooner foundered.   (171–72)

Within a space are still more spaces and memories and lives trying to be completed through the incomplete discourses and listenings of others. The bus becomes another landscape we travel into, boarded by other travelers, who initiate their journeys with "kisses and embraces / to seven relatives" (170). We watch while a "woman climbs in / with two market bags" and returns our glances "amicably" (171). We listen to—and thus come into relation with—the Grandparents' voices talking of life and death, pensions, insanity, lost children: their stories become our stories. The voices, though "not concerning us," are nonetheless "recognizable" and belong to the sensual realm we have entered. They are also voices that have survived and will be passed down from generation to generation. Our relationship with the passing external landscape has shifted to an interiorized landscape that involves human connections where everyone participates in a dialogical unfolding. Through reading—the journey mirrors reading—it is our journey and prompts our own memories. Generations, occupations, and voices both differ and supplement each other, creating a provisional—literally transient—community.

Relation and shared depth of space continue in the stanza:

> "Yes . . ." that peculiar
> affirmative. "Yes . . ."
> A sharp, indrawn breath,
> half groan, half acceptance,
> that means "Life's like that.
> We know *it* (also death)."   (172; Bishop's italics)

At this point, through the mediations of the poet, we have entered into relations with others and begin to interpret the conversation by examining the affirmative. The narrator imagines the "way they talked / in the old featherbed," moving into an entirely new space: the "dim lamplight in the hall, / down in the kitchen, the dog" (172). The movement of the narrator dreamily wandering through the Grandparents' house parallels the movement of the bus through the countryside and the eye traveling through the window into the landscape:

> Its cold, round crystals
> form and slide and settle

>   in the white hens' feathers,
>   in gray glazed cabbages,
>   on the cabbage roses
>   and lupins like apostles.   (170)

Here, as in "The Fish," the activity of observation penetrates the landscape with an empowered and experienced imagination: no one rushing past farms in a bus could possibly see the minute crystals of fog settling in the "white hens' feathers." The acts of writing and of seeing are based on the accumulation of past texts and sights—there is no original, isolate imagined artifice.

The poem almost stops after the Grandparents' voices draw the narrator into the imagined space of their house:

>   Now, it's all right now
>   even to fall asleep
>   just as on all those nights.   (172)

Observation leads to closure and loss when it is severed from the immediate flux, and evokes a representation of domestication or safety. But then the bus "stops with a jolt," for a moose "has come out of / the impenetrable wood" (172). The appearance of the moose interrupts the nearing of sleep and breaks off the possibility of closure. While all the other landscapes are known and experienced, the moose and its place cannot be penetrated by the imagination or figurative language. The self has reached a point of its own limitation; the moose re-presents the mysterious and the other. The moose appears as "Towering, antlerless, / high as a church" and "grand, otherworldly" (173), and, according to Vendler, not belonging to the world described by the poem prior to the moose's appearance: "a beloved landscape and beloved people, that which can be domesticated and those who have joined in domesticity."[15] The moose's surprising and invasive presence releases the self from the habitual and from slumber, and back into discourse to "exclaim in whispers, / childishly, softly." The moose is not the antithesis of the domesticated landscape; instead, it embodies the inherent mystery in the mundane, for the moose itself is "homely as a house / (or, safe as houses)."

Larry Levis suggests that "when animals occur in poems . . .
they are often emblems for the muteness of the poet, for what he
or she cannot express, for what is deepest and sometimes most
anti-social in the poet's nature."[16] For example, in Galway Kinnell's "The Bear," the narrator hunts and kills a bear to merge
literally with the carcass. The self is extinguished and utterly lost
in this communion with the condition of the primal: "What anyway /was that sticky infusion, that rank flavor of blood, that poetry, by which I lived?"[17] Distance, in Kinnell's poem, is reduced,
and thus any mediation between self and other is lost in a total
synthesis. In contrast, the narrator of Bishop's poem does not
merge with the animal; instead, self and other maintain a mutually distanced and mediated relation. After the interruption, the
journey continues, yet always with the traces of the past.

> by craning backward,
> the moose can be seen
> on the moonlit macadam;
> then there's a dim
> smell of moose, an acrid
> smell of gasoline.   (173)

The renewing encounter with the moose parallels the Grandparents' conversation and their affirmation of life. Likewise, the
descriptions of the landscape, revived by active observation, secure each thing's presence despite the transitory nature of experience. Indeed, the rhetoric of description assures us of the copiousness of the world and the word:

> the sweet peas cling
> to their wet white string
> on the whitewashed fences;
> bumblebees creep
> inside the foxgloves,
> and evening commences.   (170)

Observation reveals the copiousness, yet the movement through
the poem, the landscape, and the list of topological features re-

mind us of the loss we are stained by—we are marked by time, hence by the inscription of mortality within movement. Like Orpheus, the narrator looks back and suffers a final severing—the poem is a permanent record of an accumulation of departures. Nonetheless, the crossing of thresholds and horizons reveals the plenitude brought into the poet's being and language.

The presence of the moose evokes a childlike exclamation among the bus riders. The narrator finds herself unable to interpret this moment, unlike the interpretation offered of the Grandparents' affirming "yes,"

> Why, why do we feel
> (we all feel) this sweet
> sensation of joy?   (173)

The narrator can only ponder. The sight of this moose (or other) revitalizes the self and affirms the mystery in every being: thus, the process of placing continues, for we are left with a question and a trace: "a dim / smell of moose, an acrid / smell of gasoline." The celebratory moment of the appearance of the moose is dispersed like the spreading "rainbow, rainbow, rainbow" of leaking gasoline from the rented skiff in "The Fish." The poem would be far different if it ended a mere four lines earlier with "the moose can be seen / on the moonlit macadam," for we would have ended on a resonant and alliterative memory—a representation of an inviolable essence. By stretching beyond that moment, Bishop regards the sharpness of loss and the over-powering accretive force of experience and language. The "acrid / smell of gasoline," like the bus's jolting stop, denies nostalgia and the safety of domesticity, for the ordinary intrudes and limits our desire or belief in affirmation.

Like "The Moose," "In the Waiting Room" explores liminal moments and seeks to describe memory in terms of place as well as time. The poem, which opens *Geography III,* begins by geographically locating the action: the poem forms a map on which Bishop taxonomically assembles a world. Her insistence on place is demonstrated by the volume's preface of excerpts from an 1884 geography primer, whose first two lessons form taxonomic definitions through the catechismal formula of questions and answers. Echoing the meditative questions in "The Map," these lessons suggest how to read and see; they also return us to childhood, where things remain unlearned and uncertain. By addressing the place, one drives into the interior, toward the particular—if one questions and looks, rather than answers and defines. The processes of remembering and self-definition depend on the ability to situate oneself and to initiate and maintain an interrogative looking. Where the narrator sits, the waiting room, suggests the place or condition prior to crossing an initiatory threshold. The child begins to traverse various thresholds in "In the Waiting Room": she is initiated into her name as a mark of separation and she is drawn into the room her aunt occupies as well as into the pictures of tribal women in the *National Geographic,* a magazine that carries the idea of traveling and place in its very title.

Writing on "In the Waiting Room," Lee Edelman argues that the poem subverts and discredits the binary oppositions of inside and outside, male and female, literal and figurative, and human and bestial. Edelman reveals Bishop's distortion of the logic of cause and effect, which questions the mastery of a text as well as the ideologies that assert mastery and hence marginalize. Bishop's text challenges distinctions and reveals the distortions to which society subjects women by transforming them into linguistic and economic counters for exchange. Female sexuality is *pictured* as unnatural, and thus marginal, "one more figure in the language of culture." The tribal women represented in the text become representations of women in Bishop's own society; each is connected by the interiorized (repressed, unread, marginal, hidden) cry of pain—"Aunt Consuelo's voice" (160). To locate or clarify that cry is "to put it in its place," to read it "as a zero, a void," rather than to hear it as a cry "against the reduction of woman to the status of a literal figure, an oxymoronic entity constrained to be interpreted within the patriarchial text." To the distortion of African women's necks bound by wire, the narrator adds the trope "like necks of light bulbs" (159); not only does the figuration reveal a participation in the dehumanizing language and ideology of the culture but also, as Edelman notes, these figures "illuminate . . . her fate as a woman."[18] Thus language doubles back upon itself to subvert by revealing the controlling ideology. Clearly, then, language is seen as liminal or always at a point of change even while it paradoxically maintains the controlling culture.

Entering the visual frame of the photographs commences the narrator's transformation and self-definition. The narrator recognizes her own identity when she recognizes herself regarding her relation with others:

> But I felt: you are an *I,*
> you are an *Elizabeth,*
> you are one of *them.*
> *Why* should you be one, too?
> I scarcely dared to look
> to see what it was I was.   (160; Bishop's italics)

Here, in one of the most self-reflexive moments in Bishop's poetry, the narrator recognizes, first, through the mirroring gaze, that she is an "*I*": that is, a self. Furthermore, the underscored *I* is named; it is not only the subject and viewer (I-eye), but a potential object, an "it" or an "*Elizabeth.*"[19] "*Elizabeth*" becomes part of the linguistic traffic and part of the ideology of exchange. The self is seen as a name, as part of a text, and as an element in an undisclosed concordance. The name offers itself as a fact, hence as something mastered and as a marker of stability. Yet the name or signature, like the details in the *National Geographic* or the poem itself, is a trace, thus always decentered and displaced. Identity, mirrored in language, is liminal and provisional while also subject to social forces. Bishop makes one final and brilliant leap in "In the Waiting Room": she continues the self-reflexive placing by revealing her own disquieting connection with the disfigured and reified women pictured in the magazine through the alienating and indicative pronoun "*them.*"

To recognize one's identity and relation is to fall from an un-differentiated Edenic world centered around oneself and the nur-turing of oneself by the undisclosed (m)other. The narrator tells herself that she will be seven years old in three days in order lit-erally to stop the fall into instability and the loss of mastery over self and language. With the gaining of identity come unsettling existential questions: "Why should I be my aunt, / or me, or any-one?" or "How had I come to be here, / like them . . . ?" (161). The experience is estranging:

> I knew that nothing stranger
> had ever happened, that nothing
> stranger could ever happen.   (160)

In the moment of estrangement, the narrator suddenly recognizes the paradoxical quality of differentiation: to be different is also to establish a relation with the other;

> What similarities—
> boots, hands, the family voice
> I felt in my throat, or even
> the *National Geographic*
> and those awful hanging breasts—
> hold us all together
> or made us all just one?   (161)

Estrangement marks the exile from unknowing and a movement into a historical and temporal world. The poem ends by naming place, date, and the historical fact that "The War was on." These assertions, provisional as they may be, attempt to mask and re-press the unsettling discovery the narrator has made about her-self and society.

The poem moves from a spatially defined world to one tem-porally defined by the poem's calendrical conclusion, "and it was still the fifth / of February, 1918" (161). The poem charts the loss of childhood, which is suggested here as a spatially centered state. The abstraction of time replaces the solidity of the geographical fixity and locality of the poem's first line. The entry into a community of women and self-definition is countered by the beginning of time coupled with war. "Brazil, January 1, 1502" suggests the similar dialectic between the spatial fabric of the Indian women (and implicitly the speaker) and the colonists' temporality and violent abstraction, which severs and intrudes. Affirmation of self or of community is always undercut by another—but fatally stained—discourse.

In "Crusoe in England," like "In the Waiting Room," Crusoe engages in a retrospective gaze; instead of recollecting the moment of self-definition, however, he confronts the loss of self, name, and relation. Crusoe is selected partly because of the accessibility of the reference—it is a story often told in one's childhood, thus Crusoe's exile from his island suggests our own exile from childhood. Crusoe is also the traveler who manages to survive, though he chose his exile. According to Bishop, exile defines the self's existence and the poet's condition; Crusoe's life is metonymical of exile and is composed of a series of ironic losses. Crusoe is also an other and represents, for Bishop, physical, political, and cultural survival. In her poems "The Armadillo," "The Roosters," and "The Pink Dog," animals survive man-made ravages and parallel Crusoe's actions. Survival, or the maintaining of provisional connections, is the basis of self-definition or the mapping of the self.

"Crusoe in England" is an ironic self-portrait of survival where the lumbering turtles, the sea, volcanoes, and rain constantly and mock-epically hiss in the foreground. Helen Vendler and David Kalstone discuss the poem in terms of the domestication of nature as the means of "surviving in a universe of one" [20]; however, the poet sees survival as a form of supplementation and, paradoxically, of metaphoric reduction and loss: one island is supplanted by "another island, / that doesn't seem like one, but who decides?" (166). Crusoe, like Bishop's other narrators, creates tropes and thereby reveals language's movement as one of displacement, substitution, and metaphor. His seemingly offhand question "but who decides?" foregrounds the questions of meaning, literalness, and the ideologies these imply. Crusoe's original voice is no longer known; instead, his voice, lamenting his stranded condition, is riddled by irony and the underlying desire to return to what was lost but unknown at the time of his rescue. The past, islanded beyond any genius of mapmakers, becomes the impossible originary moment, "still / un-rediscoverable, un-renamable" (162). Neither Crusoe nor any other traveler can return except by means of the provisionality of memory and imagination. Crusoe complains that "None of the books has ever got it right" (162)—history and memory are implicitly unreliable. But the storyteller, like the mapmaker, can offer only an interpretation—never "right" but always new and copious.

The island's solitude was, for Crusoe, defined by the lack of humans, yet now England becomes an ironic mirror of his previous exile. Crusoe contends with his new exile and isolation by undercutting his descriptions of the lost island:

> The sun set in the sea; the same odd sun
> rose from the sea,
> and there was one of it and one of me.
> The island had one kind of everything:
> one tree snail, a bright violet-blue
> with a thin shell, crept over everything,
> over the one variety of tree,
> a sooty, scrub affair.
> Snail shells lay under these in drifts
> and, at a distance,
> you'd swear that they were beds of irises.   (163–64)

Here the notion of singularity, of "one kind," is subverted by the repetition of "everything." Crusoe, as a poet-manqué, is primarily a taxonomist who transforms the limited world (whose lack is compounded by his exile from the island) into plenitude through the colors of rhetoric. When snail shells become irises, waterspouts "sacerdotal beings of glass" (163), or gulls start into flight "like a big tree in a strong wind, its leaves" (165), memory regenerates the lost objects through figuration.

The use of metaphor fills a lack, rather than pointing to that lack; Crusoe's memory of the island yearningly tries to fill his loss of that place, to redeem and regain the supplanted island. The ironic tone—a self-reflexive gesture or turning upon the self and the text—underscores the irremediable nature of loss. Here the poem marks an acute distinction between the possibilities of metaphor and memory: metaphor, by its quality of combining disparate elements or of establishing and crossing thresholds, creates and then fills the lack while maintaining difference. Memory, however, cannot cross the threshold: the idea of loss carries with it the absolute condition of exile.

The condition of loss as an absolute emerges in the penultimate stanza. Crusoe finds himself isolated; memory is forced to acknowledge that it cannot fill the past. With this acknowledgment comes the isolation of old age and a state of exhaustion:

> My blood was full of them; my brain
> bred islands. But that archipelago
> has petered out. I'm old.
> I'm bored, too, drinking my real tea,
> surrounded by uninteresting lumber.   (166)

These lines contain the lament of the artist who has become impotent, who can no longer create new monuments, poems, or islands. He cannot imaginatively create those archipelagoes; instead, he is captive on this other island, forced to drink his "real tea." When he views the various things around him, metaphors no longer arise to create depth and relation; instead, his vision is empty and objectifying, distant and disengaged: "My eyes rest on it and pass on" (166).

Crusoe composes a portrait of the artist caught between a permanent loss and the desire to represent what was lost. The artist is at odds with the making of art as Bishop instructs us to practice it in "One Art":

> practice losing farther, losing faster:
> places, and names, and where it was you meant
> to travel. None of these will bring disaster.   (178)

Bishop's artist is doomed to be always a traveler, always an exile, and thus always aware of the margins or boundaries of experience. The artist is doomed further by isolation, by being misunderstood, or by becoming a curiosity. The Crusoe of the island was defined by solitude and self-pity; Crusoe in England, in contrast, as Mazzaro notes, is unable to accept the judgment of the museum keeper.[21] Crusoe seeks to redefine himself in terms of connections with others, even while those connections are inevitably stained by loss. Bishop's exclamation in "One Art"—"*Write* it!" (178)—expresses the role of the artist after modernism. The insistence is on the gestural and bodily *ekphrasis,* and on the necessary materiality of the survival of sign and self.

Crusoe's life, in the final stanza, becomes the object of catalogers and historians. His creations are reduced to desiccated objects to be gawked at in museums. Physically they shrink and decay: his shoes "shrivelled," the goatskin trousers "shedding," the parasol looking "like a plucked and skinny fowl" (166). Crusoe's creations, of both fancy and survival, are not durable. Durability depends upon place, context, and use. Crusoe and his creations have been misplaced or placed out of context, in exile or in the museum. Within the context of the island, Crusoe was not an artist, nor were his creations works of art. Art would seem either private, as the poem is duplicitly the reveries of a misplaced Crusoe, or defined by the ownership of things that have lost their aesthetic and practical uses and values. Crusoe remarks, when seeing his objects on display, "How can anyone want such things?" (166). Crusoe's telling use of *want* emphasizes that we possess art out of a perceived need or lack. Nonetheless, his artifacts mirror our own lost (presupposing they were once to be had) tools of survival.

Bishop argues that the notion of ownership of art obscures the production of an object and our relationship with objects. Art becomes a privileged owning of some thing; and in its privileging, the object is misplaced or fetishized as the target of the idealizing gaze. However an object is defined, once it is labeled as art its intended value or use is diminished; the object becomes an artifact or a marker in the culture and ideology it comes to rest in. Art is a relic or parergon, or as Bishop states in "The Imaginary Iceberg," "Like jewelry from a grave / it saves itself perpetually and adorns / only itself" (4). Though the one art may be loss, it would be more accurate to describe art as the production and mapping of loss. Inscribed within loss is the recollection of a provisional connection. In "Santarém," Bishop further dislodges the authority of art by opening with the disclaimer "Of course I may be remembering it all wrong / after, after—how many years?" (185). Thus even the production, the insistent but parenthetical "*Write* it!" is subject to uncertainty and erosion.

In *Geography III,* Bishop puts far more emphasis on the role of human relations than in her previous collections. "Crusoe in England" is no exception, for the poem finally focuses on the relation of Friday and Crusoe. Crusoe attempts to discredit other stories about Friday's arrival by again parenthetically stating "Accounts of that have everything all wrong" (165). Crusoe hopes to establish his own authority over language and interpretation. The memory of Friday, however, reduces Crusoe's language to declarations of childlike simplicity:

> Friday was nice.
> Friday was nice, and we were friends.
> If only he had been a woman!   (165)

Crusoe's narrative reveals that Friday's arrival reinforced Crusoe's humanness (he would no longer be the single representative) and his eroticism. The exclamation reveals a further loss and yearning: Friday is *not* a woman. Crusoe's terms suggest sexual identification, though they also create and inscribe a lack. Crusoe's gaze redefines the other as an object of desire, or here of misplaced or exiled desire. Crusoe's account masks his sexual attraction to Friday or his ambivalence about heterosexual definitions, much as Bishop has masked her lesbian inscriptions.[22] The language, for Crusoe, does not allow any further disclosure of his attraction than "Pretty to watch; he had a pretty body" (166). Crusoe's account then fails, in that his desires are mastered or silenced by the dominant ideology of language and culture. Instead, Crusoe must recast his desires into the language of the dominant culture: "I wanted to propagate my kind, / and so did he, I think, poor boy" (165). The term *propagate,* fraught with its Victorian tone and botanical usage, guards Crusoe from his passions. Bishop thus reveals the provisionality and extreme limitations in language's role of constituting truth and identity. These limitations are extended further by being the grounds of absolute loss: Friday, dead for seventeen years, is only a figure of memory.

Bishop suggests an important distinction between memory and representation. Loss, for Crusoe, is the precondition for memory. In "Poem," also in *Geography III,* the represented overrides memory. The narrator in "Poem" enters the painting and probes its horizons with her attentive looking. The narrator begins with the external features of the painting, remaining literally outside its frame, describing the painting as a neglected heirloom "About the size of an old-style dollar bill, / American or Canadian" (176). The painting "has never earned any money in its life," and thus remains "Useless and free" (176). The narrator sounds a bit unsympathetic to writers and artists who don't make money (or at least earn their keep) and are apparently useless; yet the narrator suggests, romantically and ironically, that to be an artist (hence broke and useless) is also to be free. Taking the poem as a self-portrait, we see Bishop rejecting the modernists' vision of art as playing a culturally redemptive role. Art, as an "heirloom," defines itself a constituent part of memory. For Bishop, the making of art is the revelatory concordance of memories and of the loss framing those memories.

The poem describes the production of "Poem" and the reading of a "Poem" or a "Painting." The movement of the eye-I is toward the interior, from the painting as an object to the subject of the painting and an intimate knowledge about what is represented:

> It must be Nova Scotia; only there
> does one see gabled wooden houses
> painted that awful shade of brown.   (176)

The viewer here participates in the taxonomy of looking—identifying the subject and the references. Mere description or taxonomy limits aesthetic responses and our connections with the world. Though the viewing seeks to be a complete viewing, it is never absolute, certain, or full: "low hills, a thin church steeple / —that gray-blue wisp—or is it?" (176). Like Dutch landscape art of the seventeenth-century, Bishop's art does not privilege a particular view or feature, but through the poem's accumulation considers the prospect and participatoriness of observation. Memory initiates the process of interconnection and observation. Memory transforms one dab of titanium white into a barn, thus commencing the essentially metaphorical event of looking—the movement across an abyssal threshold between discretes. Bishop here posits memory as a liminal moment swerving us from loss to a provisional interconnection:

> Heavens, I recognize the place, I know it!
> It's behind—I can almost remember the farmer's name.
> His barn backed on that meadow. There it is,
> titanium white, one dab.   (176)

Georges Braque expresses visually what Bishop's "Poem" moves toward: to paint the objects' "relationships to each other and to the space surrounding them . . . to *paint* these distances or spaces, to make them as real and concrete for the spectator as the objects themelves. . . . to convey the sensation of having walked around his subjects, of having seen or 'felt' the spaces between them," unlike Picasso's hierarchical endeavor to provide some "ultimate pictorial truth."[23] At this point in the poem, however, the painting remains an illusion for the viewer, for the viewer asks "Would that be Miss Gillespie's house?" (177). The activity of remembering, nonetheless, initiates relations:

> I never knew him. We both knew this place,
> apparently, this literal small backwater,
> looked at it long enough to memorize it,
> our years apart. How strange. And it's still loved,
> or its memory is (it must have changed a lot).   (177)

The contemplation of a particular place connects the two distant relatives: the niece and uncle, the poet and painter, writing and looking. The place, not art, is finally what is loved; even though life and memory become "so compressed / they've turned into each other" (177), the narrator comes to know the vitality of the artifice she looks at.

In the final lines of the poem, the language has turned from description and exclamation to a language of renewal:

> but how live, how touching in detail
> —the little that we get for free,
> the little of our earthly trust. Not much.
> About the size of our abidance
> along with theirs: the munching cows,
> the iris, crisp and shivering, the water
> still standing from spring freshets,
> the yet-to-be-dismantled elms, the geese.   (177)

Unlike the Keatsian condition of beauty, the viewer extends the painting beyond its frozen idealized moment: destructive forces intrude, the diseased elms will be dismantled and the geese will disappear. The painting, like the poem and memory, is a trace of something before its loss. Though Bishop insists that loss is inescapable, art offers, paradoxically, a continuity of place and object outside of time or before the invention of time. Art is then the place of infinite probings and glances of the eye, and as such it is not distinct from life—thus, like Bishop, we ask "which is which?"

Bishop seeks to create dialogical relationships with others. In her poems, not only does the poet look but the world's return of that regard and glance is at issue. The homely fish avoids the narrator's stare, the moose approaches and "sniffs at / the bus's hot hood" (172), Crusoe's knife "won't look at me at all" (166), and in "At the Fishhouses" the seal "stood up in the water and regarded me / steadily, moving his head a little" (65). This issue recalls Merleau-Ponty's discussions of Cézanne and painting: "it is the mountain itself which from out there makes itself seen by the painter; it is the mountain he interrogates with his gaze." [24] Merleau-Ponty describes the moment of mutual regard as a doubly self-reflexive moment. Bishop's poetry reveals this process of looking or the movement of placing, and so establishes a more primordial form of understanding. At the end of "At the Fishhouses," the narrator moves from the shore and its human population, to the seal, and finally to the elemental, the water itself:

> If you should dip your hand in,
> your wrist would ache immediately,
> your bones would begin to ache and your hand would burn
> as if the water were a transmutation of fire
> that feeds on stones and burns with a dark gray flame.
> If you tasted it, it would first taste bitter,
> then briny, then surely burn your tongue.
> It is like what we imagine knowledge to be:
> dark, salt, clear, moving, utterly free,
> drawn from the cold hard mouth
> of the world, derived from the rocky breasts
> forever, flowing and drawn, and since
> our knowledge is historical, flowing, and flown.   (65–66)

Knowledge for Bishop comes to be "derived" from concretes and is itself phenomenal: "dark, salt, clear, moving," the sea itself, the primordial grounding of form, formlessness, and life. In the phenomenal resides mystery: the constant and erosive flux; thus, the object can never be simply objectified or held fixed and distant. Likewise, our knowledge is "flowing, and flown"; subject to change and decay, knowledge is temporal and governed by linguistic constructions. The relation between things, such as knowledge and sea, rather than distinctions, is expressed in the final repetitive and connective music of "flowing and drawn . . . flowing, and flown."

Definition exists only in terms of relation, where each thing is linked to another, shadows the other, ebbs from the other, and overflows with the other:

> The big fish tubs are completely lined
> with layers of beautiful herring scales
> and the wheelbarrows are similarly plastered

with creamy iridescent coats of mail,
with small iridescent flies crawling on them.   (64)

The scales plaster everything here, and everything turns iridescent. Seeing links things physically and syntactically with the repetition of "iridescent." The connectedness blooms etymologically,
for "iridescent" links with the iris plant, the iris of the eye, and
the rainbow.[25] The rich descriptions link the narrator to the world
described as, analogously, seventeenth-century Dutch paintings
re-present the world. Taxonomic detailing draws the narrator (or
viewer) into the landscape and begins the process of meditative
self-reflexivity—where, as Merleau-Ponty writes, "the perception of a thing opens me up to being." Everything resides in the
events of being, in the commonality of the perceptual field of
one another. Thus, Merleau-Ponty continues, "the perception of
the other founds mortality by realizing the paradox of an alter
ego . . . by placing my perspectives and my incommunicable solitude in the visual field of another and of all the others."[26] The solitude of the poet, mapmaker, and traveler necessitates not only
active looking but also the lucid regarding of the copiousness
of others. The visual description in "At the Fishhouses," and
throughout Bishop's poetry, insists the observer enter into the
perceptual field and come into relation with others, and thus,
however provisionally, stave off isolation, silence, and death.

CHAPTER TWO

John Ashbery's
Artes Poeticae
of Self and Text

Of recent poets, none is so tellingly self-reflexive as John Ashbery, nor has any generated such an enormous and far-ranging
critical response. We are asked to invent and salvage meaning
from the myriad possibilities inscribed on the astonishing surfaces of his poems. The cornucopia of readings place us in the role
of inventor manqué—while also preserving the more traditional
roles of participant and spectator. Ashbery's poetry names its
role—and thus mirrors us as readers and critics—as one of engaged and continuous speculation. The poem exists as the other
that we must regard so that we, in turn, may glimpse our own
silhouettes. The word of a poem is an abyssal mirror into which
we ceaselessly fall. In counterdistinction to the play of mirroring
gazes, Ashbery suggests that the music of the poem can never be
contained within the frame of the word. The plethora of readings,
as with the abundance of words, arises from the music the poet's
words seek; the music, however, always remains different and
outside the logocentrism of the poem. "Self-Portrait in a Convex
Mirror" describes this supreme double bind, where speculation
folds into the mourning of the music by the poet:

That is the tune but there are no words.
The words are only speculation
(From the Latin *speculum,* mirror):
They seek and cannot find the meaning of the music.[1]

Ashbery meditates on our mortality—both in intimate voices and thematically as a cultural issue of the diminishment of significa- tion and representation. The text and the self mirror each other in their speculations and in their faltering provisionality.

The ontological difficulties[2] poetry presents appear in Ash- bery's poetry; these difficulties recall the complexity of Elizabeth Bishop's defamiliarizing glance, which dissolves the certainty of the world. In Bishop's poem "The Monument," the viewer must engage a mysterious object whose presence makes for both her- meneusis and the difficulty of hermeneusis.[3] "The Monument" is an assembled but incomplete form—there is something always left unseen or to be added—and as such it typifies the postmodern vision, which stresses performance and the reader's or viewer's role as a means of subverting signification and metaphysics.

Ashbery's project demands performance and process, but with- out Bishop's provisionally celebratory activities of observation. Like Bishop, Ashbery discovers ambiguity and the impossibility of definition, and hence suggests the extreme provisionality of presence. In Bishop's poetry, ambiguity and provisionality under- score an ironic pessimism and a profound mysteriousness that su- percedes signification. The world of things, for Ashbery, however, becomes overwhelming and creates a supreme anxiety: What are we to make of this world of "Millions of facts of distributed light" (RM 14, "Civilization and Its Discontents")? In Bishop's poetry, we continually cross thresholds and penetrate new spaces with our traveling eye, and in turn we are incorporated—if we look closely enough—into each new space. Ashbery's poetry overlays surfaces; the travels are across maps rather into a map. Hence his work emphasizes the surface and the illusions of the impenetra- bility of the whole combination of surfaces—a quality analogous to the collages of Kurt Schwitters. It is not uncommon to find Ashbery being described as a *collagiste*.[4] The concerns of Ashbery and Schwitters, however, go beyond the formal constructions of a collage.

In Schwitters's collages, relationships replace meaning, at least metaphysical and hierarchical meaning. Revealingly, Schwitters calls his works "MERZ-pictures," derived from the second syllable of *Kommerz,* or commerce.[5] Insignificant and impoverished objects are named by the meaningless and fractured *merz.* Obviously, Schwitters suggests the daily commerce we have with tickets, buttons, lumber, wires, anything from our midden-heaps and factories, our daily traffic. *Commerce* also implies histories, lost and new, as well as transactional movements among themselves and between themselves and us. These transactions illuminate the materiality of the mysterious and the transcendent. *Merz* also echoes the violent and excremental: *merde.* The first half of the twentieth-century certainly can be described in these two terms—and as Schwitters was a victim of this century, the apocalyptic reading of *merz* cogently reveals an art of salvaging, interjection, and survival. For Schwitters, the significance is the object, gesture, and moment—these are what have been rescued. The word, like Schwitters's objects, is no longer subjected to a hierarchical conception of meaning that displaces the very presence of the word, its writtenness, and its place in the script of writings.

The modernist preoccupation with the exploration of the arbitrariness of the sign found in Mallarmé, Kafka, Genet, and Beckett, reveals, as Ihab Hassan argues, the sign's muteness and even silence in a world that has slowed to an utter and unfulfilled stasis.[6] In the verbal collages Ashbery orchestrates, the dialogical relationships between signs and between the readers and signs presuppose movement and transformation. In this constant flux of signs and roles, the self becomes a prolific devourer, to borrow W. H. Auden's phrase, appropriating all that surrounds it, hence collapsing any self-definition and distinction. As we shall see, such a moment initiates further meditations on the possibility of desire, emotion, and interconnection in the world. The world is seen as an arena of representational possibilities, where each sign, each word, each assumed voice is an act of role-playing and part of the activity of replenishment. The intrusion of irony—undercutting, reversals, flattening, and self-mocking or self-critical turns—expresses the tension between the impoverishment of discourse and the necessity of replenishment. The self appropriates and decimates while also noticing and passing on this extended vision to others. Rhetorically, irony allows for the extension of the meditation, for it reflexively enjoins emotion and redirects the poem. Thus, irony, the self's trope, propels each poem. Irony marks the presence of the self and the poem's critical awareness of its tenuous making—and its potential dissolution. Ashbery's poetry thus veers near disaster—apocalyptic and ordinary—while seeking a sustaining or connecting discourse.

In Ashbery's first collection, *Some Trees,* the reader confronts the core drama in his poetry: while we expect an allegorical revelation, meaning is ever-dissolving or its approach is always fore-shortened. The poetry expresses an ongoing dialogical relation: a perpetually in-forming and dis-closing *ars poetica.* "Pantoum" employs the traditional form of a pantoum; yet, through its prescribed repetition and placement of lines, our expectations of meaning are subverted: the repetition of lines is used, not to build either a narrative or a meditation, but to orchestrate juxtapositions. Juxtaposition, especially in Ashbery's poetry, is self-reflexive and returns us to the signs themselves. And in "Pantoum," because of its prescribed authority of structure, the words and their syntactic relationships are not lost to the demands of the signified.

The dynamics of a pantoum require repetition and accumulation. Formally and imagistically, the poem's self-reflexivity creates a movement that enfolds and a music that echoes:

> Eyes shining without mystery,
> Footprints eager for the past
> Through the vague snow of many clay pipes,
> And what is in store?
>
> Footprints eager for the past,
> The usual obtuse blanket.

> And what is in store
> For those dearest to the king?   (*ST* 30)

The returning or repeated lines throughout the poem are also "footprints eager for the past," as though by repetition they should gain meaning, yet all that is in store is simply those footprints and the paths they have made. The intimation of a narrative adventure—"what is in store / For those dearest to the king?"—drops from sight and has no closure, hence no definition outside the recurrent line "Why, the court, trapped in a silver storm, is dying!" (ST 30). The narrative drama is elided, favoring only the play of telling—these are the parts of a story that gave pleasure and so are remembered and retold.

Instead of attempting to capture the subject, as does the unremitting gaze of the painter in "Sestina," Ashbery's poetry describes the performance of writing—its movements, shifts, and connections—and thus creates an expressly grammatological poetry:

> These are amazing: each
> Joining a neighbor, as though speech
> Were a still performance.   (*ST* 51)

Here, in the title poem, "Some Trees," *still* describes the complex paradox of writing: the word suggests persistence while also meaning silence and the lack of movement. Writing, too, is both ongoing and motionless. In turn, the copula is celebrated, for it is the means of linking and marks presence:

> you and I
> Are suddenly what the trees try
>
> To tell us we are:
> That their merely being there
> Means something; that soon
> We may touch, love, explain.   (*ST* 51)

The poet desires the seeming fullness of interconnection or being that the other—the trees, the world—possesses. The potential of the copula amazes the poet, who exclaims his hope and want of connection and discourse. The "still performance" of the trees or their phenomena of being as writing recalls to the poet the potential of language to form a union, a potential that we have essentially lost, but that we nonetheless try to reinvoke.

The use of parody, for Ashbery, indicates our extreme condition of living in a world overrun by meanings and representations that nonetheless diminish our presence and spirit. Among them we lose all sense of scale, as in "The Picture of Little J. A. in a Prospect of Flowers," where the writer

> cannot escape the picture
> Of my small self in that bank of flowers:
> My head among the blazing phlox
> Seemed a pale and gigantic fungus.　　　　　　(*ST* 28)

Parody and irony offer provisional control over language that otherwise seems to spin out of control. By anchoring the poem in pastoral (or mock-pastoral) tradition, by appropriating Marvell's "The Picture of Little T. C. in a Prospect of Flowers," Ashbery sketches his own ancestry or genealogy of writing as well as suggesting the erosion and redefinition of writing in that genealogy: "only in the light of lost words / Can we imagine our rewards" (*ST* 29). Rather than suggesting a return to the conventional, Ashbery emphasizes that our discourse is in a crisis if we are compelled to enact such a return and, indeed, to admit that "as change is horror, / Virtue is really stubbornness" (*ST* 29).

Parodic retrieval and defamiliarization also provide the means for pointing to the surfaceness of a poem, to the language itself. Ashbery's aesthetics, however, do not marginalize the sign but seek the sign's—and analogously the self's and the text's—presence and interconnection. The poems in *The Tennis Court Oath* experiment extensively with parody and the juxtaposition of different ranges of language:

> How much longer will I be able to inhabit the divine sepulcher
> Of life, my great love? Do dolphins plunge bottomward

> To find the light? Or is it rock
> That is searched? Unrelentingly? Huh. And if some day
>
> Men with orange shovels come to break open the rock
> Which encases me, what about the light that comes in then?
> What about the smell of the light?
> What about the moss?   (*TC* 25)

The symbolist language of this Lazarus-Christ in "'How Much Longer Will I Be Able to Inhabit the Divine Sepulcher . . .'" is subverted by the reductive and nearly nonverbal "Huh," which displaces criticism by self-reflexively commenting on the text. The interjection criticizes criticism by parodying its motives for explanation, but serves also as a juxtaposition of a completely different range of language. The poem is not questioned on the grounds of being meaningless; instead, the poem's self-criticism pursues the possibility of meaning.

The activity of self-criticism in Ashbery's work is a process of rewriting the self that continuously unfolds and accumulates. With each collection of poems, and within each poem, Ashbery's project continues to unveil the quest or the desire for presence:

> And we say goodbye
>
> Shaking hands in front of the crashing of the waves
> That gives our words lonesomeness, and make these flabby hands
>   seem ours—
> Hands that are always writing things
> On mirrors for people to see later—
>
> Do you want them to water
> Plant, tear listlessly among the exchangeable ivy—
> Carrying food to mouth, touching genitals—
> But no doubt you have understood
>
> It all now and I am a fool.
>
> (*TC* 26, "'How Much Longer Will I Be Able
> to Inhabit the Divine Sepulcher . . .'")

Language, as this *ars poetica* indicates, is transitory and always sliding away from us, thus revealing our culture's impoverished sexuality and, hence, our mortality. We glimpse ourselves mirrored only in the writing left by someone else. Fred Moramarco remarks that those "shaking hands suggest both camaraderie— our mortality links us all—and the fear and trembling that result from the confrontation with immensity of time and space."[7] Ashbery's vision of language stresses the importance of interconnection in the face of mortality. The self-reflexive mode, by rejecting a solipsistic examination of language, emphasizes the relation, not the dichotomy, of self and other. Ashbery's use of the inclusive first person plural pronoun—"our words . . . make these flabby hands seem ours"—as well as his general shifting of pronouns, dismantles the subject / object distinction. A dialogical, not a hierarchical, relationship results from taking the extreme recourse of dismantling language's inborn, incestuous referential system, which authorized the taboo of the other.

Our condition is defined by our desire for language to affirm the presence of ourselves and our world. Nonetheless, Ashbery's poems are, in Maurice Blanchot's terms, "l'écriture du désastre," or the writing of the disaster; in contrast to Nietzsche's complaint that we have words only for extremes of feelings, Blanchot writes that the opposite may be the case: "that we have no words for the extreme; that dazzling joy and great pain burn up every term and render them all mute."[8] Language is to be mistrusted; it also preserves enigmas while seeking to explain, and thus it might be considered a gift. In the closing lines of "A Last World," a mysterious letter is about to be delivered and read amidst flux, change, and apocalyptic fire:

> Everything is being blown away;
> A little horse trots up with a letter in its mouth, which is read
>   with eagerness
> As we gallop into the flame.   (*TC* 58)

The letter claims its importance as writing, as banal communication, and as law. It is a countertext to the poem and to the world.

In both text and world, everything slides toward apocalypse and undifferentiated mass: "The sky is a giant rocking horse" that then becomes the horse of delivery on which we "gallop into the flame." In this world of shifting grounds, the letter (a missive or an element of an alphabet?) is greeted with eagerness and as a sign of hope, stability, and truth. The same eagerness is found in "Rain" and in "Europe," where a letter and postcards are always on the verge of arrival. The provisionality of hope and language is emblematized by "The missing letter—the crumb of confidence" (*TC* 30, "Rain"). The letter itself is important, not its contents nor the exegetic piercing of the surface of discourse: the letter's journey parallels our own reading of these poems, where the movement across the surface remains the primary experience. Reading holds out the hope of continuity (and immortality) and is interminable, for no final revelation subsumes us.

The expected and longed-for sign or letter arrives from the silence of the white page or from the "flat sea rushing away" (*TC* 31, "Rain"), and is the event of optimism and a signal of renewal. Throughout "Rain," the image of the sea recurs as a motif of skating across surface, "over the shuddering page of sea" (*TC* 29). The sea or any surface implies a mysterious depth we are compelled to examine and interpret, to the neglect of the surface itself. Ashbery celebrates the surface by invoking its materiality rather than its traditionally vaunted transparency: it is "the great city / I build to you every moment" (*TC* 31). These poems pursue the letter, the place of inscription, and thus reinstate the sign as the precondition of speech. The poems of *The Tennis Court Oath,* through their radically multiple inscriptions, enforce their presence as collections or surfaces of graphemes.

In the multiplicity of the inscriptions come both fragmentation and recovery of the otherness of the sign. Ashbery, in his insistence on process and on the energies released through fragmentation, is an Orphic poet—not the Orpheus who sang to the beasts, but the one whose songs mirror (or arrive after) his dismemberment. Coming from the severed corpse of Orpheus, these songs describe mortality. The poet, now a mock-Orpheus, sees all attempts at revelation fail because he discovers the limitations of the performance of language: "I try to describe for you, / But you will not listen, you are like the swan" (*TC* 35, "White Roses"). The address of the poet to his lover or an audience fails, yet the poet reveals the conjunction of the erotic and the deathly inherent in writing and reading through the metaphor. The audience or lover plays the role of the ravishing god disguised as the swan—yet implicitly and paradoxically every poem is the poet's swan song; thus, the poet mirrors the silent, but fraught with potential, swan.

The long poem "The Skaters"—by far the most demanding poem in *Rivers and Mountains*—provides an important grounding for Ashbery's later poems because it maps the self's parodic returns, mirrorings, and self-portraitures. The opening lines of "The Skaters" initiate a meditative proposition the poem develops and elaborates upon. In this poem, language becomes a "kind of flagellation" (*RM* 34), which combines the erotic with punishment as well as suggesting continuous movement and propulsion. The poem rejects the notions of progression toward a transcendent absolute in favor of "an entity of sound / Into which being enters, and is apart" (*RM* 34). Within these interactions and interconnections is the mysteriousness of transformation, as when "the water surface ripples, the whole light changes" (*RM* 34). The notion of cause and effect as well as the opposition of subject and object is subverted. The universe sways back and forth in Herakleitian flux; what would seem the affected affects; the observer mirrors the observed and becomes the observed. Truth is then mutable; or, the only truth is the surface activity or the loci of intersecting utterances. Though the mysterious potential of the surface is celebrated, there remains always the ironic awareness of the mutability of the surface and hence our own mortality: "The waves of morning harshness / Float away like coal-gas into the sky. / But how much survives? How much of any one of us survives?" (*RM* 34).

Ashbery attempts to collect and fashion some discernible order from the cast-off and fallen representations. Collection evolves into a marking whose repetition and rhythm sustains our presence. The action of the skaters describes and inscribes the most clear image of play upon surface:

> Lengthening arches. The intensity of minor acts. As skaters
>   elaborate their distances,
> Taking a separate line to its end. Returning to the mass, they join
>   each other
> Blotted in an incredible mess of dark colors, and again
>   reappearing to take the theme
> Some little distance, like fishing boats developing from the land
>   different parabolas,
> Taking the exquisite theme far, into farness, to Land's End, to the
>   ends of the earth!   (*RM* 37)

The journey of the skaters, like that of the letter, always entails distance, separation, recoupling, and repetition. The skaters leave only temporary incisions of their solitary journeys and crossed paths on the ice. Like the skaters tracing the sign for infinity, we are asked to journey literally into the words, "far, into farness" or "to Land's End, to the ends of the earth!"

If the reading of the poem entails a journey into words rather than a recognition of a mimetic representation of the world, then the poem self-reflexively enfolds its own criticism and exegesis:

> It is time now for a general understanding of
> The meaning of all this. The meaning of Helga, importance of the
>   setting, etc.
> A description of the blues. Labels on bottles
> And all kinds of discarded objects that ought to be described.
> But can one ever be sure of which ones?   (*RM* 38)

The question of which ones—what is to be selected and described and what is to be left out—emerges as the central critical question, but one that the writer refuses to answer: "this is an important aspect of the question / Which I am not ready to discuss, am not at all ready to, / This leaving-out business" (*RM* 39). Selection marks presence and absence, interconnection and fragmentation, or discourse and silence. It imparts authority, as does explanation, and by definition it also excludes. This "leaving-out business" forms the surface of the poem as well as foregrounding poiesis. All criticism, then, forms an extension of the surface's inscription, for criticism is already enfolded in the text and given a place; and as elaborations of previous texts, any text implicitly questions originality. Since explanations or meanings are not readily forthcoming, our desires are deferred and, as such, unfulfilled. While stressing the activity of representation arising from emotional and social desires, the surface play of various roles or voices (the poem's narrator shifts, for example, from poet to critic to outright detractor) dismantles the twin notions of the unity of voice and of rhetorical persuasion:

> What is the matter with plain old-fashioned cause-and-effect?
> Leaving one alone with romantic impressions of the trees, the
> sky?
> Who, actually, is going to be fooled one instant by these phony
> explanations,
> Think them important?   (*RM* 39–40)

The multiplicity of voices also promotes a continual revising or refiguring of the poem. Thus the poem shows itself, deictically, to us as an incomplete collection of desire-laden gestures.

As the poem's movement defers death or closure, the poem's beginning is always rearticulated.[9] Movement pushes against the confines of representation; thus, "The figure 8 is a perfect symbol / Of the freedom to be gained of this kind of activity," as are "perspective lines . . . another and different kind of example / . . . In which we escape ourselves—putrefying mass of prevarications etc.— / In remaining close to the limitations imposed" (*RM* 47). We are caught in a paradox that disrupts the conventional dichotomies of literal-figurative or life-death. These dichotomies, belonging to an empiricist ideology, are framed in the pictorial metaphor of perspective lines that "are said to 'vanish.' / The point where they meet is their vanishing point" (*RM* 48). Though our mortality is certainly one of Ashbery's most powerful and consuming meditations, he asks us to avoid the use of oppositional models to contemplate death and survival. These models offer little that is either new or useful:

> Looked at from this angle the problem of death and survival
> Ages slightly. For the solutions are millionfold, like waves of wild
>   geese returning in spring.
> Scarcely we know where to turn to avoid suffering, I mean
> There are so many places.   (*RM* 48)

Does Ashbery here block the argument with a sentimental rejoinder reinstating optimism? Or does the return of the geese, the interjection of a natural phenomenon, point to a different set of readings that implies a different perspective of the world? Or is the poet turning upon the poem, interjecting the ironic qualification, rendering the meditation moot or exactingly insolvable? The poem, the journey, or our daily actions overflow with possibilities and memories that can arrest our movement, yet are the very landmarks we must pass in a landscape where all the details are "Filling up the available space for miles" (*RM* 49). The poet sees innumerable epistemologies clotting the landscape and crowding out central questions of self-definition, suffering, and death with their "true and valueless shapes" (*RM* 49). The poem, while subversively accumulating objects, critiques the culture that produces these shapes "that pester us with their raisons d'être." The poem self-reflexively critiques its own status in such an inflated, thus valueless, culture.

At the moment of dissolution when drama and writing appear unable to continue—the intended messages so rife with lacunae, so overdetermined, or so overused—the postman returns bearing yet another letter "in his outstretched hand," offering again the possibility of communication and interconnection and thus bridging the distances implied by closure and departure. The letter, as seen in the earlier poems of *The Tennis Court Oath,* is a moment of delivery; fittingly, it is the postman who plays this role of the deus ex machina of mock epics. The letter is the precondition to interconnection, and it is the emblem of connectedness. Ashbery parodies the desire to present the gift of intended meaning while also acknowledging the strength of that desire. Though a parody, the unopened letter or whatever the postman bears is also the gift of language—it is the poem that we open and with which we correspond. In the outstretched arm of the postman we see prefigured the englobing arm of Parmigianino in "Self-Portrait in a Convex Mirror."

The parodic returns in "The Skaters"—to boyhood pastimes, to journeys always on the point of embarkation, to exegetic departures—map the playfulness of texts. As a series of ruptured contingencies and sutured uncertainties, the poem and Ashbery's poetry in general create a drama in the texture of language. The poem is itself the secret, the meaning, the invention that we try to invent. The poem explicitly and self-reflexively reasserts its own logic by continually shifting its movement; thus, it mirrors our own designs for self-knowledge and self-definition. The secret of the poem is the sum of the space it has moved through. This existential gesture, however, is futile in attaining any transcendent knowledge. The secret can never be told. Similarly, the body, Ashbery writes, is fully present but unseen as a whole; thus, its truth is hidden: "you must shield with your body if necessary . . . / . . . the secret your body is" (*RM* 51). The poem and the body (or corpus) are before us, yet always and already other; thus, neither can ever be seen as a totality or fully known:

> Another time I thought I could see myself.
> This too proved illusion, but I could deal with the way
> I keep returning on myself like a plank
> Like a small boat blown away from the wind.　　　(*RM* 59–60)

When we recognize that language is constantly sliding—and it does so not only in Ashbery's poems, but as we would generalize from them, also in the forest of words by which we define ourselves—we also recognize that time is part of what language speaks about, namely, the nexus of death, dissolution, and transformation. Each moment must be seized, but with the knowledge of curtailed expectation or hope or with the patience of writing that recognizes that language, at least in our particularly inflated epoch, too easily diminishes emotion and intimacy:

> One seizes these moments as they come along, afraid
> To believe too much in the happiness that might result
> Or confide too much of one's love and fear, even in
> Oneself.   (*RM* 61)

Ashbery suggests that time is escaping us at a nightmarish speed, and, while overwhelmed with the consumption and production of images, we are severed from history and distracted from recognizing mortality or global disaster:

> The sands are frantic
> In the hourglass. But there is time
> To change, to utterly destroy
> That too-familiar image
> Lurking in the glass
> Each morning, at the edge of the mirror.   (*RM* 61)

Though caught and fixed in the glass, the poem, nonetheless, holds out the possibility of a transformation that is intimate and founded on interconnection: "The delta of living into everything" (*RM* 63). The moment of eloquence must also be an ethical moment of writing if it is to transform or re-vision language.

Words glisten on the page like the infinite figure eights the skaters trace. There is a mutual reflexivity; the poet's self is mirrored, and in turn, the self mirrors all the rhythms and objects found. The self seeks to establish order, correspondence, and destination, but any conclusion or fulfillment of this desire is as illusory as the seeming convergence of parallel lines somewhere on the horizon. Instead, the poem and the self pretend conclusion and definition: any moment of indeterminacy offers also provisional relations and definitions. "The Skaters" closes with an imperfect memory, or rather reopens narrative possibilities through misremembering. The night sky, like a giant magic writing pad, is the site of memory and destination: "The constellations are rising / In perfect order: Taurus, Leo, Gemini" (*RM* 63). Though the poet ironically confuses the order of the rising constellations, the confused ordering describes a movement that reinterprets the bounds of the authorized and given order of perception. Ashbery's use of stars echoes Rilke's invocation of the stars as a form of un-closing, or swerving from conclusion, as Elizabeth Sewell notes:

> Figures of the mind may be thought of as being the terminus of one end of the scale of nature. The stars, those infinitely remote elemental fiery powers, are the other. Between the two lies the whole range of form, in the energy of matter and the energies of mind. Interpretation is given for this task. So the Orpheus myth ends with two things: the affirmation of unity of all the forms in nature, between the galaxies and the mythological lyre—the power of the human mind figuring in its own characteristic function of language—which joins them, and there is also the floating, singing head, which is poetry and thinking, prophetic and unquenchable.[10]

In Ashbery's arbitrary order, what is celebrated is the materiality of words, the substance of their song. Objects of the most distant nature offer ironic hope with the repetition of their names; by misremembering the known, we navigate toward the unknown.

The far more meditative and elegiac poetry in *The Double Dream of Spring* constitutes a shift away from outright textual collages found in the earlier volumes.[11] What Ashbery has retained from those experiments is the startling awareness of rhetorical, syntactic, and tonal shifts and disjunctions, all of which leads to the uneasy apprehension that any single moment may be more than the poem's sum of moments. *The Double Dream of Spring* takes its title directly from one of the more reflexive and rhetorical of de Chirico's metaphysical paintings. De Chirico depicts a study of the finished painting we view and what is hidden by the illusion—the paint, the process of painting, and the presence of the painting itself. The study, which only outlines or abstracts the object of speculation, blocks our view of the subject; the studio, landscape, and sky, which spill from the edges of the study, are nonetheless also contained within the study: the study literally stands in place of the subject; thus, it is a metonymy for both subject and painting. Our gaze is interrupted and our desire subverted; there is no fulfilling culmination of perspective lines except in what is both tentative and patently put forth as artifice. De Chirico intercepts our gratification and parodies our impulses for conclusive exegesis. De Chirico suggests the anxiety of perception and interpretation: the certainty that seems to arise from the exegetic framed study due to its mathematical rigidity and control is undercut by its obviously incomplete state. The anxiety of incompletion recalls Ashbery's use of Louis David's study *The Tennis Court Oath,* in which the various figures are partially sketched in, partially layered onto the surface, the whole work remaining incomplete. Ashbery cites these paintings as examples for his own *ars poetica*—they become maps or tropes for our reading and for the work we read. What we read, Ashbery implies, is already an exegesis.

These *artes poeticae,* enfolded in the poems, are openings where each poem acknowledges its beginnings as "something / Nobody can translate" (*DD* 20). The opening stanzas of "Summer" evoke a plenitudinous pastoral scene whose landscape is likened to the making of the poem. Poiesis parallels a "sound like the wind / Forgetting in the branches" (*DD* 20) or a music both present and disappearing. Only afterwards is this sound put down on the page as something with an intended meaning. Writing is not questioned here so much as is the assignment of an intended, an inevitably mistranslated, meaning. Summer, like the inspiring sound, the poem, or oneself, is present only in time and for a brief time. Only a shadow of meaning is possible; though even that is "ample," it is "hardly seen." Meaning arrives posthumously, in "the sobering 'later on,' / When you consider what a thing meant, and put it down" (*DD* 20). Any vision that pretends completeness contrasts with the multiplicity, contingency, and provisionality of the moment, where all "life is divided up / Between you and me, and among all the others out there" (*DD* 20). The acute passage of time and the seemingly unbridgable divisions between the self and the other create an elegiac sensibility.

The poem inscribes us in its Herakleitian mirror: "And the face / Resembles yours, the one reflected in the water" (*DD* 20). The shifting pronoun *you*, both a disjunctive element in the poem and a carnival mask to be worn by many, creates a mystery and subverts any definition of the poem's intention and any idealization of the poem's readers. By foregrounding the ambiguity of language and self through the use of the Janus-like *you*, the poem forms a dialogue among the narrative self inscribing the language, the otherness of the "you" as that of the reader, and the mask of the writer as an other. Ashbery recasts into language its own inherent event of self-reflexive relationships.

By dramatizing language, the poet seeks to understand the past, the "corrosive mass" in which "he first discovered how to breathe" (*DD* 13, "The Task"). Both in a relatively minor poem of the collection, "Summer," and in the clearly propositional opening poem, "The Task," Ashbery sets out to establish the self in relation to the other. Caught in the ever-sliding course of time, the narrators of each poem become provisional and urbane pilgrims fully cognizant of their ironic and interminable pilgrimages. Ashbery invokes discrete moments that might subvert the inexorable movement of time:

> I plan to stay here a little while
> For these are moments only, moments of insight,
> And there are reaches to be attained,
> A last level of anxiety that melts
> In becoming, like miles under the pilgrim's feet.   (*DD* 13)

We long to retrieve past moments, since they may be sources of our identity and self-knowledge. We hope, Ashbery suggests, that by continuing to define ourselves through narratives, we will unravel the question of "where we got it wrong" (*DD* 15, "Spring Day"). But due to an inexorable movement toward completion and summation as well as to the overwhelming ornamentation, the mere idea of a personal or explicitly historical narrative is "floundering in the wind of its colossal death" (*DD* 15, "Spring Day"). This notion is not one more announcement of the death of the art, but a recognition of the limitations of personal narratives and cultural metanarratives as well as the recognition of the necessity of reinventing the essential ways we know ourselves and others.

Writing offers us its materiality and its apparent durability. We can return to writing and find "that sublime hope made of the light that sprinkles the trees" (*DD* 39, "French Poems"). Writing's diachronic and deictic movement also paradoxically diminishes us, in that through it we edge closer to the period and the consuming silence. "Definition of Blue" illustrates the anxiety arising from the presence of writing and also from the imaginative endeavor, for the poem's narrator asserts "there is no point in looking to imaginative new methods / Since all of them are in constant use" (*DD* 53). Each method, in its own use and "erosion," becomes "a medium / In which it is possible to recognize oneself" (*DD* 53). Rather than lamenting limitations, the poet recognizes that "Each new diversion adds its accurate touch to the ensemble, and so / A portrait, smooth as glass, is built up out of multiple corrections / And it has no relation to the space or time in which it was lived" (*DD* 53). The historical and political proposition that opened the poem—"The rise of capitalism parallels the advance of romanticism"—is overturned in favor of an ahistorical vision of the self and the endeavors of the individual. "Ashbery's subject," John Koethe notes, "seems possessed by an impulse, which it knows has to be frustrated, to *reify* itself," but this desire for reification yields a personality or image that "can only be a *surface*."[12] At some point, the narrator believes, the portrait or any speculation becomes a memorial to itself rather than an engaged interpretation of the self and the world. The poem, however, refuses to yield; instead, it closes with an existential, and hence historically responsible, statement that what remains is "the exact value of what you did and said" (*DD* 54).

Though "we cannot imagine the truth of it," we idealize "The kindness of acts long forgotten / Which give us history and faith" (*DD* 51, "Sunrise in Suburbia"), regardless of the proximity and ordinariness of these acts. In "Sunrise in Suburbia," Ashbery reinforces the demands of existential knowledge by arguing that such knowledge rescues one from the "old unwillingness to continue" (*DD* 49). Caught among the residue and debris of signs, the sunrise is reinvented or refigured as a moment of transformative and perhaps utterly destructive energy:

> It was the holiness of the day that fed our notions
> And released them, sly breath of Eros,
> Anniversary on the woven city lament, that assures our arriving
> In hours, seconds, breath, watching our salary
> In the morning holocaust become one vast furnace, engaging all
>   tears.   (*DD* 52)

In this visionary moment Eros, holiness, elegy, and holocaust converge in the daily offices of our lives. This moment of transition and transformation connects each of us, "engaging all tears," in a Kaddish or lament for city, country, and each other.

We destroy ourselves through Eros or desire, for desire reveals our transience, yet desire is also our only connection with others. Desire's temporality knots life and death together, which provokes our anxiety for presence. Ashbery asks in "Clouds,"

> How do we explain the harm, feeling
> We are always the effortless discoverers of our career,
> With each day digging the grave of tomorrow and at the same
>   time
> Preparing its own redemption, constantly living and dying?
>   (*DD* 68)

Ashbery's subject of speculation is always death and its supplement—life. Against this inexorable sliding or supplementation, Ashbery posits the imagination or the imagined moment "heavy with the mere curve of being" (*DD* 67). In this rewriting of the myth of Semele, the moment of Eros is shared by Semele and Zeus as well as the poet who "stood up to assume that imagination," the ominous clouds. The moment is future and past, in that it is being rewritten, as well as a moment that foregrounds Eros: "It was a solid light in which a man and woman could kiss / Yet dark and ambiguous as a cloakroom" (*DD* 67). Semele, who emblematizes ourselves, "Moves away, puzzled at the brown light above the fields" (*DD* 69) that portends the revelation of Zeus. Though Zeus will destroy Semele in this act of revelation and sexual union, the birth of Dionysus and the return of Semele from Hades are insured. The supreme mystery, the doubled moment of closure and dis-closure, enfolds the moment of desire and the possibility of poiesis.

Ashbery's long poem "Fragment"—complete in its implied incompletion—examines the motives for what we say is our desire for revelation:

> If there was no truth in it, only pleasure
> In the telling, might not others set out
> Across impossible oceans with this word whose power
> Was the opposite reverence to secret deities
> Of shame? Or absent-mindedness? Because the first memory
> Now, like patches, was worn, only as the inadequate
> Memento of all that was never going to be? Its
> Allusion not even blasphemous, but truly insignificant
> Beside that lake opening out broader than the sun!
> This, then, was indifference: it was what it always had been.
>
> (*DD* 92–93)

The unrecognized nature of the quest for and of the word is not pleasure—otherwise, more, no doubt, would have set about these tasks—but truth, or the hope that by peeling away "all past sets of impressions / . . . servitude and barbarism might shrink to allegorical human width" (*DD* 92). However, language fails in this task—or perhaps it is the human spirit that fails language. The eidetic sun is diminished by the mundane's surface, the devouring "lake opening out broader than the sun!" The word, imaged as a boat or vessel or container, "stood hieratically still / On the unread page of water" (*DD* 93) and reveals the sacerdotal nature of language's origins, "the first memory" that is now represented in an "inadequate / Memento of all that was never going to be." The power of words diminishes even while words are part of "the element of living, a breath / Beyond telling," that engenders and continues to portray "the externals of present" (*DD* 93). They provide us "with dwarf speculations / About the insane, invigorating whole they don't represent" (*DD* 93). The sadness of the impoverished word mirrors the sadness and horror of the passage of the moment. We, like words, edge closer to both life and death:

> The dance continues, but darker, and
> As if in a sudden lack of air. And as one figure
> Supplants another, and dies, so the postulate of each
> Tires the shuffling floor with slogans, present
> Complements mindful of our absorbing interest.   (*DD* 94)

Figurative speech and the speaker, the written and the writer, the dance and the dancer are all diminished: "a whole of raveling discontent, / The sum of all that will ever be deciphered" (*DD* 94). Time and language move toward endless versions and interpretations, thus toward incompleteness and abyss.

The final stanza of "Fragments" fuses the various meditations found throughout this collection and is one of Ashbery's most powerfully elegiac moments. The Orphic poet and exegete confronts his own limitations of vision, interpretation, and experience:

> But what could I make of this? Glaze
> Of many identical foreclosures wrestled from
> The operative hand, like a judgment but still
> The atmosphere of seeing? That two people could
> Collide in this dusk means that the time of
> Shapelessly foraging had come undone: the space was
> Magnificent and dry. On flat evenings
> In the months ahead, she would remember that that
> Anomaly had spoken to her, words like disjointed beaches
> Brown under the advancing signs of the air.   (*DD* 94)

The poet-exegete erases himself before the text and before experience. The final line recalls the conclusion of "Clouds," where the air was massive and corrosive, laden with Zeus. With the impending destruction of Semele, we have again reached the end of an epoch, one that is a parody of some already-lost pastoral golden age. The enjambed copula, "was," marks this hinged time, the line and age end yet continue into one another. The profound austerity and aridity of a landscape that is "Magnificent and dry" echoes Eliot's wastelands—except here an elegiac tone displaces the invocation of regenerative myth.

Three Poems marks another radical experiment in the *ars poetica* of self and text, while also turning away from the elegiac poetry of *The Double Dream of Spring*. In his earlier collections, the surface contains the tension between exclusion, the "leaving-out business," and accumulation. The surface of *Three Poems,* however, allows decentered but not foreshortened arguments to unfold, releasing language from the constraints of the poetic line; thus, the text demands that we examine anew the idea of poetry. Pushing against the limits of defined form is a concern of any poet, and is illustrated in the varieties of forms used throughout Ashbery's writings. In *Three Poems,* however, he generates the illusion of a complete or full text. The loss of the privileged poetic line expresses the loss of a particular lyric identity. The writing, in its plenitude and overrunning interpretive scriptings or (w)ritings, mirrors midrashic and sacred texts. The poems swerve us from responding to them within the genre of lyricism; more than any other of Ashbery's works, these must be recognized as *writings*.

The opening text, "The New Spirit," begins with the persona, the evoked rubric of the self, the "I": "I thought that if I could put it all down, that would be one way. And next the thought came to me that to leave all out would be another, and truer, way" (*TP* 3). The poet suggests confession, yet discards that voice as not useful for the "you," who could be the reader or the poet's rhetorical double. By discarding or "narrowing-down," the writer moves toward the condition of renunciation and selflessness. The poem assumes an instructional role, offering, not a private quest, but the quest(ion) of Everyman. The *ars poetica,* mirrored in the questioning of the line and the self as to their own anonymity and otherness, becomes each of ours, for the "you" and the "we" incorporate us in an intimate complex of confession, judgment, and definition: "For we judge not, lest we be judged, yet we are judged all the same, without noticing, until one day we wake up a different color, the color of the filter of the opinions and ideas everyone has ever entertained about us. And in this form we must prepare, now, to try to live" (*TP* 7–8). A willed self is impossible; it is always lost in the accumulation of other opinions of ourselves. We are not the author of ourselves but the creation of the looks accumulated by others. Likewise, the text is an accumulation of readings and scriptings.

In these passages come provisional expressions of affirmation: "to try to live" or "the look of belonging." Movement—in writing and being, if, indeed, the two can be split—is a generative energy drawn from the traces of the past; it is a "new merging, like ancestral smiles, common memories. . . . To end up with, inside each other, moving upward like penance. For the continual pilgrimage has not stopped" (*TP* 5). The beloved, the sexual other, the text, and otherness are sought by the self. Ashbery insists on a moral vision of our interconnectedness: "we must learn to live in others, no matter how abortive or unfriendly their cold, piecemeal renderings of us: they create us" (*TP* 13). Far more than a call for reciprocity or détente, Ashbery views the self, like the midrashic text, existentially generated or rendered from our contacts with others.

The possibility of definition of other or self remains forever elusive and subject to change. Ashbery shifts the question of intention and otherness to the readers, the "you": "It is you who made this, therefore you are true" (*TP* 3). While parodying Descartes, Ashbery reverses the hierarchies of perception: mirroring, not perception, is primary; it is the role of the observed or the other, not the self, that is creative. The text, however, does not rest with this shift of roles implied in the statement that assigns the responsibility of the text's essential presence to its readers. Discerning that no change has occurred through this simple reversal, Ashbery questions the construction of poetry and its ability to make any claims for the self or for others. The question is one of ethics, for Ashbery examines in this quest his own motives and intentions: "Is it correct for me to use you to demonstrate all this?" (*TP* 15). Ashbery defines the poet as "spectator" but also as the mirror through which watching takes place. The spectator thus must be responsible for what is witnessed or at least for the commentary:

> yet there is now interleaving the pages of suffering and indifference to suffering a prismatic space that cannot be seen, merely felt as the result of an angularity that must have existed from earliest times and is only now succeeding in making its presence felt through the mists of helpless acceptance of everything else projected on our miserable, dank span of days. One is aware of it as an open field of narrative possibilities. Not in the edifying sense of the tales of the past that we are still (however) chained to, but as stories that tell only of themselves, so that one realizes one's self has dwindled and now at last vanished in the diamond light of pure speculation.   (*TP* 41)

The poem, as part of this abundantly impoverished condition, can ironically offer "stories that tell only of themselves." The self loses its ability to make judgments because it is flooded over by the plenitude of narrative possibilities, "where everything is a way, none more suitable nor more accurate than the last, oblivion rapidly absorbing their outline like snow filling footprints" (*TP* 17). When such possibilities lack distinction or alterity, they become potentially valueless and only serve to mask the emptiness of our political and cultural condition.

"The New Spirit" ends with two visions: one the "horrible vision of the completed Tower of Babel," where all potential is exhausted, "an eternal reminder of the advantages of industry and cleverness" (*TP* 50). To attain the ideal, to assume the godhead by literally assuming the Logos, or Ur-word, describes the destructive and dangerous first vision. A completed Tower of Babel is the dream of metaphysicians, philosophers, and tyrants. The poet and quester can still turn away or trope away this vision of absolute closure. The second vision is a looking forward: even as the constellations are figures of narratives, they point beyond themselves and offer other narratives not yet figured: "Yet they were in no way implicated in the success or the failure, depending on your viewpoint, of the project, as became clear the minute you caught sight of the Archer, languidly stretching his bow, aiming at a still higher and smaller portion of the heavens, no longer a figure of speech but an act, even if all the life had been temporarily drained out of it" (*TP* 51). Furthermore, theirs is an "impassive grammar of cosmic unravelings of all kinds, to be proposed but never formulated" (*TP* 51). Though the stellar grammar may never change, it is infinite and offers us any number of new journeys or tales. Our being here, "receiving the colorless emanations from outer space" (*TP* 41), is affirmed by "just their presence, mild and unquestioning" (*TP* 51).

The self then is specular and mirrored in the world of objects. The self is not only one among others in the field of phenomena, but as John Koethe states, the self tries "to see them [emblems with which the self might try to identify] from the vantage point of the metaphysical subject, as what they really are, things among other things, and so to transcend them."[13] The enfolding of the past in the present describes the difficulty of reification: "You see that you cannot do without it, that singular isolated moment that has now already slipped so far into the past that it seems a mere spark. You cannot do without it and you cannot have it" (*TP* 84). "The System" argues that time and experience form a continual surface where each daily occurrence "gets folded over into ancient history like yesterday's newspaper, but in so doing a new face has been revealed, a surface on which a new phrase may be written before it rejoins history, or it may remain blank and do so anyway: it doesn't matter because each thing is coming up in its time and receding into the past, and this is what we all expect and want" (*TP* 102).

As a meditation on temporality, "The System" describes the movement of each moment as it eludes the present, "which is really a no-time, continually straying over the border into the positive past and the negative future whose movements alone define it. Unfortunately we have to live in it" (*TP* 102–3). Caught in time and extinguished by its passage, writing enfolds its own mortality as well as ours. The ways we choose to define ourselves "are the same, that we *have* them both, the risk and the security, merely through being human creatures subject to the vicissitudes of time, our earthly lot" (*TP* 81, Ashbery's italics). To reinvent the positions of the reader and the text implies a recasting of time; the text belongs to any number of different times, yet it is still one locus. The text can never be read fully, though to avoid extinction the text depends upon differentiation in readings to continue its discourse and to generate the energies for new discourses. Though the reader creates the text's pattern and authorization, the reader paradoxically has no control over the creation: "in reality it is you who are creating its pattern, embarked on a new, fantastically difficult tactic whose success is nevertheless guaranteed. You know this. But it will be a long time before the ordinary assurances will be able to make themselves felt in the strange, closed-off state you are in now. You may as well forget them and abandon yourself to the secret growing that has taken over" (*TP* 88). The text and self are Herakleitian, for as Charles Altieri argues, "There is no synthesis whose completeness is not a delusion, although there is also no way of quite dispelling the dream of totality."[14] Ashbery's speakers desire the delusion of a self fully defined, but in self-interrogation these dreams unravel.

The "leaving-out business" creates the delusion of the whole by piecing together recollections to fit a narrative we use to define ourselves. The repressed or the anomalies that have been left out threaten to deconstruct the text and the self. From the rubble of the deconstructive "lyric crash in which everything will be lost and pulverized" emerge "new wilder tendencies, as foreign to what we have carefully put in and kept out as a new chart of elements or another planet—unimaginable, in a word" (*TP* 104). These "new wilder tendencies" are forestalled by being "unimaginable," for "we are rescued by what we cannot imagine" (*TP* 104). By calling these tendencies—ironically, things waiting to be discovered yet already mapped in that they presuppose charts and maps and topologies of all sorts—"unimaginable, in a word," Ashbery, in a word, names our "salvation." Since everything reveals itself on the surface, the surface offers the possible paths that can be taken—thus, there is no choice but to take up one path and to give oneself over to it; hence, the imaginable traps us within its prescribed and conventional limits. Though not as expansive as that of "The New Spirit," the ending of "The System" opens outward, freed from its own coils: "The allegory is ended, its coils absorbed into the past, and this afternoon is as wide as an ocean. It is the time we have now, and all our wasted time sinks into the sea and is swallowed up without a trace. The past is dust and ashes, and this incommensurably wide way leads to the pragmatic and kinetic future" (*TP* 106). As a carpe diem, the poem encourages us to recognize that this is all "the time we have now."

Well keyed and pitched, "The Recital" performs a taut version of the same questions raised in "The System": "All right. Then this new problem is the same one, and that is the problem" (*TP* 110). In the midst of naming the overwhelming experience of life comes the dilemma of the nature of the autonomy of the present, so that "there is even a doubt as to our own existence" (*TP* 114). To free ourselves from this problematic mire, we must begin, Ashbery states, a narrowing down of our tangible experience: "It becomes plain that we cannot interpret everything, we must be selective, and so the tale we are telling begins little by little to leave reality behind" (*TP* 109). The poem, itself an interpretation or performance of the previous poems, mirrors our own ambivalent endeavors at self-exegesis: "What is it for you then, the insistent now that baffles and surrounds you in its loose-knit embrace that always seems to be falling away and yet remains behind, stubbornly drawing you, the unwilling spectator who had thought to stop only just for a moment, into the sphere of its solemn and suddenly utterly vast activities, on a new scale as it were, that you have neither the time nor the wish to unravel?" (*TP* 115).

Ashbery asserts the vastness of any discrete moment and the mysteriousness of the linguistic present. We are active spectators in an ever-evolving drama or passage where "the voyage always ends in a new key, although at the appointed place; a note has been added that destroys the whole fabric and the sense of the old as it was intended" (*TP* 116). Maintaining any form of value is frustrated by constant demands for change. Art fails because we subject it to our demands for idealization, transforming it into a fetish: "Perhaps no art, however gifted and well-intentioned, can supply what we were demanding of it: not only the figured representation of our days but the justification of them" (*TP* 113). Ashbery, like Adrienne Rich, probes the ethics of art through the self-reflexive moment of the *ars poetica*. While Rich proposes a new common language, Ashbery's poetry, particularly in *Three Poems,* maintains a far more speculative and conditional position. What is at issue, the possibility of salvation through the intervention of the text, is seen (or read) as a monolithic and timeless dilemma that marks our failure—Ashbery's insistence on this persistent condition is indicated in the repeated use of "always."[15] While writing toward a desired salvation, writing always and already creates the condition of inescapable erosion of self, value, and writing itself.

Reflecting the primacy of the Herakleitian movement, the final paragraph invokes the motif of the sea so as to foreground the transcient and transformative place of inscription. The surface is the place of energy and change as well as of repetition: "A vast wetness as of sea and air combined, a single smooth, anonymous matrix without surface or depth was the product of these new changes" (*TP* 118). The world and the self have no ethical distinctions; though Ashbery notes that the "scarcely noticeable bleakness" is transformed "into something both intimate and noble," he also laments "there was no longer anyone to care in the old sense of caring" (*TP* 118). The poem forms an inclusive "matrix," self-reflexively embracing its own criticism and limitations. "The Recital," as a coda and a reification of the previous poems, is heard, but its idea remains unanswered, still "something to be acted out and absorbed" (*TP* 118).

Self-Portrait in a Convex Mirror shifts from the midrashic texts of *Three Poems* to a series of interrogative self-portraits contained in the title poem and in such poems as "Grand Galop," "As One Put Drunk into the Packet-Boat," and "As You Came from the Holy Land." Ashbery continues his exploration of the surface, where one discovers the mirrored *artes poeticae* of self and text. The voice throughout *Self-Portrait in a Convex Mirror* becomes more personal, suggesting an autobiographic concern, unlike the disjunctive and *collagiste* methods of his earliest collections or the later elegiac and argumentative poetics.

"As One Put Drunk into the Packet-Boat" begins the collection; the Rimbaud allusion serves as an indication of certain differences and affinities Ashbery has with Rimbaud's own poetics of correspondence and indeterminacy. The poem reveals the interlinking energies of observation that subvert the dichotomy of subject and object and thus suspend definition:

> A look of glass stops you
> And you walk on shaken: was I the perceived?
> Did they notice me, this time, as I am,
> Or is it postponed again?   (*SP* 1)

Postponement of the definition of the self paradoxically creates both anxiety and the possibility of discourse. The poem looks forward to Parmigianino's self-portrait and Ashbery's dynamic, interrogatory relationship with it in "Self-Portrait in a Convex Mirror." Drunk on language, we commence in time and in the midst of a simile to be put on the packet boat about to head out to sea. The textual surface or sea is where the dismembered Orphic poet—and Orphic reader—resumes the song:

> I felt the stirrings of new breath in the pages
> Which all winter long had smelled like an old catalogue.
> New sentences were starting up. But the summer
> Was well along, not yet past the mid-point
> But full and dark with the promise of that fullness,
> That time when one can no longer wander away
> And even the least attentive fall silent
> To watch the thing that is prepared to happen.   (*SP* 1)

Unlike an invocation of writing as sibylline utterances disseminated and lost, as expressed in W. S. Merwin's poetry, Ashbery invokes writing as an emotional engagement. These "stirrings" in a season "dark with the promise of that fullness," invoke both the atavistic relationships with the phenomenal world that Merwin often explores and a gesture or intimation of a future that is to be anagogically understood.

The old catalogs, of Whitman's and Ashbery's detailings of America, are found to be unwieldly and stale. While Ashbery feels these newly inspired stirrings, he also realizes that they presage the possibility that the performance of writing will give way to "That time when one can no longer wander away" (*SP* 1)— when the carnival ends and with the closure of poem, word, and life. The narrative of such closure (self-reflexively the poem's entrapped and entrapping script) becomes impossible:

> But I was trying to tell you about a strange thing
> That happened to me, but this is no way to tell about it,
> By making it truly happen. It drifts away in fragments.
> (*SP* 19, "Grand Galop")

To reveal but not to conclude, as in Scheherazade's narrative seduction and veiling, creates this paradox, which subverts the notion of a full word central to logocentric philosophy.

"Self-Portrait in a Convex Mirror" is Ashbery's most explicit *ars poetica* of self and text as well as arguably his most central poem, due to the relative accessibility of the thematic issues and rhetorical turns.[16] The meditative act of self-portraiture mirrors Ash-

bery's speculations and links him to Parmigianino's self-portrait.
The convex mirror, Parmigianino's means of self-speculation, dissolves the edges of confinement and allows for discourse. This
blurring of edges subverts the painter's desire for discovering
presence through exclusion:

> The glass chose to reflect only what he saw
> Which was enough for his purpose: his image
> Glazed, embalmed, projected at a 180-degree angle.
> The time of day or the density of the light
> Adhering to the face keeps it
> Lively and intact in a recurring wave
> Of arrival. The soul establishes itself.   (*SP* 68)

The text, like the portrait, enshrouds the soul; the soul is "a captive . . . / . . . unable to advance much farther / Than your look as
it intercepts the picture" (*SP* 68–69). As the emblem of corporal-
ity and mortality, the unsettling, anomalously rendered hand of
Parmigianino—"Big, but not coarse, merely on another scale, /
Like a dozing whale on the sea bottom" (*SP* 70)—seems to punc-
ture the sphere, but it is firmly an architectural component or
parergon[17] necessary for the whole:

> It must join the segment of a circle,
> Roving back to the body of which it seems
> So unlikely a part, to fence in and shore up the face
> On which the effort of this condition reads
> Like a pinpoint of a smile, a spark
> Or star one is not sure of having seen
> As darkness resumes.   (*SP* 69–70)

The hand of the artist is the margin we cross, leaving life outside.
Deictically, Parmigianino shows us the hand of the artist which
made this artifact that survives beyond the time of the maker.
The hand is rendered unnatural and grotesque—a corpse like all
else lying in time and space outside the frame. "Roving back to
the body," the hand creates an illusion of depth, and by its place-

ment reveals the mystery of the portrait's repose and the reflection of the identification founded by this artifact. Parmigianino's hand suggests pictorial depth while also forming a mediating shield, a surface on which all details are encrusted and where we posit our own responses. Parmigianino's eyes "proclaim / That everything is surface. The surface is what's there / And nothing can exist except what's there" (*SP* 70). The eyes also proclaim a linkage with our selves, for as we speculate we are mirrored and trapped by the domain of the surface.

The use of the mirror as the controlling conceit of this poem belongs to a literary and visual tradition that is an implicit aspect of any reading of the poem. The mirror traps the viewer, like Perseus's shield or Narcissus's pool, forming the surface that mediates the connection between one and another. The reflection is a place of self-interrogation as well as the intersection of looks, as in Velazquez's *Las Meniñas*. Those viewed within the mirror and outside it, in *Las Meniñas,* join at the illusionary mirror in the depths of the canvas, on the unseen surface of the painting, and beyond, in a space dictated by the measure of perspective. *Las Meniñas,* Ashbery's poem, and Parmigianino's self-portrait confound the desire to make a single, determined, and unprovisional reading or representation. This "accumulating mirror" (*SP* 73), as a metaphor for art, reveals Ashbery's ambivalence about the sustaining and humanizing possibility of art that confronts the demands of the present moment. The past had meaning, for "Long ago / The strewn evidence meant something" (*SP* 71); however, "today is uncharted, / Desolate" (*SP* 72), impossible to be gauged or assessed. Ashbery's gaze at Parmigianino's portrait forms a frightening self-judgment:

> I see in this only the chaos
> Of your round mirror which organizes everything
> Around the polestar of your eyes which are empty,
> Know nothing, dream but reveal nothing.   (*SP* 71)

Ashbery's response to the self-portrait forms a critique of metaphysics or the "enterprise of returning 'strategically,' ideally, to an origin or to a 'priority' . . . in order to then think in terms of derivation, complication, deterioration, accident, etc." [18] The portrait itself excludes and so seeks to give priority to its own image:

> Impossible now
> To restore those properties in the silver blur that is
> The record of what you accomplished by sitting down
> "With great art to copy all that you saw in the glass"
> So as to perfect and rule out the extraneous
> Forever.   (*SP* 72)

Though the portrait itself excludes, the response or interconnection with the poet forms an inclusive dialogue in which other texts and views are included. Each observer—Ashbery, Vasari, Freedberg, and the readers—supplements the otherness of the portrait. The travels of the eye are not arrested by the portrait's apparent englobement; instead, we add to the portrait because our looking is metaphoric and generative. Thus, a simile can swerve us away from the sequestering surface of the painting or our illusory atomistic selfhood, and instead open up a landscape "alive with filiations, shuttlings; / Business is carried on by look, gesture, / Hearsay" (*SP* 75). Figurative language extends the edges of the surface to expand and ironically englobe all possibilities.

Parmigianino's and Ashbery's creations want to "siphon off the life of the studio, deflate / Its mapped space to enactments, island it" (*SP* 75). Ashbery finds himself in the dilemma of a spectator being supplanted or "compromised / By the portrait's will to endure" (*SP* 79). The artist is both at the mercy of his or her work and a spectator of the work. Criticism and theory posit certain laws and methods in order to describe art (and experience) as a "mute, undivided present," having "the justification of logic," and which "exists at the expense of all the others" (*SP* 80). The composition, however, is accidental and provisional: the artist finds "He has omitted the thing he started out to say / In the first place" (*SP* 80). The artist's task is "Life-obstructing" (*SP* 80), since it arrests and constrains the artist's regard of others. What the artist "wanted so desperately / To see come into being" (*SP*

80) is defeated by the accidents of the artistic process. The work existing is an abberration, though one that takes control; the artist is a failed Pygmalion, one whose sculpture is the self's own obliterating seduction.

The impossibility of full knowledge of intention and meaning reflects Ashbery's interest in the portrait as he moves away from a close inspection of it and then circles back to it in order to regard it from a new angle. Being a spectator, he has "been given no help whatever / In decoding our own man-size quotient and must rely / On second-hand knowledge," and in fact "no one else's taste is going to be / Any help, and might as well be ignored" (*SP* 81–82). Ashbery discerns art and theory's complex relationship, one whose dynamics can never be completely posited and defined because such a procedure or "telling" would somehow intrude, "twisting the end result / Into a caricature of itself" (*SP* 80). Threatening to be lost to the exegesis (as you are now reading), the poem suggests exegesis risks the marginalization of what it purports to examine. However, like the relationship of the viewer and the representations in *Las Meniñas,* neither can be confirmed without the other:

> This otherness, this
> "Not-being-us" is all there is to look at
> In the mirror, though no one can say
> How it came to be this way.   (*SP* 81)

The other text always prompts us onwards, yet in so doing, it erases itself while it encapsulates us as fragmented mnemonic permanences.

"Self-Portrait in a Convex Mirror" does not end, but subsides literally into "time," the last word. The poem and the poet desire knowledge of life and its interconnectiveness; in fact, Ashbery modestly argues that "it seems likely that each of us / Knows what it is and is capable of / Communicating it to the other" (*SP* 77). Interconnection is "Love . . . / . . . shadowed, invisible, / Though mysteriously present, around somewhere" (*SP* 77). Time has eroded love and filled the landscape and language with our cast-offs and residues, as described in "Street Musicians," the opening poem of *Houseboat Days:*

> Our question of a place of origin hangs
> Like smoke: how we picnicked in pine forests,
> In coves with the water always seeping up, and left
> Our trash, sperm and excrement everywhere, smeared
> On the landscape, to make of us what we could.   (*HD* 1)

There seems no way of understanding our histories except by the accumulation of our own debris. Memory and writing here intercede, for both preserve this moment of connection, however diminished or primal, as another trace, another place of origin anchoring our identities. The poem—like any sign—is an intersection of death, memory, and the desire for connection. The poet, disguised as one of the street musicians, declaims "I cradle this average violin that knows / Only forgotten showtunes" (*HD* 1). Who is this poet but Orpheus, condemned now to gather not only his scattered remains but ours as well. The poet's role is that of a *collagiste* who implicates us, at every turn of phrase, in his seditious acts that allow us to continue:

> For progress occurs through re-inventing
> These words from a dim recollection of them,
> In violating that space in such a way as
> To leave it intact.   (*HD* 67, "Blue Sonata")

Poets and critics share in the necessity of invention. Ashbery's *artes poeticae* are emblems of invention and reinvention of the poet and poetry. In "Syringa," Ashbery explicitly invokes the myth of Orpheus, particularly the aspect focusing on renewal or re-membering after fragmentation or dismemberment. The poem's title points to still another emblem of poetry, the reed, or what Syrinx was transformed into so as to escape being raped by Pan. The narrative of Syrinx is displaced by the story of Orpheus—her story is alluded to only at the end of the poem. Ashbery, thus, suggests there are two modes of poetry. On the one hand there is the Orphic, whose

> music passes, emblematic
> Of life and how you cannot isolate a note of it
> And say it is good or bad.
> You must
> Wait till it's over.   (*HD* 70)

Ashbery, however, regards Orpheus with some approbation, depicting him as a comic-book figure in the opening lines and questioning the culture that allows the elitism and self-serving endeavors of the artist who acknowledges that "Stellification / Is for the few" (*HD* 71). On the other hand, there is the music of Syrinx, of whom only a name remains—the signature of both the poet and her now fragmented and dispersed poems that leave only these "hidden syllables" (*HD* 71) of her name. Or does Syrinx represent the demand that art transcend its artifice, to move from something loved to life itself? To invoke that utter transformation, as Syrinx did before Pan could seize her,

> Is to become the tossing reeds of that slow,
> Powerful stream, the trailing grasses
> Playfully tugged at, but to participate in the action
> No more than this.   (*HD* 70)

Though these grasses appear now as passive elements in nature, as David Bromwich notes,[19] they are all that is left of an apocalyptic encounter. Ashbery locates a pastoral idyll on each side of the catastrophe. Syrinx, but for her name, has disappeared; similarly, Semele, in "Clouds," was seen wandering "puzzled at the brown light above the fields" (*DD* 69): what is left unwritten, unseen, is the moment of chiasmas. This moment of transformation is what the poet must write towards. Disappearing with the rise of the Apollonian mind and Orphic natural histories, Syrinx's music represents the juncture of the sacred, violent metamorphosis, and of violence forestalled by invocation.

Writing is an ironic signature, in that we elegiacally write our "own mark grotesquely with a stick in snow" (*HD* 85, "Fantasia on 'The Nut-Brown Maid'"). We write in order to speak, in order to forestall death: urgently the poet insists "What I am writing to say is, the timing, not / The contents, is what matters" (*HD* 85). The movement of the poem—its writing—is literally "what matters." Ashbery argues that the poem must have "a sense beyond . . . meaning" (*HD* 5, "Collective Dawns")—both a rationale and a physical lushness. Similarly, Ashbery describes our lives as a rebus in "The Wrong Kind of Insurance," which is painted in "Terrific colors, magnificent and horrible, / Close together" (*HD* 49). Though we paint our lives with the colors of rhetoric, "We too are somehow impossible, formed of so many different things, / Too many to make sense to anybody" (*HD* 50). Each detail englobes vast knowledges that, in our epoch, are beyond control—in that sense, poetry has relinquished its status as the site where the narratives that define the culture are inscribed.

In the long, polyvocal poem "Litany," in *As We Know*, Ashbery argues that criticism has failed to understand both the poet and poiesis. He observes that to see things "*In* approximately *the same way as the writer or artist / Doesn't help*" (*AW* 33–34; Ashbery's italics), for the critic does not pursue the task of being an artist. Ashbery rejects criticism that takes only itself as its subject in order to master language. Nor does he accept a criticism "*too eager to criticize us: we / Could do that for ourselves, and have done so*" (*AW* 34; Ashbery's italics). Instead, he calls for criticism to

> *make the poets more aware of*
> *What they're doing, so that poets in turn*
> *Can stand back from their work and be enchanted by it*
> *And in this way make room for the general public*
> *To crowd around and be enchanted by it too,*
> *And then, hopefully, make some sense of their lives,*
> *Bring order back into the disorderly house*
> *Of their drab existences.*   (*AW* 33; Ashbery's italics)

The poet demands that art should provide order and charm to our existence, and furthermore that art has the ability to do so. We dream that poetry might have such a power; and certainly through the acts of self-interrogation, poets like Ashbery and Adrienne

Rich seek to reimagine the inventiveness and power of words. Poetry remains a form of enchantment and mystery, for though "Poetry has already happened," it is transformative in that it is the
"agony / Of looking steadily at something" not really there but
"far beyond" (*AW* 37–38). Ashbery suggests that "Grace, in the
long run . . . is what poetry is" (*AW* 38). Grace has a doubled
meaning, for it is both transformative and ornamental, "useful
and useless at the same time" (*AW* 39). Then poetry, envisioned
as grace, is supremely paradoxical in that, while potentially prais-
ing, it also breaks expectations and metaphysical laws.

"Paradoxes and Oxymorons" argues that a poem is inherently
the mirror of the reader by concluding "The poem is you" (*S* 3). The
poem achieves this transformation, however, only through the process of its being; though the poem may end up being you (the
reader, the writer, the page), the poem is first "talking to you" (*S* 3).
The poem, even as a definition of being, is never possessed: you
may "have it but you don't have it" (*S* 3). What exists outside the
poem—the author, the intention, the meaning—is a shadow that
is set "softly down beside you" (*S* 3). Meaning, arrived at through
interpretation, is a form of play or "A deeper outside thing, a
dreamed role-pattern, / . . . Open-ended" (*S* 3). Indeed, the collection's title, *Shadow Train,* underscores the description that
the movement of interpretation is one of shadowing the poems.
The poems also form a shadow train; not only does each poem
conform in structure in this collection, but each poem is a translation of experience in that what "happens modestly . . . . / . . . is
translated into something / Floating up from it, signals that life
flashed, weak but essential" ("The Vegetarians," *S* 50). The poem
forms a complex relation with the reader that allows the reader to
establish a conditional self-identity. As the copulalike mirror and
the shadow of the self, the poem is distinct but dependent on the
formation of the presence of the self. While marking the presence
of the self, the rhetorics of mirroring and shadowing act to conceal
the self—the poem writes over the author and creates an artifice
that makes self-definition increasingly impossible, yet the illusion of it all the more present. In "Frontispiece," this paradox is
made explicit: "It must be there. And so we turn the page over /

To think of starting. This is all there is" (*S* 46). These last two lines of the poem suggest something of the dilemma of a book with no beginnings and the vertigo of the final period. To what does *This* refer: the abyss beyond the ending or the interminable beginning or the absence of the book whose presence "Frontispiece" (in medias res in this collection) marks?

To dismantle the artifice, to shred it and thus possess the self, is an impossible task, but "We are all soiled with this desire, at the last moment, the last" (*S* 22). In "Drunken Americans," Ashbery argues that each moment of self-definition is "thin, unsatisfactory / As gruel, worn away more each time you return to them" (*S* 22). In fact, to "rip the canvas from its frame" is an ironic act of self-destruction and certainly a prescription for death. Death or the end of discourse constitutes another shadow train running throughout the collection and his poetry in general. The reification of the self, not in language, but in pictorial terms denotes the mistrust with which our culture regards words and the desire our culture has to maintain a static, conservative vision of itself.[20] There is no avoiding the desire for absolute identity; it is as rooted as fate, for it arrives, at the very latest, at the "last moment." Ashbery suggests that this is not only an individual's psychological desire but also one that defines our culture—we are inescapably the "Drunken Americans" who revoke transformation, dreams, and language. The poem, thus, implicitly describes the destruction of the poetic voice or the act of poiesis, for the title recalls the chaos that surrounded the dismemberment and destruction of Orpheus and Syrinx. The cultural and psychological demands for coherence and definition are in opposition to the impulses of lyricism and, more fundamentally, the heteroglossia of writing.

The poet's significance is that he or she is the last one (though perhaps once the first) to forge language into the possibility of being an authentic mirror of our condition:

> And I see once more how everything
> Must be up to me: here a calamity to be smoothed away
> Like ringlets, there the luck of uncoding

> This singular cipher of primary
> And secondary colors, and the animals
> With us in the ark, happy to be there as it settles
> Into an always more violent sea.   (W 50, "Proust's Questionnaire")

Ashbery's stance is ironic—the poet is modest. The task grows more trying and the looming of fate more pronounced. Poetry is, then, the place for criticism—if we are to escape the bound and self-created images of ourselves that increasingly sever each of us from the world. *A Wave* continues an uncoding of mortality— poetic and personal—and an articulation of poetry as criticism begun in *Self-Portrait in a Convex Mirror*. In "Litany," Ashbery suggests our failure in self-criticism would liken us to a *"Narcissus . . . born blind* [and who] *still daily / Haunts the mantled pool, and does not know why"* (AW 35, Ashbery's italics). The failure of self-criticism is an ongoing cultural disaster not limited to our era, but which stretches throughout the epochs. The apocalypse is always in the periphery of time (it marks time) and it is already inscribed in our grammars. "Meanwhile, great fires / Arise, as of haystacks aflame," Ashbery writes, but more troubling is that our "graciousness in living / Conspires with it" (W 2, "Rain Moving In"). Through a poetics of self-reflexivity, we fashion a place for ourselves within the fabric of discourse; our identities are provisional, but they constitute a dialogic universe: "Blurred but alive with many separate meanings / Inside this conversation" (W 32, "The Path to the White Moon"). Though we are makers of "marvelous graffiti" (W 69, "A Wave"), Ashbery suggests in the title poem of *A Wave* that as we have created ensnaring systems, so too "Are we set free on an ocean of language that comes to be / Part of us. . . . / Preparing dreams we'll have to live with and use" (W 71, "A Wave"). Knowing we are part of language's protean and polymorphous surface rescues us, or provisionally sustains us when confronting daily erosions and finding disaster in each sidelong glance.

"Fiery Iconography": Language and Interconnection in the Poetry of Adrienne Rich

Though Adrienne Rich's poetry poses questions about the self-reflexivity of writing, it also significantly redirects our responses in order to foreground the issues of power, tradition, and the institution of language as a medium of exclusion. By seeking a "passionate" and "lucid" language,[1] Rich breaks with convention, offers ideological dissent, and demonstrates reflective and critical self-definition: Rich has been writing towards a "fiery iconography" (*PSN* 12, "For the Conjunction of Two Planets")[2] that seeks to recast the poem and thereby initiate the re-reading of the self and the transactions of self and history. Her work has become strenuously self-critical and has pursued vigorously the articulation and elaboration of a vision of connection that is perhaps more obvious in hindsight, when examining her early poetry. Though *Leaflets* (1969) marks the beginning of her sustained examination of these issues, her development as a poet has always mirrored and chronicled her personal changes. Her earliest poetry, nonetheless, describes a critical response to the condition of women and of that shared but unacknowledged world of women. While many of her central themes are present in her first collections, her critical definition of herself as a woman poet and the inclusion of her critical self-reflections, however, are only latently present. These elements became present when Rich sought to identify the interconnectedness of women through the idea of motherhood as the primary and unifying experience that, if separated from the institutions that both idealize and closet it, allows for self-definition and transformation. Later, Rich identifies herself in her poetry as a lesbian and then defines lesbianism and the lesbian continuum as instruments for political change and as essential for describing the cultural, historical, sexual, and political intensity or connectedness between women.[3] Found throughout Rich's poetry, but never separate from these issues, are her meditations on the condition of language. Rich redirects the discussion of language from the eroded tracery of John Ashbery's apocalyptics to a language responding to and responsible for its condition and the conditions it creates.

The feminist visions of community, connection, and history are central to Rich's poetry and hence demand not only the language of textual criticism but also a critical vocabulary that explicitly considers political and historical concerns (while grounded in the material of writing), for Rich's poetry has examined increasingly the institutions of power and the circumstances of powerlessness. Before we turn to the poetry, the distinct difference of Rich's poetry compared to the poetry of Ashbery or even the more politically explicit poetry of W. S. Merwin should be emphasized. In part because her poetry chronicles her own changes, it has been read as a barometer of the culture's life and thought. More explicitly, women read Rich to learn what she is thinking about language, racism, militarism, her Jewish heritage, and the ways of defining oneself. Though some may argue Rich's are restricted interests, what Rich attests to are of utmost concern to the culture—feminism is not a narrow theoretical endeavor but a praxis applicable to the entire community. Indeed, Rich seeks to envision the very possibility of community instead of a corrosive society split by institutions that empower and silence.

That Rich is one of the most public of our poets is demonstrated by the fact that her poetry is read by those who do not otherwise consider themselves readers of poetry. Her essays have widened her contacts with readers, while also serving to extend arguments often found in the poems. The shift from book reviews to both more topical and more theoretical essays coincides with the emergence of her self-conscious public voice. Her essays punctuate the overall fabric of her poetry; neither subordinate nor outside her poetic concerns, the essays nonetheless constitute a wholly different voice and endeavor. As a public poet, Rich writes occasional poems that have often caused critics to label her work as propaganda.[4] Such charges misrepresent Rich's stated belief that a poet is the voice of the community, a voice for the voiceless.[5] Nor should Rich's occasional poems[6] be viewed as a failure of aesthetic control; rather, the steady convergence of political and personal commitments—the intrinsic part of the feminist project—necessitate poems that are directed to foregrounding an issue as directly and publically as possible. The assuming of the public voice demands a responsibility to one's community or one's audience, who seek to be represented and made present through the poet's language. While her poetry defines self and ethos, it also recovers and maintains language, connections, and histories.

Rich's poetry, by proposing a dissenting critique of language, subverts the insistence upon decorum[7]—or foregrounds aesthetic conventions and necessitates the reader's own critical response to those conventions. Rich's work parallels Ashbery's in that both undercut the twin and twined notions of a monolithic reader and a monolithic aesthetic. Rich moves us from aesthetic responses to ethical considerations; thus, her poetry self-reflexively examines image and representation, the heart of decorum and law. Rich's poetics, as Rachel Blau DuPlessis writes, is "a signal of frustration with convention and a sign of ideological dissent, a desire to rewrite culture by the critical examination of the 'natural': that is, by uncovering that which our current social and linguistic practices exclude."[8] Charles Altieri argues that Rich's project is "to make the margin a place where identity and identification can and must be informed."[9] Her poetry, however, argues that the margin can never be a home; the task of writing is to transform the premises that create and allow the division, exclusion, and silence described by the margin.

In an interview with Wendy Martin, Rich describes the influences surrounding her first collection of poems, *A Change of World:* while a student at Radcliffe College, she did not see a woman teacher for years and learned poetic craft from the male poets she read as an undergraduate.[10] "Aunt Jennifer's Tigers" portrays a woman who "suffers from the opposition of her imagination," and who, as Rich has written, "was a person as distanced from myself as possible—distanced by the formalism of the poem, by its objective, observant tone—even by putting the woman in different generation."[11] The poem signals the poet's desire to connect with other women and their histories, for it retells Aunt Jennifer's circumscribed life. Aunt Jennifer, embroidering Blake's prophetic tigers, is trapped in the mesh of patriarchy and its contract of marriage. The tigers foreshadow the emergence of Rich's "fiery iconography" (*PSN* 12). The constraint of language, however, illustrates the inherent forces of domination and separation. The highly stressed lines, end rhymes, and alliteration point to poetic traditions that are as domineering and authoritative as "The massive weight of Uncle's wedding band" (*PSN* 4). The language, particularly that of Eliot, Auden, and Lowell, "Sits heavily" on the poet and on the poets of her generation. Although Rich has imagined this woman as from a previous generation, they are close relatives: an imaginary aunt close enough for Rich to scrutinize—and to be glimpsed in the mirror.

Throughout Rich's first volume, *A Change of World,* she tentatively revokes the strictures pressed on art and passion. In "Stepping Backward," the poet asks,

How far dare we throw off the daily ruse,
Official treacheries of face and name,
Have out our true identity?   (*PSN* 8)

The poet maintains we "at last renounce that ultimate blue / And take a walk in other kinds of weather" (*PSN* 9). To idealize is to remove oneself from the domain of the human, where the imagination's and history's actions take place. Art is named the "common interchange" (*PSN* 9); thus, Rich underscores transaction, exchange, and the desire for connection as the defining practice of art and art as a locus for defining the condition of the self. The condition of the self and the artist is provisional and necessitates an ethos founded on self-instruction and survival: "These are the things that we have learned to do / Who live in troubled regions" (*PSN* 3, "Storm Warnings").

The poet, as the explorer of the condition of the self, confronts in this collection the difficulty of change and the need for the energies of transformation found in writing. Self-interrogation begins, but it is circumscribed and distanced by the very art of the poem, described in "At a Bach Concert" as

This antique discipline, tenderly severe,
Renews belief in love yet masters feeling,
Asking of us a grace in what we bear.   (*PSN* 7)

A Change of World reveals the emergence of a private self in an instituted and conventional language. The necessity for and risk of change is indicated in the opening line, which prefigures a much later title poem: "Like divers, we ourselves must make the jump" (*PSN* 10). Rich uses the conceit of the springboard to describe the energy that "makes the body shoot / Into its pure and irresistible curve" in the will to transform—"a force beyond all bodily powers" (*PSN* 10). The poem describes a romantic urging toward transformation and the relinquishing of self-identity in the momentary flight of imagination.

The Blakean junction of will, passion, politics, and poetry is invoked in "For the Conjunction of Two Planets," a poem that prefigures "Orion" and "Planetarium":

> Is any light so proudly thrust
> From darkness on our lifted faces
> A sign of something we can trust,
> Or is it that in starry places
> We see the things we long to see
> In fiery iconography?   (*PSN* 11–12)

As in Blake's prophetic works, there is a looking toward the future: the collection closes—yet opens—on a threshold. Rich hopes to re-vision language into a passionate and lucid presence, "present to us in sensuous form," in the figurations of "fiery iconography." Through re-vision (a seeing again and anew),[12] language becomes fiery in its anger and alchemical in its transformative powers.

The Diamond Cutters probes transitoriness and estrangement as conditions imposed on women:

> There is a mystery that floats between
> The tourist and the town. Imagination
> Estranges it from her. She need not suffer
> Or die here. It is none of her affair,
> Its calm heroic vistas make no claim.   (*PSN* 16)

The narrator is as distanced from her subject as the woman being described is distanced from the town or established culture: "Here she goes untouched, / And this is alienation" (*PSN* 16). Such opening lines as "We had to take the world as it was given" (*PSN* 15, "Ideal Landscape"), "Those clarities detached us, gave us form, / Made us like architecture" (*PSN* 15, "The Tourist and the Town"), or "I write you this out of another province / That you may never see" (*PSN* 33, "Letter from the Land of Sinners") express enforced or imposed isolation. Unlike Elizabeth Bishop's travelers, who desire interconnection and provisionally attain it through the mapping of their imaginations as well as their land-scapes, the narrator in "The Tourist and the Town" precludes these possibilities for "We have no choice: / We are only tourists under that blue sky" (*PSN* 16). The blue—"that ultimate blue" of "Stepping Backward"—imposes itself again as idealization, domi-nance, and authority.

While this terrific sky blazes throughout *The Diamond Cutters,* Rich begins a self-defining critique of her own condition: "To work and suffer is to be at home. / All else is scenery" (*PSN* 16). In "Au-tumn Equinox," Rich uses a veiled autobiographical structure to illustrate the depersonalizing demands of the father and of mar-riage; self-critically, the narrator sees herself transposed as her mother, "Correct and terrified on our wedding-day, / Wearing the lace my mother wore before me" (*PSN* 24). Through generations of repetition, women's roles have become more confined and en-shrouded: "aunts around us nodded like the Fates / That nemesis was accomplished" (*PSN* 24). The narrator uses her life as an ex-emplum; during this night walk Rich indicates the changes she must make herself—thus, she redefines poetry as a process of self-interrogation.

In "Villa Adriana," Rich reinscribes the quest narrative as the means for self-definition:

> We come like dreamers searching for an answer,
> Passionately in need to reconstruct
> The columned roofs under the blazing sky,
> The courts so open, so forever locked.   (*PSN* 21)

The self, as a secret "so open, so forever locked," is further veiled as the search probes the congruent architectures of memory and the unconscious. "Villa Adriana," like "Springboard," prefigures "Diving into the Wreck"; however, the parallels with the later poem are more certain, for the poet's demands have shifted from imagining the paradigm of a willed energy to a "need to recon-struct / The columned roofs" and recover the remains of an elu-sive past:

> And some of us, as dreamers, excavate
> Under the blanching light of sleep's high noon,
> The artifacts of thought, the site of love,
> Whose Hadrian has given the slip, and gone.   (*PSN* 21)

Not the result of time and process, this wreck has been so since its beginning, for its origin was that of disaster: Hadrian "might have seen it as today we see" (*PSN* 20). The shattered villa marks the "site of love" of Hadrian and his favorite boy lover, Antinoüs, and in turn, Rich overlays the place with her own name. No longer the palace for Antinoüs, it marks the poet's desire and discontent. The moment, historical and personal, becomes an androgynous equation; "I am she: I am he" (*DW* 24). Here, however, androgyny, if this term can be applied usefully, is not expressed as an explicit form of political and social realignment and redefinition. The transposition of "Adriana" and "Antinoüs" allows Rich to mask her identity and record only the mute wreckage. This ambivalence reveals the risks that any disclosure of the self entails as well as the difficulty in finding a language not already shattered in which to locate and define oneself.

Poetic risk-taking, begun in Rich's work of the late 1950s, is doubly important: Rich not only breaks poetic decorum but also breaks the poetic code by defining herself as a woman writer with a woman's consciousness.[13] This identification grew from her participation in the development of the feminist project that places the personal into the arena of history. In the title poem of her third collection, "Snapshots of a Daughter-in-Law," alienation, confinement, and repression are again confronted, but now within a personal vernacular. The immediate and direct statements forming this new poetry do not lose any eloquence, nor do they shift into the elegiac relationship with history exemplified by Robert Lowell's poetry: instead, they task history with informing the present moment. Rich, fully aware of the continuity and power of the past's institutions, "fears that the past will rob her present," David Kalstone writes—unlike Lowell, with his legacy of Pound and Eliot, who fears the present will plunder and sack the past.[14]

The weaving of the historical and the personal is not only the signature of Rich's poetic method, as Cary Nelson argues,[15] but is a necessary demand of her entire poetic endeavor and a form of survival. "Snapshots of a Daughter-in-Law" explores the historical continuum of women as well as the persisting repression of that continuum. The poem enters into a dialogic relation with both history and the condition of the individual. Rich asserts that poetry be dialogic and diachronic—language cannot be idealized; rather, it must be recognized as a function of time and history as well as offering the hope of interconnection through its very structure of exchange. While recalling Pound's and Eliot's use of allusions, the poem reveals the necessity of making present the continuum of women's voices and conditions. The poem revolves around Dickinson's line, "My life had stood—a Loaded Gun." That line, metonymical of "Snapshots of a Daughter-in-Law," marks the status of the imagination—and particularly a woman's—and the edge at which the narrator, a woman, has lived, as well as marking the violence posed in such an unnatural stasis or confinement. Dickinson's line, like Rich's poem, also proposes the explosiveness of the life and imagination of women, who have been cornered and relegated to corners of history and writing.

The use of citations and the stanzaic arrangement provide an album of photographic stills that record and interrogate the role of women and, self-critically, the poet's task. Rich empowers her own dissenting script by placing it in a continuum of dissent where each allusion or snapshot records a moment of dissent. The poem also merges a critique of modernism with a critique of a millennial-old ideology through the allusion to Yeats's Leda: "A thinking woman sleeps with monsters. / The beak that grips her, she becomes" (*SDL* 22). As DuPlessis argues, Rich turns back on itself Yeats's question, "Did she put on his knowledge with his power / before the indifferent beak could let her drop?" and shows an "ambivalent judgment about the possession of phallic power and knowledge."[16] No matter how caustically she exposes the double bind in which the dominant culture has placed women, Rich participates in a rhetoric that is marked by that dominant culture. Her poem becomes an ironic or paradoxical *Wasteland,* in that she must use the apparatus of allusion and authority belonging to the dominant culture to criticize the doxology of that same rhetoric and culture. While Eliot and Yeats invoke and hope to maintain their vision of the dominant culture, Rich appropriates their rhetoric to dissent.

Each snapshot makes apparent the conflict between the circumscribed lives of women in a masculine culture and the traditional impositions of poetic decorum. The condition and representation of women in the discourse of men offers "no pure fruition, but a thorn" (*SDL* 22). Rich describes her condition as "iron-eyed and beaked and purposed as a bird, / dusting everything on the whatnot every day of life" (*SDL* 22). This disfiguration and repression by the demands of the patriarchy has literally turned women into harpies, Medusas, and petrified objects in the iconography of the dominant culture.

"Snapshots of a Daughter-in-Law" closes by looking toward the future. By looking into the sky,[17] Rich seeks out the essential nature that has been distorted through an oppressive ideology:

> Her mind full to the wind, I see her plunge
> breasted and glancing through the currents,
> taking the light upon her
> at least as beautiful as any boy
> or helicopter,
>   poised, still coming,
> her fine blades making the air wince
> but her cargo
> no promise then:
> delivered
> palpable
> ours.   (*SDL* 24–25)

The terrific sky of domination disappears, and the poem opens to arrival and possibility. Rich's audience—that is, the one inscribed in the poems—is women, not an amorphous universal reader. In speaking of women and to women, Rich makes present and "palpable" the future of "all that we might have been, / all that we were—fire, tears, / wit, taste, martyred ambition" (*SDL* 23). The poem attempts to unite dispersed selves "In a random universe, what more / / exact and starry consolation?" (*SDL* 34, "Double Monologue").

"Snapshots of a Daughter-in-Law" demonstrates, as Claire Keyes suggests, that Rich "cannot reconcile *what* she is (a poet) with *who* she is (a woman). She won't be able to effect this reconciliation until she finds new terms for power, and ultimately a new language capable of embracing female energy and power."[18] Concluding with a utopian representation underscores this problem, for with such a vision Rich relinquishes the demands of history and time. Such utopian speculations, while offering hope, risk diminishing self-examination and responsive connection with others. The assertion of a utopian image at the poem's close must put into question the condition of the self or one's own identity, particularly if self-definition is only known through the transactions of history and language.

The issues of the survival of the self and self-definition and the appraisal of idealization continue to be examined in the collection *Necessities of Life:*

> Is it in the sun that truth begins?
> Lying under that battering light
> the first few hours of summer
> I felt scraped clean, washed down
>
> to ignorance   (*FD* 59, "The Corpse-Plant")

Again, under the terrific gaze of the sky, the woman is subjected to the battering rays of an eidetic image of truth. Yet she too is an emblem, for in traditional iconography the unveiled woman represents essential form, idealized beauty, proportion, or truth. Thus, the narrator is battered by any representation of truth. Her own self—not as truth, the Athenic figure springing from the solar but sterile and abstracted womb of Zeus—cannot participate in the discourse of men. Neither she nor her ghostly but unveiled representation are allowed into discourse. She is then both secondary and external (a springing forth from Zeus) and the impossible center (the gazed-at fetish). To counter this force of abstraction necessitates a re-visioning of language, self, and seeing.

These poems seek "now and again to name / over the bare necessities" (*FD* 56, "Necessities of Life"), to elucidate connections and self-identity. Rich's elegy for her father, "After Dark," turns away from death, despite the destruction the father wrought. The poem reconfronts the father-daughter relationship; in it Rich voices Lear's desires for reunion and escape. By confronting the father's death—both personal and symbolic—the poet confronts her own capacity for destruction and death:

> Now let's away from prison—
> Underground seizures!
> I used to huddle in the grave
> I'd dug for you and bite
>
> my tongue for fear it would babble
> —*Darling*—
> I thought they'd find me there
> someday, sitting upright, shrunken,
>
> my hair like roots and in my lap
> a mess of broken pottery—
> wasted libation—
> and you embalmed beside me.   (*FD* 69–70)

Unlike Sylvia Plath's "Daddy," this poem displaces anger with the desire for reunion and retrieval—of going back to the wreck. The overlay of childhood wishes and of Iron Age fertility rituals [19] is an act of self-revelation and suggests that the atavistic power of prehistoric rituals continues to inform one's imagination and history. The symbolic authority or law of the father is recognized in this archaeology of childhood as a death wish and the denial of one's own identity. To wish for the father's power, defined here as specifically sexual, is to destroy oneself or to sacrifice oneself to ritual and institutions of power authorized by the father.

In her elegy, "Halfway," to her maternal grandmother, Rich

concedes her own mortality and her longing to learn from the past as told by women. Here, Rich points to the direction the strongest of her future poetry will take; poetry is the site of exchanges and hence is the place of realigning the relationships that define oneself and one's culture:

> To sit by the fire is to become another woman,
> red hair charring to grey,
> green eyes grappling with the printed page,
> voice flailing, flailing the uncomprehending.
> My days lie open, listening, grandmother.   (*FD* 73)

The poet recognizes she is at a threshold of revelation. Unlike Ashbery's liminal moments, which teeter toward apocalypse, Rich envisions a potential cornucopia:

> Masses of birds revolve, blades
> of a harvester.
> The sky is getting milkily white,
> a sac of light is ready to burst open.   (*FD* 73)

Though the combination of images of birds and harvester blades recalls the image of the woman / helicopter at the end of "Snapshots of a Daughter-in-Law," the two poems are distinct in that "Halfway" grounds itself in the natural world and personal recollections. By sitting by the fire, Rich embraces the symbolic energies of fire that, like language, should weld and transform. Writing and telling are distinguished—though the printed page remains abstract, unlike the immediacy of telling, what is written is recognized as empowering. The poet in "Halfway" likens her life to a book whose "days lie open," waiting for the stories to be transposed onto the page or held in the memory of the audience.

Self-reflection generates the revisionary sloughing of past or imposed portraits, as in "Moth Hour":

> A million insects die every twilight,
> no one even finds their corpses.

> Death, slowly moving among the bleached clouds,
> knows us better than we know ourselves.
>
> I am gliding backward away from those who knew me
> as the moon grows thinner and finally shuts its lantern.
> I can be replaced a thousand times,
> a box containing death.   (*FD* 74–75)

Rich underscores the dynamics of change: it is an irreversible process, like death, for the old self or identity is gone before one knows it. Thus, one is "already reaching toward an empty space" (*FD* 75) where someone once was. The self mirrors language, as both are traces of an originary moment that remains unknown, in that we have always been retreating from it. Rich posits this meditation about language in the cyclical and natural metaphor of lunar phases—Will we return or regain a full knowledge of ourselves and our language?

While envisioning "a dream of language / unlived behind the clouds" (*PSN* 137, "Postcard"), Rich describes the ontological difficulty of writing as a form of solitary confrontation within the institution of patriarchy:

> and I am afraid
> of the language in my head
> I am alone, alone with language
> and without meaning
> coming back to something written years ago:
> *our words misunderstand us*
>
> wanting a word that will shed itself like a tear
> onto the page
> leaving its stain   (*FD* 198–99; Rich's italics)

The language Rich describes is not a deictic language nor is it one that is comprehensible in itself or comprehending of her—it is "without meaning." This scopic version of language eclipses the body and the diachronic with the demand for the ideal or abstract. She envisions a phenomenal language, or one "leaving its stain," but words nonetheless slide out of control and away from a defined presence. What is wanted is "a word that will shed itself" or transform the abstract into the physical and the emotional.

Language, in *Leaflets,* changes hands and is handed out, thus gaining durability and duration. As a medium of interconnection, language emerges as the collection's central concern and exists in a state of emergency, as expressed in this collection's title poem:

> I want to hand you this
> leaflet streaming with rain or tears
> > but the words coming clear
> something you might find crushed into your hand
> > after passing a barricade
> and stuff in your raincoat pocket.
> I want this to reach you
> who told me once that poetry is nothing sacred
> > —no more sacred that is
> than other things in your life—
> > to answer yes, if life is uncorrupted
> no better poetry is wanted.   (*L* 55)

The narrator sacralizes the language of poetry by demanding to know "how can we use what we have / to invent what we need" (*L* 56). Any moment of self-definition is provisional, since words are subject to change in their diachronic condition: "These words are vapor-trails of a plane that has vanished; / by the time I write them out, they are whispering something else" (*L* 62; "Ghazals: Homage to Ghalib"). The erosion of language seems a particularly technocratic or industrial condition, as suggested by the metaphor of the plane's vapor trails. A natural or phenomenal language, by contrast, would not be subject to erosion, nor would it be an instrument of oppression. The writer's intention gives way to the reader and to the words themselves, which are "whispering something else." This line emphasizes an underlying complaint that language escapes the bounds of the author's intent. Words gain a power of their own; they take flight from the diffuse script—a vapor trail that disperses into the sky or page—to whisper in their own or in others' voices. Not monolithic, language undergoes constant dispossession, transformation, and rupture: "For us the work undoes itself over and over: / the grass grows back, the dust collects, the scar breaks open" (L 64, "Ghazals: Homage to Ghalib"). The place of writing dramatizes itself, for suture and rupture come to describe writing. Rich seeks to recover language's ability to heal itself and transform itself, and thus to provide the medium for change of self and culture: "Only where there is language is there world" (L 21, "The Demon Lover").

We are defined by what we produce: that is, language; thus, Rich's poetry criticizes the sovereignty of engendered language and the authority it exerts. Rich sees, nevertheless, in the inherently mutable quality of language the possibility of personal and political transformation: "I wanted to choose words that even you / would have to be changed by" (L 42, "Implosions"). Writing, though laden with intention, is also the responsibility of the reader: "When they read this poem of mine, they are translators. / Every existence speaks a language of its own" (L 75, "Ghazals: Homage to Ghalib"). Rich describes her writing as subject to necessary reinterpretation: "If these are letters, they will have to be misread. / If scribblings on a wall, they must tangle with all the others" (L 75). Writing forms an overlay of other writings, and in this tactility writing is experiential yet provisional: "When you read these lines, think of me / and of what I have not written here" (L 61, "Ghazals: Homage to Ghalib"). What is written emerges from a particular and personal context while also displacing that context. Rich insists on writing as a dialogic activity; thus, it forms the basis of interconnection.

Interconnection works as a social and cultural force as well as describing the connotative and durational quality of language. As in "Dwingelo," the frequent use of stellar imagery illustrates the scale on which interconnection works. "Dwingelo" embraces the site of observation, its sources, the floating "never, still arriving" you, and the cosmos:

> To wait is the password; and to listen.
> In Dwingelo you can hear it whisper,
> the void in the radiotelescope.

> There too the singing of your nerves is gathered,
> becoming graphic on a sheet of paper
> not unlike this one here.   (*L* 18)

And, like the later poem "Planetarium" or the early poem "For the Conjunction of Two Planets," the cosmos gathers in the body. The poet becomes connected with the cosmos without constellating or idealizing herself. Her movement is made visible and graphic through her writing. The poem, in its final line, emphasizes a community of selves—the writer, the poem, and the readers—who seek to limit distance through the invoked discourse of the poem; thus, it posits an ethical imperative in order to point to community and discourse. Through the final self-reflexive turn, Rich emphasizes that her poetry is not only a poetry of experience but also a necessary sharing of personal experience and the placing of the poet and the reader in the ongoing formation of reality.

Experience, paralleling what Rich desires for language, must be transformational: "I tell you, truth is, at the moment, here / burning outward through our skins" (*L* 65, "Ghazals: Homage to Ghalib"). From the journallike notations of "Ghazals: Homage to Ghalib," Rich demonstrates that her poetry is exploratory: "From here on, all of us will be living / like Galileo turning his first tube at the stars" (*L* 76). The enjambment of this couplet stresses the liminal moment: women are on the verge of recovering the world and history, Rich hopes, outside the constrictions of the patriarchy. Enjambment and liminality, however, also indicate a distance and separation from two versions of the self—one present, "living" and looking; the other, future and desired. The stars point toward risk and exploration where "Even to hope is to leap into the unknown" (*L* 76), as well as into confrontation with one's daimon:

> Calmly you ache up there
> pinned aloft in your crow's nest,
> my speechless pirate!
> You take it all for granted
> and when I look you back

> it's with a starlike eye
> shooting its cold and egotistical spear
> where it can do least damage.
> Breathe deep! No hurt, no pardon
> out here in the cold with you
> you with your back to the wall.   (*L* 12, "Orion")

In "Planetarium," Rich writes "What we see, we see / and seeing is changing" (*WTC* 14). Throughout the pivotal collection *The Will to Change,* Rich emphasizes the centrality of observation to self-definition's processes of interconnection and transformation. By connecting ourselves with nature and others, seeing forms a dangerous activity linked intimately with writing, transformation, and identity: "the eye bleeding with speech" (*WTC* 48, "Images for Godard"). What the poet witnesses demands to be recorded. Likewise, speech wounds the specularly defined self, for speech displaces the body as the privileged mark of presence. With any use of language, however, Rich insists on ethical or self-defining responsibilities: "If I thought of my words as changing minds, / hadn't my mind also to suffer changes?" (*WTC* 22, "The Blue Dhazals"). As an ethical observer and transmitter, the poet must be the eyes of the community, eyes that recall and heal the community:

> I am an instrument in the shape
> of a woman trying to translate pulsations
> into images   for the relief of the body
> and the reconstruction of the mind.   (*WTC* 14, "Planetarium")

The transformation of the representation of women includes the recovery of texts and histories of women. *The Will to Change* opposes the ideology that seeing, naming, and writing comprise strictly a masculine prerogative. In "Planetarium," Rich re-sees the skies, and thus refigures and re-visions them. In the poem, the scales of body and cosmos converge:

> I am a galactic cloud so deep   so invo-
> luted that a light wave could take 15

years to travel through me   And has
taken
(WTC 14)

Spacings and ruptured lines and words self-reflexively show the poem's movement as tactile and physical—registered first on the page, not in speech. The tactility inscribes the reader through the conjunction of visual and aural chiasma and realignment. Like Caroline Herschel's or Galileo's telescopes, Rich's poem draws language and the world common to women from abstraction and obscurity into proximity.

The poet must criticize "the oppressor's language" (*WTC* 18, "The Burning of Paper Instead of Children") while simultaneously taking on the task of remaking language from "this lettering chalked on the ruins / this alphabet of the dumb" (*WTC* 46, "The Photograph of the Unmade Bed"). By examining the idea of the image, Rich analyzes domination in language. The alternating blocks of lines in "The Photograph of an Unmade Bed"—like photos in an album—create visual tensions and emphasize the physicality of language. Yet photographs and poems differ, for in a photograph Rich claims "The image / isn't responsible / . . . It is intentionless" (*WTC* 45). She suggests that language based on images fails because of the degree to which an image *appears* to have no intention, though it implicitly appropriates meanings and values and is easily appropriated. Rich, instead, will posit discourse (which may be composed of discrete images, but which maintains exchanges within and outside its frame) as the model for language. (It should be said that this description of photography negates the semiotic transactions of a photograph and essentially renders it valueless.) The image has no transactions with time or history; it is disembodied and idealized—as such, Rich suggests that photography be the metaphor for the discourse of men. The photograph remains a copy of a solitary and initial "thrust in the dark / to see if there's pain there" (*WTC* 45). The camera's way of seeing is one of penetration and violation, rendering lifeless the observed. Rich literally replaces this deadening gaze of the photograph with its analogue in language.

The photograph stares us down, pinning both the viewer and the photographed to a wall. The gaze's defining function is to appropriate, hierarchize, and control; the camera's gaze is that of a watchtower in a police state. In "Pierrot Le Fou," Rich attempts to describe language in filmic terms, having rejected the stilled images of photographs. The poem's six scenes or divisions, the use of abrupt line breaks, dropped lines, and stanzaic patterns, parallel cinema's montage construction and jump cuts. The glance, or an ongoing regard that never concludes, is explored as a new poetic. We take in parts, never the whole, when glancing: thus the glance proposes movement, body, time, showing and making.[20] The glance re-visions language and perception to emphasize and recover their diachronic movements. Charles Altieri argues that *The Will to Change* was "probably a mistake" because "the juxtapositional, notational style was so successful in capturing the flow of unconsciousness that it could not produce any of the counterpressure by which one establishes individual identity."[21] This judgment fails to consider the deictic quality of Rich's style and the implicit intentions of any style that could be considered "notational." The historical context of both this poetic and Rich's volume form a counterpressure to an aesthetical, social, and linguistic ideology that consumes the individual identity or demands identity assume a mask. Rich's deictic poetry here seeks to subvert the dominant ideology that denies the human scale, history, and movement of language.

"Images for Godard" foregrounds the poetics of self-reflexivity: "the notes for the poem are the only poem" (*WTC* 49). Since the "moment of change is the only poem" (*WTC* 49), the poet and the reader become inscribed in the very moment and gesture of the text. Rich emphasizes that language, and in particular the endeavor of writing and reading poetry, should be transactional and always locate itself on the boundary or the space between phoneme and meaning, signifier and signified, reader and author, context and text. Nor can any of these pairs be isolated; instead, they are connected, and due to this connectedness they are capable of change.

The filmic analogue or model is most extensively and success-fully explored in "Shooting Script." Importantly, the poem ques-tions its own transformative possibilities: "Entering the paper airplane of the poem, which somewhere before / its destination starts curling into ash and comes apart" (*WTC* 61). The title sug-gests incompletion specifically because it is a version or a plan for a film not yet made and that may turn out entirely different. The poet becomes a role player, the self a mask, the poem a script. Though the poem is a newsreel of items describing a destructive culture, the poem also examines language and poetry as impli-cated in that destructive culture. By restricting and repressing its inherent heteroglossia and polysemy as well as its materiality, language becomes logocentric and patriarchial; then the "mo-ment of change" seems impossible because of "the subversion of choice by language" (*WTC* 61). The poetics of the open field—one of association and a decentering of intention—are in conflict, however, with Rich's political and ethical demands of language. We must assume an ethical relation to language if self-definition and political change are to take place. Rich discovers, as we do through the process of the poem's own movement, that language's transformative power lies in its projection toward a future through the ongoing, discursive transactions of language.

By re-visioning the durational and historical movement and re-lations of language, Rich subverts the power of the synchronic im-age—which has been described as the essential level of the vio-lence of sexism and capitalism.[22] Any privileging of the image risks the severing of relations and interconnections. The image no longer re-presents (makes present again) but defers or dis-places presence. The image becomes the object of appropriation; in counterdistinction, Rich's use of imagery seeks to form rela-tions and to participate in interchange. Imagery illuminates the potential for immanence and transformation; whereas in, for ex-ample, dominant cinema, the image is withdrawn from discourse or interconnectedness and is indentured for the maintenance of the status quo. Though Rich does not refute the seemingly inher-ent erosive condition of language, she nonetheless envisions that language can be durational (historical and diachronic), recover relations and form connections, and attempt to attain (or sustain) a phenomenal nature.

The reinvention of the representation of women as well as the spectator's position and the spectator's response to seeing must take place. Language creates and controls official versions of history; therefore, it is the means for opposition and dissent. Though "Someone has that war stored up in metal canisters, a memory he / cannot use," the representation and the represented "would not be the war I fought in" (*WTC* 62). Not only is the world common to women marginalized through its representations in the dominant culture, but it is not situated in terms of women as respondents—readers or viewers. In a project as important as open dissent, Rich proposes to recover the "other films" that "have been there all along" (*WTC* 26, "Pierrot Le Fou"). The role of the readers extends the process of self-definition; their participation in the poem is part of Rich's re-visioning of language. Montage, association, and rupture necessitate the inclusion of the reader, in that the reader must consider the relationship of parts and paths toward a reading. Marked by provisionality, interpretation can no longer assume authority, especially as authority always carries patriarchial appropriation within itself. Interpretation, as synthesis, creates an image that, as an idealization, reconciles space and time in a totality, and thus denies any diachronic movement.

The Will to Change forms both a consideration of cinematic possibilities for poiesis and a rejection of those possibilities. It considers two distinct diachronic possibilities as the means of re-visioning a language that had become overwhelmingly synchronic and fetishistic. Rupture, distance, and opposition—typical cinematic structures—form one diachronic poetic at work in her poetry. Like the glance, the diachronic forms a discourse that cannot be complete, ideal, or an object of utter commodification. The diachronic poetic subverts the image / woman as object of appropriation and idealization. As the title implies, *The Will to Change* charges the poet and the reader with the ethical necessity of personal transformation and political redefinition. At the heart of both *will* and *change* is a re-visioning of language. By closing the collection with departure, finishing her "last meal" in her "old neighborhood," and "[knowing]" in every distortion of the light what fracture is" (*WTC* 67, "Shooting Script"), Rich points to her future tasks. Language must be, moreover, unfractured light, a "fiery iconography," the means for the examination of self and place: "the prism in your pocket, the thin glass lens, the map / of the inner city, the little book with gridded pages" (*WTC* 67).

In *Diving into the Wreck,* language has been burned off, leaving situation, event, and statement. The self-defining poetics of "Pierrot Le Fou"—"To record / for that is what one does" (*WTC* 28)—form the core poetics of *Diving into the Wreck.* Indeed, in the title poem, Rich writes:

> I came to explore the wreck.
> The words are purposes.
> The words are maps.
> I came to see the damage that was done
> and the treasures that prevail.   (*DW* 23)

Susan Van Dyne argues that these poems reveal a split between the poet who "almost obsessively urges community and commitment" and the poet who celebrates "an exhilarating solitude and easy suspension." [23] In such poems as "When We Dead Awaken" or "The Mirror in Which Two Are Seen as One," suspension does not deny connection but affirms the identity of self through the empirical process of observation and critical reflection.

The "I," however, in "Diving into the Wreck" is a disembodied marker and does not establish an identity or ethos. The narrating "I," instead, forms a mask at once allegorizing the condition of the individual in the quest for self-knowledge and the history of the feminist project. "Diving into the Wreck" fails in restoring intimate relations; instead, its logic parallels the early poem "Villa Adriana," where the personal is veiled. Rich has organized her parable around moments of liminality: the diver begins her quest by leaving the boat (a microcosm of society) to enter the "deep element" of the ocean. The "sun-flooded schooner" (again the intimation of the dominating "ultimate blue" of "Stepping Backward") is vacant; the symbol of society is empty—there is no "Cousteau with his / assiduous team" (*DW* 22). The second liminal moment comes when the diver is about to enter the wreck:

> I stroke the beam of my lamp
> slowly along the flank
> of something more permanent
> than fish or weed   (*DW* 23)

The diver has left the specific but empty culture of the schooner, has dived out of one element into another that is polymorphic, in constant change, and does not resist language's heteroglossia— the oceanic is not only immense and primordial but also rich in discourses "among so many who have always / lived here" (*DW* 23). The diver leaves the mediating oceanic medium to enter the wrecked mirror of the schooner she has left floating above her. The fusion of pronouns—"I am she: I am he" (*DW* 24)—marks the third liminal moment, where language is recast into an androgynous form founded on a transformation of modes of definition and empowerment. The poem suggests that the primary site for initiating political and social transformations is in the language— and particularly the language used in identification: "And I am here, the mermaid whose dark hair / streams black, the merman in his armored body" (*DW* 24). The final liminal moment occurs with the diver focusing on the "book of myths / in which / our names do not appear" (*DW* 24). She has journeyed to the center of the wreck, to the ship's log, or the book of myths, to discover the cause of the wreck—the exclusion of her name, of women's names, of their discourses, from the text, dicta, or mythos of culture. By allegorizing her personal and political condition, Rich asks us to read *otherwise*—not between the lines, nor only hermeneutically, but as the diver, the other for whom the schooner is an empty bark.

The persuasive power of "Diving into the Wreck" lies in its ability to employ the mythic structure of quest and discovery. While mythic structures primarily establish distinctions, Rich attempts to redirect the mythic structures of the quest and the gift as the means to "find our way / back to this scene" (*DW* 24) of the wreck or the trace of the world's and language's condition prior to the storms that led to the foundering and diaspora. Though the poem may invent a new woman who is both the hero and the treasure of the quest (and thus the poem critiques the patriarchical myth of woman-as-gift),[24] the reliance on the mythic structure erodes Rich's vision—if mythic structure is seen as always and already constructing a static and conservative version of historical reality so as to reduce the world to a system of exclusive norms. The question is whether mythic structures in themselves depend on the mechanics of distinction, deferral, and hierarchy, which in turn politicize the world. Rich obviously seeks to escape this by reaffirming her desire for the primordial and originary condition: "the wreck and not the story of the wreck / the thing itself and not the myth" (*DW* 23).

Rich has previously tried to reinvent herself and her language through the invocation of myth, probably in the earlier poem "I Dream I'm the Death of Orpheus" from *The Will to Change*. What is the death of Orpheus—the death of a particular form of lyricism? a particular ideologically defined discourse? the anger of the Thracian women? the poetry of the Bacchantes? Or is it Eurydice, the unnamed and the one lost to sight or at best peripheral, but whose ghost necessitates poetry:

> I am walking rapidly through striations of light and dark thrown
>   under an arcade.
>
> I am a woman in the prime of life, with certain powers
> and those powers severely limited
> by authorities whose faces I rarely see.
> I am a woman in the prime of life
> driving her dead poet in a black Rolls-Royce
> through a landscape of twilight and thorns.   (*WTC* 19)

In this homage to Cocteau's *Orpheé*, the self and the other are recast as mutually reflective masks:

> a woman sworn to lucidity
> who sees through the mayhem, the smoky fires
> of these underground streets
> her dead poet learning to walk backward against the wind
> on the wrong side of the mirror   (*WTC* 19)

Rich casts herself as a solitary who must read the "map of the future, the road radiating from the / initial split" (*WTC* 67, "Shooting Script"). She must become essentially the poet whom she guides back to the world; thus, writing heals the split between Orpheus and Eurydice and the abyss between poem and inspiration (where the poem marks the relinquishing of inspiration), as well as forms the medium for healing the institution of opposition and division. The poem thus describes a dream of androgyny and the task of recommencing from the wreck.

"Diving into the Wreck," however, is undercut or loses its critical edge by masking Rich's engagement with the phenomenal world (both historical and personal) with the turn to myth. The poem distances the reader from the poet as well as severing the poet from the narrating "I"; thus, self-definition and interconnection are unfulfilled. Each time Rich turns to myth (either as reference or as structure), she cedes her own language and identity. Myth leads to the fusion in the poem, where "I am she: I am he"; as a necessary political step, Rich is later to reject the concept of androgyny, in that it erases history and identity based on difference:

> There are words I cannot choose again:
> *humanism   androgyny*
>
> Such words have no shame in them, no diffidence
> before the raging stoic grandmothers: . . .
>   (*DCL* 66, "Natural Resources," Rich's italics)

These words are not permeated with "the fibers of actual life / as we live it, now" (*DCL* 66); thus, they have little power. The oversimplification of these terms elided the examination of the categorization of masculine and feminine as well as ignoring the institutionalization of power in privileged categories. From the vision of androgyny in "Diving into the Wreck," Rich turns to the examination of lesbianism and motherhood, while arguing for a poetry founded on historical and personal interconnections.

"Diving into the Wreck" expresses the desire to recover lost origins and the world before the schismatic language of the oppressors, while also healing these divisions of gender, if we argue she has successfully subverted the mythic structure and that the dive itself does indeed trace the transformation of myth in the moment of re-visioning:

> First the air is blue and then
> it is bluer and then green and then
> black I am blacking out and yet
> my mask is powerful
> it pumps my blood with power
> the sea is another story
> the sea is not a question of power
> I have to learn alone
> to turn my body without force
> in the deep element.   (*DW* 23)

The poem reflects the poet's solitary task of self-definition as well as the work of recovery of that which has been repressed throughout cultures. The poem, in effect, turns to myth for the will to change or the self's assent to dive into "the deep element." In this sense, the poem has become didactic, for Rich turns herself into an exemplum by donning a "mask [that] is powerful" and that "pumps [her] blood with power."

The criticism of the distant and solitary "I" is not limited to only the title poem. Though "Diving into the Wreck" suggests a utopian hope through a vision of androgyny, it also foregrounds the isolation and solitude of women. In "Merced," emotions are seen as attenuated and abstracted; the poet herself has withdrawn (or is literally borne away by postindustrial technology) from the pedestrian world of Amsterdam Avenue, to literally map the ethical collapse of the city, a microcosm of the culture:

> I look down at the city
> which meant life to me, not death
> and think that somewhere there
> a cold center, composed
> of pieces of human beings
> metabolized, restructured
> by a process they do not feel
> is spreading in our midst
> and taking over our minds
> a thing that feels neither guilt
> nor rage: that is unable
> to hate, therefore to love.   (*DW* 36–37)

The airborne voice recalls the earlier images of the helicopter as deliverer (*SDL* 24) and soul (*FD* 57). Here, however, the poet wheels away, as if only through distance can the suffocation of spirit be escaped.

"The Phenomenology of Anger" and "Meditations for a Savage Child" accomplish personal testimonies. By glancing and assembling, ethos and poem form and inform each other. The anger of the poet—in response to a world of neglect, confinement, and abuse—is mapped through the use of short, jarring statements and violent shifts of narrative direction. "The Phenomenology of Anger" contains (in both senses of the word) its own anger: "How does a pile of rags the machinist wiped his hands on / feel in its cupboard, hour upon hour?" (*DW* 27). The denial of one's own rage constitutes another form of denying one's presence as well as distancing oneself from action. The denial of anger is a further internalization of the oppressor's methods and institutions, prompting frustration, impotence, and depression[25]: "Madness. Suicide.   Murder. / Is there no way out but these?" (*DW* 28, "The Phenomenology of Anger"). The oil-soaked rags become the stuff of Rich's writings, for in them is her genius of anger, another form of her "fiery iconography."

Anger forms an ethical energy if it can be transformative; through anger the narrator enables herself to define herself and to recover what has been oppressed—personally and politically. Anger is transformed into the desire for bearing witness and refusing silence. Rich interrogates the language to determine the meaning and the bounds of "Madness.   Suicide.   Murder." Language, Rich insists, is historically defined, and in its configurations we recognize ourselves as inhabitants of this particular century:

> You show me the poems of some woman
> my age, or younger
> translated from your language
>
> Certain words occur: *enemy, oven, sorrow*
> enough to let me know
> she's a woman of my time   (*DW* 40, "Translations"; Rich's italics)

These stanzas reassert the necessity of testimony and underscore the ethical demand for interconnection: the words "*enemy, oven, sorrow*" are passed from woman to woman, as if they were stones that could be held, still warm from handling, durable and understood. Language sheds its authority and distance once it has been shifted from the abstract domain to the intimate or womanly scale. The sign or word accedes to the place of an object, a durable presence and history.

"Meditations for a Savage Child," the final poem of *Diving into the Wreck,* self-reflexively and deictically records the activity of reading and reflecting on Itard's account of the Wild Boy of Aveyron. The tension between quoted text and the narrator's sections form a drama; the boy and the poet shadow each other and share the condition of oppression: "When I try to speak / my throat is cut" (*DW* 59). Language itself oppresses, for it demands our dependence on the things named, our inclusion in its ideology, and our conformity to its representations: it is used to commodify experience, to name "things / you did not need" (*DW* 55). Language, as a mark of some original wound or alienation, maps our separation from nature, the alienation of sexes, social and political schisms, and the distortion of reproduction. Language, as Rich suggests in this poem, is also the place of healing or suturing: language wounds; the scar is "a hieroglyph for scream" (*DW* 59).

The overlays of scar tissue "white as silk" trace the ambivalent, doubled nature of language:

> Go back so far there is another language
> go back far enough the language
> is no longer personal
>
> these scars bear witness
> but whether to repair
> or to destruction
> I no longer know   (*DW* 58)

As in the previous collection, Rich critiques language and desires to re-vision its production and power. Rich proposes to share voices, to generate a dialogic discourse, rather than arguing for either a personal (or private) voice or a public voice. "Diving into the Wreck," unlike "Meditations for a Savage Child," may map the quest for the sharing of voices, but the question remains whether the use of a mythic structure used by and constituting the oppressor's institutions can indeed be transformative, especially when the poem neglects to criticize the motifs of quests and gifts so central to patriarchial myths and narratives.

The poetics developed in her ghazals and such poems as "The Shooting Script" and "Meditations for a Savage Child" lead—stylistically and thematically—to the poems in *The Dream of a Common Language*. These poems respond to the conditions of human life and move specifically toward a passionate re-presentation of and a lucid attention to the lives of women. In particular, Rich inhabits the voices of other women. The poems expand the reflexive use of language, which mediates the impulse to describe the self in idealized terms. Reflexivity foregrounds the relation of the self as creator and respondant to language. The title of the collection suggests the vision of a dialogic discourse and indicates a radical shift from her earlier volumes, which are critiques of the "oppressor's language" (*WTC* 18). Rich reveals the desires of this new poetic in "Origins and History of Consciousness":

No one lives in this room

. . . . .

Without contemplating last and late
the true nature of poetry. The drive
to connect. The dream of a common language.   (*DCL* 7)

The room is a room of one's own and a public room, the poet's
mind and self and the readers' selves; it forms a shared and inter-
textual space that cannot be closed or silenced. Discourse is this
shared space or common language no longer governed by the
"myths of separation," and it is never possessed by any one participant. Thus, Rich inhabits—as we as readers (or more strictly
women readers) do—these heteroglossic rooms and the presence
of others.[26] The insistence that the implied audience is composed
of women may be argued as a separatist tactic, but it must be recognized as a result of extending Rich's own self-re-vision as a
woman-poet; such self-definition specifies political and cultural
contexts in order to address most immediately particular mem-
bers of the reading audience who have not often been addressed so
directly. The poems' generally dramatic structure emphasizes
Rich's desire to converse with discrete and responsive voices;
thus, in order to be read, the poems necessitate the reader's self-
reflective participation.

  The Dream of a Common Language redirects the notion of a
lyric poetry to include and acknowledge language as a social
discourse:

If in this sleep I speak
it's with a voice no longer personal
(I want to say   *with voices*)
          (*DCL* 4, "Phantasia for Elvira Shatayev"; Rich's italics)

The plenitude of discourse is revealed through the polyvocality
of such poems as "Phantasia for Elvira Shatayev" and "Paula
Becker to Clara Westhoff." The other inscribed in discourse revokes unicity found in conventional and structuralist formulas of

language. The inclusion of the other instead insists on the social
and heteroglossic movements of language. Part of Rich's ethical
writing and the ethics of self-definition is an engagement with
one's own otherness or soul that is "dragged down deeper / where
it cannot hear me" (*DCL* 35, "Twenty-one Love Poems"). Thus,
Rich attempts through the act of writing to narrow the distances
and to heal the isolation expressed in *Diving into the Wreck*.

   "Sibling Mysteries" relocates the mythic within the context of
intimate relations whose domains are kinship, sisterhood, memory, and dialogue. The poem desires to recover the freedom of the
secret writing shared in childhood between two sibling sisters.
Rich is again diving into the wreck, but here she has dropped the
mask and predicates the poem's drama on the urgency of dialogue:

> Remind me how the stream
> wetted the clay between our palms
> and how the flame
>
> licked it to mineral colors
> how we traced our signs by torchlight
> in the deep chambers of caves   (*DCL* 47)

"Sibling Mysteries" establishes a span of memories that connect
those of childhood to collective, chthonic, and interior memories,
or "earth-deposits   of our history" (*DCL* 3, "Power"). Unlike
the much earlier poem "After Dark," which interrogates death
and the authority of the father, "Sibling Mysteries" marks the
sources and traces of interconnection among women. Memory
forms a palimpsest of writings that leads us through texts to an
originary relation or text—keeping in mind that language is always a shared event. The poem is anchored in the Mysteries of
Eleusis, which celebrated the reconciliation of oppositions through
the reunion of mother and daughter as well as the recovery of nature from its defamation by culture. To re-member is to reunite
and express again the plenitude of relationships and identities—
as sisters, daughters, and mothers. The poem risks, however, the
negation of shared discourse by the force of the mythic identifica-

tion. The poet is torn by these two very distinct visions of language: the originary and mythic or the dialogic and heteroglossic. Though self-definition and interconnection form in language,

> we are translations into different dialects

> of a text still being written
> in the original

> yet our eyes drink from each other
> our lives were driven down the same dark canal   (*DCL* 51)

A description of language that insists on an originary moment or relation results in authorization and the subsumption of the intimate into governing categories. The dramatic condition of the poem—the poet insists on conversation—keeps it from wholly assenting to a poetics privileging mythic authority.

In addition to implying dramatic dialogues with others (exemplified by "Phantasia for Elvira Shatayev" and "A Woman Dead in Her Forties"), Rich's inhabitation of voices and lives illustrates her dialogical modeling of language and the inherent desire for interconnectedness within that model of language. "Twenty-One Love Poems" grounds these proposals for discourse in a lyric sequence that revokes the patriarchial language in the everyday world and emphasizes lesbianism as a threshold for change:

> No one has imagined us. We want to live like trees,
> sycamores blazing through the sulfuric air,
> dappled with scars, still exuberantly budding,
> our animal passion rooted in the city.   (*DCL* 25)

Set in the "sulfuric air" of a violent and deathly city, this sequence of poems emphasizes the energies needed for interconnection as a means for survival and self-definition:

> two people together is a work
> heroic in its ordinariness,

the slow-picked, halting traverse of a pitch
where the fiercest attention becomes routine
—look at the faces of those who have chosen it.   (*DCL* 35)

The poem's sequential structure composes glimpses that foreground the process of self-reflection. The poem moves from the
alienating cityscapes to a "country that has no language / no
laws," where what "we do together is pure invention" (*DCL* 31).
The language Rich envisions mirrors the awareness of each other's
bodies: "Whatever happens with us, your body / will haunt mine"
(*DCL* 32). Though Rich rhetorically asks, "was the failure ours?"
(*DCL* 33), the poem maps the necessity of critically searching for
self-knowledge as well as arguing that women define themselves
not wholly in terms of opposition but through the lesbian continuum. Such self-definition recasts language and forms a necessary step toward political change. In "Twenty-One Love Poems"
Rich names herself by interrogating the solitude inflicted upon
her by the city as the most concentrated site of the oppressor's
language: "Close between grief and anger, a space opens / where I
am Adrienne alone. And growing colder" (*DCL* 34). This self-
reflexive moment recalls Elizabeth Bishop's self-discovery and
self-naming in "In the Waiting Room"[27]; Rich, however, expresses
the difficulty of maintaining connectedness—sexual and spiritual—between women.

Though "Language cannot do everything," it is only "these
words, these whispers, conversations / from which time after
time the truth breaks moist and green" (*DCL* 19–20, "Cartogra-
phies of Silence"). Language has the potential of supplanting the
regimes of silence; such a language, as Rich emphasizes in "Natural Resources," is the work of retrieval:

The miner is no metaphor. She goes
into the cage like the rest, is flung

downward by gravity like them, must change
her body like the rest to fit a crevice

to work a lode
on her the pick hangs heavy, the bad air

lies thick, the mountain presses in on her
with boulder, timber, fog

slowly the mountain's dust descends
into the fibers of her lungs.   (*DCL* 60–61, "Natural Resources")

The poet mines for language and uses language to search out the
other, "a fellow-creature / with natural resources equal to our
own" (*DCL* 62). The miner—unlike, though echoing, the diver—
probes and explores history, "the dark lode [that] weeps for light":

My heart is moved by all I cannot save:
so much has been destroyed

I have to cast my lot with those
who age after age, perversely,

with no extraordinary power,
reconstitute the world.   (*DCL* 67)

As the title indicates, "Natural Resources" redefines culture by
emphasizing the occupations of women—the otherwise unacknowledged work done day in and day out that creates civilization.

In "a voice no longer personal" (*DCL* 4, "Phantasia for Elvira
Shatayev"), Rich recognizes herself as a public poet, speaking
within a social discourse and of a particular continuum. These recent poems do not depend upon allusions, but embrace or inhabit
particular voices. The inhabitation of other voices, or the re-
presenting of voices through one's own, triggers self-examination
and self-definition, for in discovering what characterizes others,
Rich uncovers and ascertains her own character:

I know now the kind of work I have to do.
It takes such energy! I have the feeling I'm

> moving somewhere, patiently, impatiently,
> in my loneliness. I'm looking everywhere in nature
> for new forms, old forms in new places,
> the planes of an antique mouth, let's say, among the leaves.
> I know and do not know
> what I am searching for.   (*DCL* 42)

Rich further emphasizes the interconnective dialogic process by constructing this poem, "Paula Becker to Clara Westhoff," in the form of an epistle, so that the words are not only passed between two persons but are also preserved to be read and remembered by others. In its re-visioning, language mirrors and is constituted by the phenomenal world; thus, language both preserves and interconnects:

> These things by women saved
> are all we have of them
>
> or of those dear to them
> these ribboned letters, snapshots
>
> faithfully glued for years
> onto the scrapbook page   (*DCL* 65–66, "Natural Resources")

We disintegrate into traces, but like an archaeologist Rich salvages what remains in order to piece together life that was itself always "rootless, dismembered: knowing it makes the difference" (*DCL* 75, "Transcendental Etude").

A *Wild Patience Has Taken Me This Far* continues to establish interconnectedness between women: "*Nothing but myself? . . . My selves.* / After so long, this answer" (*WP* 8, "Integrity"; Rich's italics). Poems such as "For Julia in Nebraska," "For Ethel Rosenberg," "Culture and Anarchy," "Mother-in-Law," "Grandmothers," "Heroines," and "A Vision" contend

> that history
> is neither your script nor mine
> it is the pictograph

from which the young must learn
like Tom Outland, from people
discredited or dead
that it needs a telling as plain
as the prairie, as the tale
of a young girl or an old woman
told by tongues that loved them

(WP 17–18, "For Julia in Nebraska")

Rich creates poetry that is imperishable and shared, like a pictograph. The script cannot be appropriated nor can it overrun others. Rather, as a public poetry, Rich's work has increasingly become the naming of names. In "Culture and Anarchy," unlike Matthew Arnold's work from which the title is borrowed, Rich does not establish a doxological approach to history and consciousness. Arnold emphasizes the orderly progress of mankind through clear intelligence and firm obedience, thereby allowing the dominant ideology to maintain control. Arnold's methodology is another way of reducing the world to exclusive categories, denying the plenitude that Rich, following Dickinson and Whitman, sees:

Anarchy of August: as if already
autumnal gases glowed in darkness underground
the meadows roughen, grow guttural
with goldenrod, milkweed's late-summer lilac,
cat-tails, the wild lily brazening,
dooryards overflowing in late rough-headed
bloom: bushes of orange daisies, purple mallow
the thistle blazing in her clump of knives,
and the great SUNFLOWER turns   (WP 12)

Lives and names burst like these flowers across the page:

Matilda Joslyn Gage; Harriet Tubman;
Ida B. Wells-Barnett; Maria Mitchell;
Anna Howard Shaw; Sojourner Truth;

Elizabeth Cady Stanton; Harriet Hosmer;
Clara Barton; Harriet Beecher Stowe;
Ida Husted Harper; Ernestine Rose

and all those without names
because of their short and ill-environed lives
False dawn. Gossamer tents in wet grass: leaflets
dissolving within hours,
spun of necessity and
leaving no trace   (*WP* 13–14, Rich's italics)

By literally saving these names of women abolitionists, Rich
hopes to stanch the loss of the memory of their lives. Names anchor us in social and political contexts while also forming the last
trace of presence (though a trace that is infinitely repeatable); to
remember the names or to name oneself (as Rich did in "Twenty-
One Love Poems") is to stem the erosion of history and language.
Though a name separates and distinguishes, it also indicates relations and memory and thus maintains or extends a continuum.

The poems in *A Wild Patience Has Taken Me This Far* weave
interconnections between land, the personal, the public, and history that are as inextricable as "the matrices we weave / web
upon web, delicate rafters" (*WP* 18, "For Julia in Nebraska"). In
this weaving, moments of contemplation, minute details of nature, and ordinary activities converge with something other, distant, future:

I slice the beetroots to the core,
each one contains a different landscape
of bloodlight filaments, distant rose-purple
striations like the oldest
strata of a Southwestern canyon
an undiscovered planet laid open in the lens
                                    (*WP* 15, "Culture and Anarchy")

Two vastly different scales converge under close and attentive observation. The canyon (recalling the "gorges unexplored since

dawn" [*DCL* 31] in "Twenty-One Love Poems") is pictured again in the final section of "Turning the Wheel": here Rich journeys toward "a fissure   to the female core," nearing "the edge   to meet the face / of annihilating and impersonal time" (*WP* 59). These canyons, she knows, "wear / a famous handwriting / the river's still prevailing signature" (*WP* 59). Rich, however, refuses to complete the journey. Like the diver, she is alone on the highway nearing this site symbolizing sexuality, violation, death, and gender. The site is literally still being written on and worn down. "Feeling too alone" (*WP* 59), Rich refuses the journey to the originary site for intimate and political reasons: the mythic quest cannot be undertaken, as the diver's once was, in solitude; others must be present to share any revelations.

In "Sources," the opening poem of *Your Native Land, Your Life,* Rich undertakes a solidly autobiographical self-examination; thereby, she actively shuns the demands of a mythic structure or intent. Rich seeks the phenomenal sources of her memories and poetry in the "Shapes of things: so much the same / they feel like eternal forms" (*NL* 3). Earlier poems and contexts are echoed by such specific details as "queen anne's lace, with the drop of blood" (*NL* 3). The poem revolves around the central question "*From where does your strength come?*" (*NL* 5; Rich's italics); she provides this provisional answer:

> I refuse to become a seeker for cures.
> Everything that has ever
> helped me has come through what already
> lay stored in me.   Old things, diffuse, unnamed, lie strong
> across my heart.
>   This is from where
> my strength comes, even when I miss my strength
> even when it turns on me
> like a violent master.   (*NL* 4)

This strength, like Dickinson's "loaded gun," is the same power of language. As a "violent master," language as strength is ambivalent, for it burns in and burns out of life. It is also the violence of the laws of the father—the fathers of poetic influence; her father, Arnold Rich; the symbolic authority; and the patriarchy. Rich, like Blake and Dickinson, harnesses this strength by knowing its sources of power: "real energy flowing and of power in the best sense—not power of domination"—comes through the "access to sources."[28]

The recovery and discovery of the sources of power and survival has been one of the central concerns in Rich's poetry, her prose theory, and her own life. In "Sources," she confronts her Jewish heritage, her dead father and husband, and the history of her New England landscape. These are also the histories of survivors, which prompts Rich to examine her own condition as also that of a survivor:

> All during World War II
> I told myself I had some special destiny:
> there had to be a reason
> I was not living in a bombed-out house
> or cellar   hiding out with rats   (NL 7)

These lives, she states, "must have been strategies no less / than the vixen's on Route 5" (NL 7). Though the image of the vixen represents a guiding and nurturing motherhood, it primarily suggests the necessary will and desire for one to make her way and to convey that knowledge of passage to others. This strength of will is necessary for those "who want an end to suffering, who want to change the laws of history, if we are not to *give ourselves away*" (NL 25; Rich's italics). Through the invocation of personal memories, Rich maintains an autobiographical voice, yet it is a voice anchored in the public discourse and the forces of history as they act upon and define the self.

Seeing in the "diaspora-driven" and "the 'New' Englanders who hung on / here in this stringent space" (NL 11) strategies and examples for her own survival, Rich knows how necessary it is to examine history, for "in the beginning we grasp whatever we can" (NL 6) to find the makings and remnants of cultures. Writing in

"North American Time," Rich argues that the force of history directly impinges upon language—thus, she critiques writers who believe they can be exempt from the political moment: "Poetry never stood a chance / of standing outside history" (*NL* 33). We have the choice of writing or remaining silent; furthermore, we are defined by our mortality (our passing) and our words (our remains),

> We move   but our words stand
> become responsible
> for more than we intended   (*NL* 33)

Though "this is verbal privilege" (*NL* 33), it requires ethical knowledge. The word is the mirror of the self; what is written is more than a trace of presence, in that it has power. The power of words is paradoxical, for what we write "can be used against those we love" (*NL* 35). Writing is also limited by self-knowledge: we are always writing toward knowledge, the words are always about to arrive, but never is the writing complete nor can the words be found:

> You who think I find words for everything,
> and you for whom I write this,
> how can I show you what I'm barely
> coming into possession of, invisible luggage
> of more than fifty years, . . .
> (*NL* 97, "Contradictions: Tracking Poems")

Unlike "Culture and Anarchy," which records the names of women abolitionists and feminists (where slavery mirrors the marginal status of women), or "Turning the Wheel" (a geographic and historical movement "to the female core / of a continent" [*WP* 59]), "Sources" is Rich's most eloquent and sustained entry into history through the direct and deictic questioning of her own connections to place and history. The poem best expresses the duration of contemplation, rather than arising out of a moment or a single event—in this it is a diachronic self-reflection. While

"Sources" explores the origins of poetic energy (that which allows survival and interconnectedness), Rich also catches herself, as in "Homage to Winter," contemplating mortality: looking "backward along the hem of "[her] whole life," she is still trying to learn "how to live, what must be done / though in death you will be complete" (*NL* 71). Relentlessly, Rich questions the capacities of language and those who write poetry in this epoch: Would writing be "honest work" even "if we knew the children were all asleep / and healthy,"

> would we give ourselves
> more calmly over   feel less criminal joy
> when the thing comes   as it does come
> clarifying grammar
> and the fixed and mutable stars—?   (*NL* 68, "Poetry: III")

The privilege of the writer—when there are so many who are unable to read yet are still subjected to the various discourses in our society—is seldom addressed in poetry other than Rich's. Writing holds the power of transformation, but that power is interpreted only by those who can afford to read.

In "Sources," Rich re-visions culture while also arguing that the making of a poem is an act of survival; the basis of each of these processes is interconnection:

> I have wished I could rest among the beautiful and common weeds I can name, both here and in other tracts of the globe. But there is no finite knowing, no such rest.   Innocent birds, deserts, morning-glories, point to choices, leading away from the familiar. When I speak of an end to suffering I don't mean anesthesia. I mean knowing the world, and my place in it, not in order to stare with bitterness or detachment, but as a powerful and womanly series of choices: and here I write the words, in their fullness:
> powerful;   womanly.   (*NL* 27)

Rich closes "Sources" with the act of writing. She points to the gesture of writing as belonging to time and to its durability and presence through time; thus, writing must be reimagined as a phenomenal event anchored in the world as "rockledge   soil insect   bird   weed   tree" (*NL* 26). Writing means setting down her story, and thus defining herself; to do so forms a testimony and examination of one's self in relation to others. Rich proposes a new poetics, not only of private definitions of self but of confronting one's character or ethos in one's own time and in the times and places of others, knowing full well one cannot assume another's place, but that one must try to respond to the other fully, lucidly, and passionately.

CHAPTER FOUR

W. S. Merwin's
Poetics of Memory

In W. S. Merwin's poetry, we are always on the threshold of some disquieting revelation. Each being—as much as beingness is recognizable in the wastelands Merwin evokes—is the last member of a tribe, using a language (lyric and social) that is both utterly personal in its imagery and public in its description of impending extinction. Merwin's poems are *writings* that are themselves verging on extinction; his work evokes a poetic grammar, which corresponds with a vanishing natural world. What are these writings of telos? Do they point to a desire for nothing or silence: the point at which form is broken? Merwin suggests the poet is always at the point of silence: the poem will break off, the listener or reader will depart, or the narrator will fall silent because language no longer is connected with the natural world.

In Merwin's poetry, the interrogating regard of silence demands that we read the always and already vanishing alphabets and scripts of the world:

> Now all my teachers are dead except silence
> I am trying to read what the five poplars are writing
> On the void   ("A Scale in May")[1]

Silence, associated with solitude and profound isolation, can describe the vatic resonance of a prophet in a wilderness: "Silence / is my shepherd" (*CL* 116, "Signs"). Silence, then, can guide us, for in a purely existential sense, silence is the only possible essence we might have: it is the only thing we cannot accumulate or lose. As the place from which we emerge, silence is "Born once / born forever" (*CL* 116).

Silence, however, can only be not-being and the lack of discourse between the self and others. Because discourse is the difficult seeking of fullness, we must enter into, rather than extract from, the text or poem. The response is then to go on a pilgrimage or journey—one of Merwin's prevalent motifs. Though Merwin and Elizabeth Bishop share the theme of the journey, Bishop's travels pose questions about our relations to a phenomenal world, whereas Merwin's pilgrimages desire a recalling of a theophanic world. In "Rime of the Palmers," we read without sounds or "sing, and without words, / An air of promise" (*FF* 11). The palmers move "Between stillness and time" to reveal that "Our motion is our form" (*FF* 10). The palmers—like ourselves, for in our interrogation of the palmers they come to mirror us—seek out what has been lost of themselves:

> And what do you remember
> This morning and light?
> —We go (may wonder
> Send and receive our feet)
>
> Half-remembering
> Where our bones were hid
> And the wind at evening
> There where hunger died
>
> And the evening wind
> That everywhere and sorely
> Turned and complained
> As we came away.   (*FF* 11)

Our nearly depleted memories nevertheless will guide us back to our lost bones, back to plenitude, "where hunger died," and thus away from deadening silence. This is a retreat to plenitude and, as Charles Altieri notes, is modeled on the mystical *via negativa*, rather than on the affirmative visions of such romantics as Blake or Yeats.[2] What must be emphasized is that the mystical *via negativa* leads to several forms of an ironic presence. First, presence may be affirmed in the "nothing that is." This is a space outside the poem and a space the poem does not admit to approaching, despite the journeys undertaken. Second, presence surfaces as the poem itself. The poem does not mirror immanence, but is immanence being eroded by silence. The poems, *writings* as *utterances,* express a language not split apart by conventional separations of writing and speech, body and spirit. Significance does not lie beyond words, but is the process of writing and of hermeneusis.

Merwin's poetry moves close to the abyss where language and memory end, the domain of silence. In contrast to the erosion of language, memory offers a provisional stay against the abyss. Memory always forms a dialogue with one's self, because memory is always *other*. We are made many by the remembering of the past; thus, memory is the re-vision and accumulation of pasts, so much so that to distinguish between versions, each of which is more or less correct, is difficult. Therein lies plenitude: the proliferation of versions or re-visions gives memory its dialogic and midrashic textuality. To make word, text, event, self, and world full again is the desire of memory. Thus, memory is a re-membering, or reassembling, of dispersed and severed parts.

Memory must then partake of an Orphic quality, for what is left of the singer and the song is but a fraction of the whole; the rest of the corpus has been lost, washed under and away. Resurrection and recognition through naming comprise the principle energy of a generative, Orphic memory. Memory is also to be considered writing's method of overcoming silence. The memory of the full word or of the sacred and consecrated, hence secret,[3] text arises from the atavistic desire to reinscribe the originary text.

Merwin's use of memory is essentially Augustinian, as Altieri

notes, in that memory exists nowhere, yet is the key to presence.[4]
Coinciding with this model of memory, however, is the Augustinian description of the world as book, where we must remember
how to read and where hermeneusis is the midrashic continuing
of the book or the energies of the world's writing; hence, this
memory of writing represents the possibility of plenitude:

> On dim gestures does the mind
> Exorcise abandoned limbs,
> Disbodied, of that other land
>
> Estranged almost beyond response,
> A bleached and faintly relevant
> Signature to sir the sense
> In veteran usage and intent.
>
> One dreams fixed beasts that drowse or wonder,
> Not blinking; by the stream a few
> Poplars and white beeches where
> Exhausted leaves, suspended, through
>
> The distant autumn do not fall,
> Or fallen, fired, are unconsumed,
> The flame perduring, the still
> Smoke eternal in the mind.   (*FF* 3)

"Anabasis" provides a version of the Greek retreat in Asia Minor,
recorded by Xenophon in his *Anabasis*. The event is, however,
disclosed only through the self-evident reference contained in the
palimpsestic title. Set in a past tense and using an impersonal
voice severed from experience and time, emotion and involve-
ment are dissipated:

> The remnant of all passage lies
> Cold or distorted in the brain
> As tall fables of strangers, as
> Lisped visions of other men.   (*FF* 4)

Memory, or the "remnant of all passage," is seen as provisional and fallible, a "cold or distorted" gesture or mark remaining before silence. The narrative, like the retreat, is a version covering the same ground with new footprints over the old, each path only a remnant of the other, older ones. The tension between silence and the making of language is shown in the extreme desolation of a seascape in "Anabasis II": "We turned from silence and fearfully made / Our small language in the place of night" where "We float leeward till mind and body lose / The uncertain continent of a name" (*FF* 9). We float homeward, like Odysseus, losing our names, which once gave us identity but also divided us from the others.

Memory provisionally recovers what has been lost and, like an anabasis, crosses over the ground, covering it with the tracks of its presence always already past. Memory traverses and works against or beyond forgetfulness, definition, and repression. The "Lisped visions of other men" remain housed in our memories. The return through these memories, to where interconnectedness endures, is a necessary and re-creative act. For Merwin, memory and language coincide in that both are nothing, yet both express an ineffable presentness. Though memory is a shadow, it does provide a second look, and in the looking-again reality multiplies, as an offering, a discoursing, a flowering.

Our relationship to our remembered selves forms a self-enclosed mirroring where there is

> No landscape but a demeanor of distance
> Where interchangeably the poles are death
> And death, as in an opposition of mirrors
> Where no beginning is, no end, I have lived
> Not recognizing, for as long as knowledge.   (*FF* 115, "Canso")

Merwin recognizes our deathly double bind, which memory and language describe while provisionally bridging and ironically forming distance: "a name with which to say emptiness" (*FF* 143, "The Prodigal Son"). Silence results from the prohibition of discourse, for it is always beyond and within the final period, the last interpretation, and the first breath. What does it mean to fall silent except to pronounce distance, to fall away from discourse, from others, and from being? To fall silent is to become extinct.

In "The Annunciation," Merwin describes the moment of Annunciation as a silence "That closed like a last clap of the thunder / And was perfect" (*FF* 150). Merwin invokes silence as a paradox, which breaks the conventional laws of cause and effect or logic. Though silence arguably points to mysticism, silence is always an embedded component of language, and the institutions language mirrors. Merwin's task is to remember language before the invocation of an authoritarian and denaturalizing ideology, one that Adrienne Rich has called "the oppressor's language."[5] In contrast, the language that must be remembered would be "Like no man and no word that was ever known" (*FF* 150). Mary's anxiety, "if I could only remember / The word, if I could make it with my breath" (*FF* 153), describes the tenuousness and ineffability of the otherness of language. "The poet," Altieri argues, "can no longer make the adequate word with his breath, nor so readily imagine the darkness redeemed in a spiritual light; he can only put out the false words of limited consciousness and point beyond them to an absence he evokes but does not describe."[6] Thus, the poem forms an *ars poetica* demonstrating the difficulty of inspiration. The poem is itself a recounting or remembering—thus a supplementation—of the loss of the vision, rather than a re-creation of the vision. Merwin's poetry moves further from any acknowledgment of the immediacy of vision, and deeper into the loss and the distance from that originary silence, void, or darkness.

Merwin's poetry moves along the edges of silence, intimate with death:

> last messages written on the white petals
> appear as they wither
> but in whose language
> how could we ask   (*CL* 104, "Last People")

In Merwin's explorations of the last language, flowers bloom but also wither, foreclosing any hope, any pastoral or scenic idealization. The "last messages" are written in an unknown language we cannot begin, in our estrangement, to address. Silencing and forgetting are mutilations, what Geoffrey Hartman calls "a 'blinding' of the ear and an ultimate defense against the unquiet imagination."[7]

The subversion of silence begins interpretation. Crossing thresholds toward the strange and away from the familiar (which needs no interpretation), interpretation describes two traditions of language. Interpretation, first, marks language as a medium that veils; thus, language must be pierced in order to arrive at a meaning. Interpretation, however, can also inscribe language as "not something to be penetrated or opened up but, on the contrary . . . what everyone (even without knowing it) manages to keep hidden—a sort of unspeakable danger like the lie that threatens to turn into the truth." We should view Merwin's poetry as marked by the midrashic character of writing: the parable—and writing itself—"does not convey a meaning to an audience, rather it conveys the audience to the meaning. . . . its hiddenness is not to be dispelled by understanding but requires to be preserved, for hiddenness is an essential part of that which is to be understood."[8]

Interpretation erases silence in its discourse with and toward the always hidden; likewise, it makes familiar and recollects discourse. Discourse, however, must not fill up space with empty markers or consumeristic catalogs. For Merwin, authentic discourse depends on memory, which forms a palimpsest and provides a key to the mystery of the present. Both memory and discourse connect us to the world, so that we find ourselves, in the poem "The Animals," "tracking over empty ground" animals we have never seen and "with no voice // Remembering names to invent for them," asking "Will any come back" (L 3). The paradox of the presence of the nonpresent is the paradox of memory. Language does no exist in the future, but rather its domain is always that of the past and of memory. There will be new signs, but they do not exist until they have surfaced, and once surfaced they are linked to the signs that have been displaced. Silence exists at the

end of language's chains of signification, but the generation of
signs pushes against silence and the death of language.

In "Learning a Dead Language," Merwin locates memory in the
word itself:

> There is nothing for you to say. You must
> Learn first to listen. Because it is dead
> It will not come to you of itself, nor would you
> Of yourself master it. You must therefore
> Learn to be still when it is imparted,
> And, though you may not yet understand, to remember.   (*FF* 176)

The poem not only describes the process named in the title but
forms Merwin's *ars poetica*. The poet cannot simply assume the
native tongue, for such a language, buried in its utter familiarity,
is also a dead language. Neither passively received nor made
one's own, language must arise from, release, and share sensual
plenitude. As Gerald Bruns argues, the poet, or any participant in
discourse, must seek out the ways to reinvent language and thus
rescue it from death.[9] To language's Orphic self, the poet returns
breath, the secret inspiring. The poet remembers the grammar
and order, and above all remembers to incorporate the passion
and memories into this language. Then,

> What you come to remember becomes yourself.
> Learning will be to cultivate the awareness
> Of that governing order, now pure of the passions
> It composed; till, seeking it in itself
> You may find at last the passion that composed it,
> Hear it both in its speech and in yourself.   (*FF* 176)

Passion both inspires return and lies beyond return. Re-membering language is the means by which we are rescued from silence,
for it bridges the gap between ourselves and passion:

> What you remember saves you. To remember
> Is not to rehearse, but to hear what never
> Has fallen silent. So your learning is,

> From the dead, order, and what sense of yourself
> Is memorable, what passion may be heard
> When there is nothing for you to say.   (*FF* 177)

Merwin invokes the modernist vision of a collective tradition and memory as well as a postmodern personal vision. To remember is a personal act that does not redeaden or "rehearse," but renews "what passion may be heard / When there is nothing for you to say."

Poetry, through memory, crosses thresholds at the risk of blindness and loss: "you fall on your knees and try to call to them / far in the empty face" (*W* 107, "Glass"). Poetry argues for the retrieval of the eyes, self, and language. To lose discourse, to forget the words, is to be sentenced to death:

> If you, if you my word and so my life
> And so the mode and vessel of my death,
> Should die before me, I would not go
> —Although turned phantom by your truancy—
> Calling the earth of you; neither, impelled
> By what pain soever, with a zeal
> As of an antiquarian, cull, compose
> At last a vacancy of you and there become
> An impresario of emptiness
> Swaying before defection. What are the patterned
> Potsherds to him who knows what wine there was?   (*FF* 112–13)

In this stanza, from the second of three poems titled "Canso," Merwin addresses the empty word with the same urgency one might use to address a lover: "If you, if you my word and so my life." The poem, like its namesake, the Provençal courtly love poem, constitutes intimacy and exchange between the word and others. Evoking the motifs of containment and plenum, the word— wine or blood of the communion—must be recovered and be made present again.

The poet's search for the secretive but cornucopic word is a searching for the origin of all signs:

> There must be found, then, the imagination
> Before the names of things, the dicta for
> The only poem, and among all dictions
> That ceremony whereby you may be named
> Perpetual out of the anonymity
> Of death.   (*FF* 114)

The "dicta" pronounce creation, and only at that moment is the word itself cornucopic. By reinvoking the modernist vision of the homeomorphic myth, Merwin's early poetry suggests modernist preoccupations with and beliefs in affirmation. Here the originary dicta form laws or pronouncements that make language an object of symbolic exchange. Naming, the reenactment of the original dicta, forms a ceremony of affirmation and perpetuation of them. The ceremony maintains discourse in a ritualized and not a personal form, nonetheless keeping it from falling into silence or the "anonymity / of death." The invocation of the intimate pronoun "you" subverts the complete and impersonal institutionalism:

> Creation waits upon
> The word; but you in silence are the conception
> And the consent of speech, the metaphor
> In the midst of chaos, whose word is love.   (*FF* 117)

Through the desires for the provisional "you," language emerges from silence. Merwin insists on the imagination, defined through negation, as a beginning, "a rocking cradle not yet rocking / Where yet no cradle is" (*FF* 118). These ornate poems are far more affirmative than are his later poems, because they invoke the imagination and its dependence on love. Even so, affirmation is undercut and limited, for Merwin self-reflexively turns to the reader and states, "You know the story, its dénouement" (*FF* 120).

The word, in its provisionality, evokes a "celebration of a permanence. . . . The articulate dance, the turning festival" (*FF* 117). The "articulate dance" describes the movement of discourse that always includes the other. This Orphic self-reflexivity—

where "Orpheus is poetry thinking about itself"[10]—is also reflected in the way that the "articulate dance" and the "turning
festival" refer back to themselves as the poem itself. The poem
is a "turning" of language, a troping, while following the well-
defined steps of consistent lines and stanzas. The dancer remembers past steps with each new dance; similarily, the reading of
text is a remembering of the old words in a new way. "Canso"
ends with an Orphic pronouncement:

> Death is by definition a terrain
> Of no return save to itself, where all
> Appearances are voices calling, "Look
> Now, oh look if now only"; is a face whereon
> To look is to know loss; and what if I
> Sould [*sic*] turn but once, and you vanish? The song is nothing
> If not a resurrection.   (*FF* 120)

Death is the silence we fall back into and so lose our distintive-
ness. Death and silence result from the failure of self-reflexivity
as well as when there is no link between the seer and the seen.
In this failed state—where "to look is to know loss"—we witness
the vanishing of Eurydice: there is finally a gap, threshold, or silence that cannot be crossed; thus, we are profoundly separate.
Eurydice represents, however, the point toward which art and desire tend.[11] The endeavor is marked by necessity and failure: if we
should turn and hence break the law governing exchange, we lose
not only the gift—the desired—but also our own selves. Paradoxically, however, it is this very breaking of the law that allows for
poetry. The only hope of regaining the self, and the other by supplementation, is through language. The "song is nothing / If not a
resurrection." Merwin's ambivalent relation to modernism is suggested in this poem, for it resurrects the beloved and other texts,
as well as recalling Eliot's theme of the Easter drama with its
sources in the Osiris myth.

The poems of the "Bestiary" section in *Green with Beasts* describe a time of presence before loss and the subsequent necessity
of a provisional and reconstituting memory:

> not summer, not the idea of summer,
> But green meanings, shadows, the gold light of now, familiar
> The sense of long day-warmth, of sparse grass in the open
> Game of the winds; an air that is plenitude,
> Describing itself in no name; all known before,
> Perceived many times before, yet not
> Remembered, or at most felt as usual.
>
> (FF 135, "White Goat, White Ram")

We are in a world even before the pastoral golden world, in an Edenic world where there has been no fall and where there is thus no time, memory, or iconoclasm. It is the world of the beasts, who "wait / Beyond our words, beyond earthquake, whirlwind, fire" (FF 137). The poem identifies us as the fallen, having lost the "green meanings" or the arche-writing. We now recognize our previous mystery only through desire:

> There is no need
> Even that they should be gentle, for us to use them
> To signify gentleness, for us to lift them as a sign
> Invoking gentleness, conjuring by their shapes
> The shape of our desire, which without them would remain
> Without a form and nameless. For our uses
> Also are a dumbness, a mystery,
> Which like a habit stretches ahead of us
> And was here before us; so, again, we use these
> To designate what was before us, since we cannot
> See it in itself, for who can recognize
> And call by true names, familiarly, the place
> Where before this he was, though for nine months
> Or the world's full age he housed there?   (FF 136)

The animals mark the time before our division. Our desire to return to this pristine state only distances us further by appropriating the animals to define our desire, "which without them would remain / Without a form and nameless." Like Orpheus, we ascribe names to the animals, but they are not the "true names," for we cannot know, "familiarly," where we were before this "desire."

The distance is compounded, for the animals return our regard (and our's is solely a selfish regard) with apparent indifference:

> Of the moment before him in which you stand
> Is a ghost's shimmer, its past gone out of it, biding
> But momently his vigil. Walk past him
> If you please, unmolested, but behind his eyes
> You will be seen not to be there, in the glaring
> Uncharactered reaches of oblivion, and guarded
> With the rest of vacancy. Better turn from him
> Now when you can and pray that the dust you stand in
> And your other darlings be delivered
> From the vain distance he is the power of.   (*FF* 134, "Dog")

The indifference of the dog's stare unsettles us; in it, as in the gaze of the Sphinx, we glimpse our own powerlessness and mortality. Though we name the other, we also vanish into its name, which, like the dog's stare, entombs us, swallows us, and erases us: "in them you are not there." Merwin uses the unrelenting stare to wholly reflect our relation to them: "It is the sign / We make of them, not they, that speaks from their dumbness / That our dumbness may speak" (*FF* 137). Language separates us from the other and grants us provisional identity. Language becomes our self-made prison and the medium in which our memories conjure the impossible originary moment of interconnection:

> Listen: more than the sea's thunder
> Foregathers in the grey cliffs; the roots of our hair
> Stir like the leaves of the holly bush where now
> Not games the wind ponders, but impatient
> Glories, fire: and we go stricken suddenly
> Humble, and the covering of our feet
> Offends, for the ground where we find we stand is holy.
> (*FF* 137–38, "White Goat, White Ram")

The holly bush, emblematic of resurrection, is associated with Sir Gawain and the green knight, the holly-king, and the seven days of creation.[12] The poem describes the desired recovery of the spiritual through the recognition of the loss of the knowledge of interconnection or arche-writing. Even in the face of the destructive force of "the sea's thunder," the spiritual knowledge "foregathers" before the primal sea of chaos thunders.

Merwin achieves a language in extremis, where the demands made upon it to be authentic and collective arche-writing force language to reinvent itself by casting back toward the originary:

> I wish no voice
>
> Remembering names to invent for them
> Will any come back will one
>
> Saying yes
>
> Saying look carefully yes
> We will meet again   (L 3, "The Animals")

At such a visionary moment one has no personal voice or self; rather, the poet is the one who remembers others. We emerge from "All these years behind windows / With blind crosses sweeping the tables" to track "Animals I never saw" (L 3), and thence hope they will return to us uttering the affirmation "yes" and directing us to "look carefully." The poet must assume the role of the holly-king—or any figure of resurrection. Though Merwin evokes mythic figures and motifs, his concerns remain those of postmodernism described by Ihab Hassan: "the Denaturalization of the Planet and the End of Man" corresponds to the erosion of language, so that "we no longer know what response is adequate to our reality."[13] Merwin's use of mythic imagery does not propose the collective, unconscious order of Eliot's use of symbolism, but is a form of the retrieval of interconnective readings. As sites of readings, these images are hermeneutic rather than hermetic or coded.

In "December among the Vanished," the wandering poet waits in a broken hut "with a dead shepherd / And watch[es] his lambs" (L 45). The poet preserves the mystery within names, and in so doing takes on the burdens the culture has neglected. Though the poet provisionally replaces the dead shepherd, he cannot assume the empowered and visionary role of a new shepherd: the "encroaching distances" deny any "vista of openness," instead, as Cary Nelson writes, "Everything is penetrated by loss," and though we long "to reach out and care for the lambs," we are "also part of that flock whose shepherd is dead."[14] Reduced to an interminable but powerless role, the poet can only "watch" over the lambs. Sheltered inside the "knitted walls" of the hut, the carcass of lambs, or the cadaver of language, the poet shelters his own depleted self:

> I think all this is somewhere in myself
> The cold room unlit before dawn
> Containing a stillness such as attends death
> And from a corner the sounds of a small bird trying
> From time to time to fly a few beats in the dark
> You would say it was dying it is immortal   (L 48, "The Room")

The poet's writing dies once it reaches the stillness of the page, and yet is immortal in the interminable poiesis of witnessing and sounding a "few beats in the dark."

Memory and language link the self to others; however, because language is fallen, the self turns to memory to renew the links provisionally: "Coming late, as always, / I try to remember what I almost heard" (MT 41, "The Poem"). The title signals that this poem is Merwin's ars poeticae; there is no other subject but the poem as an existential poiesis. We are always "coming late," being the most recent or the last of creations; and being late, we are closed from the world and removed from the anagogical mysteries. What one is left with is language and memory, both of which point to the loss of the keys to inspiration and a full language:

> How many times have I heard the locks close
> And the lark take the keys
> And hang them in heaven.   (MT 41)

The nearness of connection with the other causes the speaker to "try to remember." But, as Altieri writes, the speaker "ends up only with another wound, a fictive unknowable heaven that continues to generate desire ('how many times') but not to satisfy it."[15] The poet is caught in an interminable and liminal moment. The liminal, described in Merwin's iconography through such images as doors, windows, shadows, and eyes, is a dialogical and dialectical moment in which one describes and desires the absent other.

In "Invocation," the poet arrives repeatedly at the same remembered place:

> Here I am once again with my dry mouth
> At the fountain of thistles
> Preparing to sing.   (*MT* 40)

The poet and his language, like the fountain (a traditional neo-Platonic image of plenum, inspiration, and transcendent linking), have gone dry, becoming barren, divisive, and inauthentic. Eliot's "Burial of the Dead" is evoked in "Invocation," where the "day hanging by its feet" (*MT* 40) recalls Eliot's tarot reading and the absent Hanged Man, as well as his landscapes of heat and dryness. Merwin, in crucial distinction from Eliot in this poem, does not describe any implicit unicity achieved through the falling together of myths into a symbolic order. Merwin insists that the remains of language allow him to be "preparing to sing." Language, as desire, offers hope or at least counters despair. Despite Merwin's bleak landscapes and increasingly spare language, the poetry posits a personal vision based on the materiality of signs; this distinguishes his poetry from the impersonal and authoritarian symbolism of Eliot's modernism, which sought to dispose of the reflexive and material sign.

The diminishment of language, however, diminishes the self:

> We say good-bye distance we are here
> We say it quietly who else is there
> We can say it with silence as our native tongue
> > (*MT* 79, "She Who Was Gone")

When we assume silence "as our native tongue," we face an existential and ungenerative solitude. This is the silence into which discourse falls after it has ended, after the final stop or period in which meaning gains control of speech and fixes it. Crucial here is the insistence on the dialogical nature of language. At stake for Merwin are the energies of transference between the one who speaks or writes and the one who listens, reads, or understands. With silence as our now-familiar tongue, we can only "remember the sound of the snow at night / Brushing the glass towers / In the time of the living" (*L* 57, "The Mourner"). At the final period or abyssal white space all motion ceases: we could imagine the speaker assuming one of Beckett's restricted spaces, where distance, on the one hand, has vanished ("good-bye distance") and, on the other hand, expresses the profound measure of our isolation ("distance we are here"). The floating caesura in this line allows a reduced language to do more because of its ambiguity, but because of this ambiguity language becomes only provisionally meaningful.

In "Daybreak" (*MT* 97), the poet recognizes the limits of his own language, the poetic language, and enters the shriven populace. The future of speech or of the written line is a deadening silence if either fails in generating connections. The reader is asked to participate in the reinvention of language, to fill the gaps of silence the culture has created through the severing of connections. Remembering is the means of reinvention; as Altieri notes, "memory restores man to his home in process."[16] Poetic or authentic language comes only when one is faced with the loss of Eurydice, when "An open doorway / Speaks for me / Again" (*MT* 97). Language does not arise from silence, but silence is the dangerous supplement of language. The poet always inscribes the double bind of language and silence, word and speech, light and dark, and presence and death. The process is not one of opposition, but of supplementation and deferral. The poet joins this procession, finding himself part of a tradition or lineage of poets who heal language by language: words are "homeopathic, curing like by like in the manner of Spencer's 'myrrh sweet bleeding in the bitter wound.'"[17]

The process of renewing language must be continuous or else language would atrophy. This interminable process, however, reveals the impossibility of crossing the last threshold and recovering or re-membering the cornucopia. The mirroring or doubling "again" at the beginning and end of "Daybreak"—recollecting the repetition of sunrises and sunsets—foregrounds the cyclic movement of the poem and poetry's origins as an inscription of cycles. Though there is a joy in repetition—like the joy of sexual play or child's play—along with the anticipation of return and of a sedimentaton of order, repetition reinforces the familiar and excludes the secret. The poet is outside of the natural order of diurnal cycles and is aware only of its qualities of repetition. The lack of punctuation, which began to appear in *The Moving Target,* allows for an openness, a hope that the final word will not arrive. Yet in "Daybreak," this openness collapses into repetition—a dangerous form of entrapment rather than a process of memory. To remember is to desire the resumption of our relation with the other and thus to overcome loss, whereas repetition asserts the magnitude of loss regardless of memories.

Memory forms a palimpsestic common ground; the poem becomes a sibylline place, as in the closing poem of *The Lice,* "Looking for Mushrooms at Sunrise":

> When it is not yet day
> I am walking on centuries of dead chestnut leaves
> In a place without grief
> Though the oriole
> Out of another life warns me
> That I am awake   (*L* 80)

The oriole, which speaks "Out of another life," breaks the solitude and silence with a language that has been lost in the course of our separation from nature. Though the poet and the natural world are separate, there remain some ambiguous, unnamed, and atavistic connections:

> The gold chanterelles pushed through a sleep that was not mine
> Waking me
> So that I came up the mountain to find them

> Where they appear it seems I have been before
> I recognize their haunts as though remembering
> Another life   (*L* 80)

Memory draws the speaker into the morning, to climb the mountain, much like an earlier pilgrim climbing out of the night of the underworld toward the yet unseen sun. An early morning walk becomes self-reflexive, the world points toward older links between him and itself, while his memory traces back through itself to attempt to reestablish the past and lost cornucopic relationships. This final poem of *The Lice,* like each final poem from *The Moving Target* to *Opening the Hand,* involves an Orphic moment of threshold, of coming out into the world at daybreak or commencement, of transformation, of waiting for the singing to begin, or of refulfilling one's atavistic gift. Thus, each collection opens into the next, the last poem becoming the first poem to continue the desire for return.

Memory can only initiate return; yet return, like memory, depends on language. In contrast to the prevailing spareness and the theme of the almost inexorable movement toward extinction in Merwin's work, "The Well" contains the prospect of the potentiality in all things, for the water contains all its songs that have been neither released nor lost:

> Under the stone sky the water
> waits
> with all its songs inside it
> the immortal
> it sang once
> it will sing again   (*CL* 37)

The protean water will be drawn out of its secrecy, revealing that the well is "a city to which many travellers / came with clear minds" (*CL* 37). We must enter into its own element, for it is like a text "imagined to contain all that can be said, and a good deal more besides, since it recedes into the unspeakable source of all that can be put into words."[18] The midrashic process of reading—

indeed, of perception—describes an undisclosed meaning, a secret pointed to but not named:

> Echoes came in like swallows
> calling to it
> it answers without moving
> but in echoes
> not in its voice
> they do not say what it is
> only where   (*CL* 37)

Through the very activity of reading, we discover that we are among the "travellers" whose "clear minds" mirror the buried arche-song that "is nothing / If not a resurrection" (*FF* 120):

> It is a city to which many travellers
> came with clear minds
> having left everything even
> heaven
> to sit in the dark praying as one silence
> for the resurrection   (*CL* 37)

Cities turn into palaces of memory through which we travel; as such, they are labyrinths winding into either revelation or imprisonment. "The Well" thus offers a contrasting vision to Merwin's earlier poem "The Child," where

> I regard myself starting the search turning
> Corners in remembered metropoli
> I pass skins withering in gardens that I see now
> Are not familiar
> And I have lost even the thread I thought I had
>
> If I could be consistent even in destitution
> The world would be revealed   (*L* 37)

The earlier poem invokes the motif of Theseus journeying into the labyrinth or the maze of figuration. The poet regards himself as an Orpheus whose song has been lost and as a Theseus whose thread has been severed. Yet do we traverse the mnemonic otherness of the underworld; or is it the world of light we journey in, now transformed beyond any re-membering? We have left childhood, crossed its thresholds into a metropolis, losing the green world of childhood. At best, we retain through the self-interrogating regard, a provisional memory of what has been lost. The world has been dismembered, and only parts of it—and only the most external of those—remain.

In "The Child," Merwin stresses the "regard" that he notes is a process in which "the distance begins to dissolve between the seer and the seen. They are seen as one." [19] The child regards himself and his world as neither familiar nor strange but as deadened. In contrast, "The Well" describes the elemental and spiritual realm that "answers without moving / but in echoes." This resonance parallels and describes the traces or memories beckoning an absent presence: "Echoes come in like swallows / calling to it" (*CL* 37). Writing, the absent presence, supplants and breaches speech or song. Though writing is the originary ground—Orpheus "could hear only what he could write" (*CL* 115, "Memory of Spring")—writing remains a radiating echo of something beyond definition. Writing, for the first composer, is solitary and necessary; furthermore, creation becomes self-creation, as much a movement into an interior space as a movement outward into song.

The pilgrimage into the interior is found throughout *The Carrier of Ladders*. Though both Elizabeth Bishop and Merwin travel toward the interior of the text and the self, Bishop's journeys uncover the ambiguities of definition and the generative nature of language. Merwin, in such poems as "Snowfall," "Footprints on the Glacier," "As Though I Was Waiting for That," and "Ascent," confronts the other through the contemplation and the recognition of death:

> Some time in the dark hours
> it seemed I was a spark climbing
> the black road
> with my death helping me up

a white self helping me up
like a brother   (*CL* 69, "Snowfall")

In this recommencement he has not plunged into total communion, for distance still exists: "a bell rings in some village I do not
know / and cannot hear" (*CL* 69). Simultaneous with the disquieting lack of any certainty of perception or definiteness, we are
greeted with an assertion of knowledge and belief in some common human activity. What we know and what we experience are
severed; instead we know by not knowing: "Every year without
knowing it I have passed the day / When the last fires will wave
to me" (*L* 58, "For the Anniversary of My Death"). Nevertheless,
since "in the sunlight snow drops from branches / leaving its
name in the air" (*CL* 69), the vanishing name is set into relationship with the world of things and implies a provisional interconnectedness and a shared discourse. "Snowfall" doubles back on itself through the meditation on death to explore the possibilities of
communion. "Brother," the final word and stanza of "Snowfall,"
unifies the poet (including his memories of kin and death) and the
snow slipping off the branches in a moment of minute observation.
     Through division and systematization, dialectical and dialogi-
cal interconnections with others have been destroyed: "oh objects
come and talk with us while you can" (*CL* 107). This urgency and
necessity, the inverse of Ashbery's vision of the impoverished
abundance, resounds throughout the "Third Psalm: The September Vision." Each verse opens with "I see" in order to emphasize
the witnessing of the poet's extreme separation:

I see tongues being divided
          and the birth of speech
          that must grow
          in pain
          and set out for Nineveh   (*CL* 107)

Only by entreating objects to come and talk with us while there is
still time and language can we escape our depleted condition
where "there was never a silence like this" (*CL* 107).

Writing is Eurydice; like her, its presence is our loss; "before me in the dusk an animal rose and vanished / your name" (*CL* 131, "Letter"). Eurydice, once seen again, vanishes—her original form is lost in the moment of return or reiteration:

> you have been with me also in the descent
> the winter
> you remember
> how many things come to one name
> hoping to be fed
>
> it changes but the name for it
> is still the same
> I tell you it is still the same   (*CL* 131)

The name, Eurydice, remains in our memories. But where she stood—that moment of writing, full of its own meaning—fills with silence or with our memories. The word inscribes loss and reiteration; Merwin seeks to push writing into speech through reiteration. Likewise, the reiteration of memory is the desiring of the presence of the remembered. The phrase "I tell you" repeats throughout "Letter," indicating the urgency of the poet's task. Furthermore, the poem, while epistolary in its address, emphasizes the material image of writing, the letter. The letter, as seen in the later poem "Kore," is generative: it is literally the place where silence is broken.

Merwin's vision of language remains ambivalent; nevertheless, he seeks to avoid a metaphysical or systematic definition of language. To define the energy of language is to constrict experience, in that language is the mirror of ourselves and the world. Though Merwin closes *The Carrier of Ladders* with "In the Time of Blossoms," a poem that invokes a time of regeneration, the blooming of the ash tree, Ygdrasill or world-tree, and the foliation of language, he also sees in "The Pens" the erosion of language and of memory:

> In the city of fire the eyes
> look upward

```
there is no memory
except the smoke writing writing wait
wai
w                                    (CL 101; Merwin's italics)
```

The world undergoes, not a purgatorial fire, but a fire of extinction. Because our civilization has set the fires, our writing originates from our destructive ideologies and provisionally records the destruction through the material and violence we have created.

In *Writings to an Unfinished Accompaniment,* Merwin envisions the continuing erosion of language and memory:

```
but no memory no tree
even your sparks dust
toward the last                         (W 62, "One Time")
```

Though continuously erasing itself, this distanced voice also contains a self-conscious longing for a return to an interconnected world:

```
Have you seen
my memory
the flame far from the candles
                               (W 17, "To Be Sung while
                                            Still Looking")
```

Far more compact than his earlier poems, these poems point to themselves as texts isolated and fragmented on the page. Similarly, the title of the volume suggests an incompleteness and that these notes toward a poem are the poems themselves. Like Adrienne Rich, Merwin emphasizes that writing is transitory, hence it is diachronic and deictic. Merwin focuses on the temporality of writing, akin then to music; thus, implicit in this meditation on time and presence is a confrontation with death. The title implies that writing is a supplement to the performance of the music or speech—yet, only from these scripted notes will music or speech be performed. Conversely, the writings are transcriptions of the recognition and response to inspiration. The unfinished accompaniment, Richard Howard writes, is "life itself," or more specifically the poet's life.[20] These texts indicate the provisionality of life, of the poet's role, and of writing itself.

The poems self-consciously give up description, which is the self's capacity to contemplate or what Roland Barthes calls the "methodical inventory of the attributive forms of divinity."[21] What occurs in Merwin's poetry—and *Writings to an Unfinished Accompaniment* is the culmination of this particular process—is a self-reflexive giving up of the self:

> and the eye must burn again and again
> through each of its lost moments
> until it sees   (*W* 46, "A Purgatory")

Remembering "each of its lost moments," the eye of the poet as well as the "I" of the poet's signature share the desire for fulfillment: "until it sees," the vision "has just passed out of sight." To "burn again and again" erases the self through the alchemical element of fire. To see again, the eye must burn through or transform all "the selves that we remembered" (*FF* 7, "Anabasis II"), to recover an atavistic memory. Merwin discloses his own ambivalence about both the possible direction for a poetry under its own erasure and for the continuation of vision through such a poetry. The diction Merwin has allowed or restricted himself to by necessity of his vision has become self-parodic and distant. Memory's flame remains "far from the candles," so that we can only long for the fire—inspiration or energy—to return to the source.

Prophetic memories and atavistic writing converge in "Sibyl." The oracular Sibyl who composed her divinations on leaves mirrors the Bachelardian concept of the unconscious inspiration upwelling from the earth,[22] while the inscribed leaves compose the dispersed elements of a once leaf-laden but now barren tree. The figure of the Sibyl merges with that of the poet through the self-reflexive "you," which refers back to the narrator as though from a self-examining and external view:

the same wind that tells you everything at once
unstitches your memory
you try to write faster than the thread is pulled
you write straight onto the air
if it's summer

with your empty needle   (*W* 53)

The Sibyl emblematizes the dilemma of all writers: we inscribe a
silence or an abyss with every word set on the page. Each word
marks what remains outside our grasp because we cannot say
fully what we mean and, because we write with an "empty needle,"
we deplete the cornucopic word.

Merwin's Sibyl also emblematizes writing as a metaphoric
weaving of words into a shroud: words and allusions spin discourse farther into life before Atropos cuts the thread. The poet,
like Penelope, weaves and unweaves to weave again the death
shroud of Laërtês. Writing "unstitches your memory," and pulls
forth the threads of traces; unless pulled out and rewoven, when
the thread has run its course, the accompaniment will end. The
poem further suggests the simple fear of an artist of extinguish-
ing him or herself, having been drained of memory and writing. Always and already a death sentence, writing moves inex-
orably toward death, regardless of all of language's turnings and
flowerings.

The Wordsworthian ethos of the child as the teacher of the
father also occurs in "Sibyl," when the poet self-reflexively reveals "Your whole age sits between what you hear / and what you
write" (*W* 53). The return to the unindividuated preconsciousness
of early childhood is intimated at the moment of inspiration
or "the voice coming closer." This approach, however, is accom-
panied by winter, a conventional emblem of completion—both of
seasonal cycles and of one's life. The poet's life is self-reflexively
traced on his palms, for his words are written "if there's light
enough / straight onto hands" (*W* 53). But at this moment the
poem ends, for if we are to accept the concept of language as sig-

nifier separated from the signified, then language as we imagine it ceases once the separation ceases. The poem ends in utter silence, the end of language's chain of signification, the end of the tracings of life—in other words, death.

The poem's end has vanished; whiteness displaces the potential yet unwritten final refrain "if it's winter," which would have completed the inscribed seasonal cycle. Absence subverts our expectations and forces us to draw upon our own resources and memories to recover what has been silenced in this lacuna. To fill in the abyss is to complete and close the familiar cycle, but to engage the silence of the abyss is to remember the origins of our loss.

Exhaustion of spirit and body—where language has lost its Orphic power and the harpist's fingers no longer draw forth the rain in the sardonic and epigrammatic "Old Boast" (*W* 13)—encroaches on the poet's pilgrimage and quest. All around the poet, life and language disappear; the most inanimate objects lose their energy, and the poet seems to falter endlessly or to become lost:

> still I go on hoping
> as I look for you
> one heart walking in long dry grass
> on a hill
>
> around me birds vanish into the air
> shadows flow into the ground
>
> before me stones begin to go out like candles
> guiding me   (*W* 106, "The Search")

In a search that is interminable and always liminal, we pursue what vanishes yet what is present: the secret, the beloved, the ambiguous, and the undisclosed "you." The possibility of moving toward the secret, indeed entering into a secret, is vanishing. In "Spring" the future—toward which the interminable pilgrimages are directed—holds the possibility of recovering the things lost, the arche-writing, the originary song:

everything in the world has been lost and lost
but soon we will find it again
and understand what it told us when we loved it   (*W* 42)

Not only will there be renewal, but this renewal is always recurrent, for the "world has been lost and lost." The repetition suggests that the world has been either recovered again and again or
has been lost beyond loss. The ambiguity energizes hermeneusis
as a midrashic writing—we are forced to invent "meaning," knowing full well that our inventions are provisional. The thawing of
"cold lakes / from which our eyes were made" (*W* 42) inscribes the
return of spring, a writing we too will be able to see and read fully
once we "understand what it told us when we loved it."

"Gift," the closing but liminal poem of *Writing to an Unfinished
Accompaniment,* is a prayer to the "Nameless One O Invisible" to
return and

be my eyes
my tongue and my hands
my sleep and my rising
out of chaos
come and be given   (*W* 112)

Prayer will give the body, senses, and life back to the poet, who
stands as our representative. Although inspiration is entirely
personal and limited, since the poet "must be led by what was
given to [him]" (*W* 112), poetic inspiration also leads the poet to
be consumed and exhausted by the demands of inspiration. The
poet mirrors the natural world's cycles or is in symbiotic relationship with them, for Merwin continues,

as streams are led by it
and braiding flights of birds
the gropings of veins the learning of plants
the thankful days   (*W* 112)

The book, of the poet and of nature, is the gift that is complete—
"what does it not remember in its night and silence" (*W* 112)—
and thus holds all the undisclosed secrets. Merwin describes, not
affirmation, but an ambivalence and a provisionality residing in
the very moment of inspiration.

The Compass Flower, a collection that swerves toward narrative and elegy and away from the work of the previous four collections, contains the *ars poetica* and love poem "Kore," one of the
most important of Merwin's liminal poems. The key element of
the myth of Kore is the traversing of thresholds—from the world
of light to the underworld—as an image of separation and return.
Kore, however, is displaced by Merwin's intimate address to a
lover, which creates an intersection between the personal and the
mythic. The myth is re-visioned so that both the presence and
the absence of the other form the focus of the poem. Like Orpheus,
the speaker recognizes Kore's and his own presence through the
absence the poem seeks to fill. The return of Kore is assured only
through the poem, only in language. The poem emerges literally
from language, thus indicating the liminality of language and
that language is the primary arena for the poem's drama. As the
song is embedded in each minuscule of the Greek alphabet, the
poet is held within the other's smile:

> α I have watched your smile in your sleep
>   and I know it is the boat
>   in which my sun rides under the earth
>   all night on the wave of your breath
>   no wonder the days grow short
>   and waking without you
>   is the beginning of winter   (*CF* 49)

The metaphor extends and travels, carrying us into language and
into the loss inscribed by language.

The breaking of the "law" by the poet of "Kore" parallels the
impatience that, in Maurice Blanchot's version of the Orpheus
myth, produces the inspired gaze that Orpheus turns upon Eu-

rydice. The breaking of the law is inspiration; but "inspiration means the ruin of Orpheus and the certainty of his ruin, and it does not promise the success of the work as compensation, anymore than in the work it affirms Orpheus' ideal triumph or Eurydice's survival."[23] By regarding the letter in "Kore," we break bread with the letter and enter into language or song. In doing so, we paradoxically leave behind the letter—we literally marginalize it. If to write, as Blanchot suggests, we must already be writing, then to read we must already be reading, a process that "resembles the irrational impulse by which we try to open eyes that are already closed, open them to life; this impulse is connected to desire, which is a leap, an infinite leap, just as inspiration is a leap: I want to *read* what has nevertheless not been written." To read is not only to venture into a "cadaverous emptiness" but to greet "the presence—hidden though it is—of what must appear . . . to converse each instant with this Lazarus."[24] Or this Kore.

The poem, with its rubrics of Greek minuscules, points to its own inscription and the figure of Kore, who represents the fulfillment of the script and the vitalization of language. An implicit tension, however, exists between the script (of both poem and alphabet), which moves from the letters alpha to omega, and the cyclical and regenerative nature of Kore. The alphabet is not inherently cyclical in comparison to the movement of the seasons or Kore's terms of agreement with Hades. The script, in fact, is the deadening of Kore; thus, sensuousness and passion necessary to the cornucopic letter become fixed. The stanzas themselves become figurations of a natural language; the atavistic and archaic speech that remains is only a trace in the letter. Without interconnection language deadens; however, within language there is always mnemonic potential to recover and renew passionate relations with the other.

In "Kore," Merwin distinguishes between two forms of memory. The poem rejects memory that represents simply the conscious and sentimental past:

π I trust neither memory nor expectation
   but even the white days of cities
   belong to what they do not see
   even the heart of the doubters' light is gold   (*CF* 53)

In addition to the sentimental past, the equally sentimental quality of expectation is rejected. The poet seeks an active seeing, one
that would establish the presence of the always and already vanishing Kore: "I burned up all the matches in the night / to look at
you" (*CF* 54). The poet's desire for Kore, the atavistic memory, is
foregrounded by his breaking of the laws that restrict or deny the
awareness of one's body:

I reach for you with my eyes
I call you with my body
that knows your one name   (*CF* 55)

At the moment the poet reaches with his eyes, he actively and at-
tentively sees the other. The poet knows Kore's "one name," yet
maintains its secrecy by leaving the name unuttered and thus not
present. Only when Kore has returned, and thus is present, can
her name be present—otherwise the name is a mark or a cadaver.

Nevertheless, seeing is a provisional exchange and an affirmation:

even when you are not with me
in the flowerless month of the door god
you look at me with your eyes of arrival   (*CF* 53)

Janus, the god of thresholds with his two faces, one looking each
way, emblematizes thresholds and the two-way path of seeing.
Furthermore, seeing denotes arrival, the state of coming into
union and embracing, and thus the diminishing of separation. Of
course, with "arrival" there is always an implicit departure; in
departure, however, "your eyes of arrival" would be present again.
The poem ends with the paradox of the present already being
absent:

ω   The shadow of my moving foot
    feels your direction
    you come toward me
    bringing the gold through the rust
    you step to me through the city of amber
    under the moon and the sun
    voice not yet in the words
    what is spoken is already
    another year   (*CF* 56)

The poet seeks the originary that has been lost, yet through desire and memory it is made present again in a voice that is not yet
a voice. Kore approaches in "The shadows of my moving foot" or
in the tracery of the poetic line, or through the tracery of autumnal forests, "the city of amber" where Sibyl's leaves are dispersed
by the wind. The ending, the omega, opens into the interminable
approach of the desired. At the moment of the final enjambment,
we leap and cross another threshold into "another year." What is
longed for is already past, yet always ahead.

Extending from the thematics of desire, memory, and language
in "Kore," *Finding the Islands* consists essentially of love poems
in which memory joins the present so that experience is not lost:

    I want to remember clearly
    from the beginning
    come and greet me   (*FI* 69, "Winter Storm")

Merwin proposes that in the moment of ecstatic presentness everything becomes transparent, much in the way that Roland Barthes
describes the haiku: "articulated around a metaphysics without
subject and without god, [the haiku] corresponds to the Buddhist
Mu, to the Zen *satori,* which is not at all the illuminative descent
of God, but 'awakening to the fact,' apprehension of the thing as
event and not as substance." The site of reading exists as a moment of utter presentness—not as a substitute or as a metonymic
event. In the poems, in *Finding the Islands,* as in haiku, "time is
without subject: reading has no other *self* than all the haikus of

which this *self,* by infinite refraction, is never anything but the site of reading."[25]

The self-reflexivity of "infinite refraction" is not an affirmation but an assertion of presence, it is simply *that,* "or better still: *so!* it says, with a touch so instantaneous and so brief (without vibration or recurrence) that even the copula would seem excessive, a kind of remorse for a forbidden, permanently alienated definition"[26]:

> We stood in a garden by a wall
> and the evening star
> took us by surprise   (*FI* 49, "Living Together")

The element of the unremarkable being remarked upon has no originary moment, nor does the poem offer any commentary. We do not penetrate the poem, rather we explore simply a flatness, or what Barthes calls *matte.* Because there is no "deepening" of language, we approach each stanza as a momentary experience; our reading becomes a seamless "adequation of signifier and signified."[27] The interconnectedness that was longed for in "Kore" emerges:

> I travel on and on
> until there is only you
> my homeland and morning   (*FI* 45, "Turning to You")

The effect of each stanza is to fall silent, not, however, in the silence of the period—the silence of closure and death—but to an attentive presentness. The halt of language "is not a matter of crushing language beneath the mystic silence of the ineffable, but of *measuring* it, of halting that verbal top which sweeps into its gyration the obsessional play of symbolic institutions. In short, it is the symbol as semantic operation which is attacked."[28]

Each stanza reflects all the others; thus, they are like the Kegon or Hua-yen doctrine of a net of jewels that creates a myriad of mirrorings.[29] The intention, the desire for presentness of self and language within a collective whole, however, is a naive gesture, especially given the ambivalence toward any sustained or authentic experience of interconnection expressed in Merwin's earlier poems. The poems of *Finding the Islands,* however, succeed insofar as they do because they emerge from the previous discourses and are transparent in their desire. The impossibility of a full language, nonetheless, is reflected in the extreme momentariness and ephemerality of these poems. The vision is not sustainable, the simplicity of the language does not allow an extended attentiveness. The passage of attention and our (and the poet's) failure to remain engaged in the deepening of the mundane or of presentness indicates our estrangement.

Finding the Islands, though attempting to heal memory (and its inscription of loss) and presence, revokes memory. Desire arguably overruns memory and creates what John Ashbery described as the "still performance"[30] of mere and momentary presence. Each stanza forms a discrete moment that in its stillness becomes intimate to the point of being unreadable, if we construe reading as a hermeneutic activity. Language, like memory, constantly displaces itself, covering and recovering its tracks; Merwin shifts from this vision of language to one that is extreme in its self-containment and refusal of metaphor. In addition, *Finding the Islands* refuses to undertake cultural and personal crises addressed in the previous collections. To revoke memory or push it toward disappearance demonstrates Merwin's desire for a language that is immediate and iconic. Because this poetic denies the energy of forming connections, Merwin returns to probe memory as a familial space of connection in *Opening the Hand.* The metaphoric title of this collection suggests a gesture of greeting and revelation. By opening the hand, we might reveal what was hidden inside the closed fist or secreted in the wrapping palm's lifelines. The title is a metaphor of hermeneusis—one of continuity or "opening." What seems undisclosed is what the hand holds: Is it empty or does it hold a secret? Will it grasp our own hand or fail to make contact? Will the hand open or flower? When the fist opens, it changes from an expression of possible violence and closure to one of offering and connection. By opening our hands we reveal what was written on our palms (or in the cards), in our inmost selves.

Opening the Hand contains a melancholy similar to that en-
countered in *The Compass Flower*. The failure to link with others
concerns both collections, which seek, through a discursive poetry, to reestablish ties. The earlier poem "St Vincent's" [*sic*]
suggests many of Merwin's later concerns of style and theme in
Opening the Hand. "St Vincent's" is a meditation on the nature
of perception and presence as well as a cataloging of what the
observer has seen and hence decided to record or remember.
Mysterious details, once forgotten in their familiarity, are seen
again. If "Kore" could be termed a private and ecstatic mnemonic
poem, then "St Vincent's" is a public poem moving toward the
intimate by means of sustained and attentive looking. The poet
has "seen the building drift moonlit through geraniums," has
"seen the nurses ray out through / arterial streets" as well as "no-
ticed molded containers stacked outside / a delivery entrance on
Twelfth Street" (*CF* 35). The disciplines of the hospital—from
the mundane routines to the study and disciplining of the human subject, in Michel Foucault's terms[31]—remain impenetrable,
hence the external features are mapped and posited as a metaphor for the interior. The hospital is metonymic of the city that
subjects us to prescribed order; the poet who seems outside the
panoptic scrutiny of the hospital (an arena of examinations) is
nonetheless left a powerless subject of the hospital's, and implicitly the culture's, monumental shadow:

> smoke rises from the chimneys do they have an incinerator
> what for
> how warm do they believe they have to maintain the air
> in there   (*CF* 36)

The observer next calls into question the accuracy of his own perceptions, thus forming a self-interrogation:

> several of the windows appear
> to be made of tin
> but it may be the light reflected   (*CF* 36)

As Elizabeth Bishop's poetry illustrates, description and observation are provisional, since the observer is unable to ascertain the

truth. The poem shifts again, when the observer no longer looks, but imagines what might be possible though never affirmed: "I have imagined bees coming and going / on those sills though I have never seen them." Once the threshold of the visible is crossed, observation becomes speculation.

The final line—"who was St Vincent"—questions the very name and hence the very presence of the other. The question is, moreover, a desire to remember and move through the palimpsests of the name. It suggests that the name has been emptied of history and meaning. Without a remembered history the name is a cadaver. The informed name is the vital mystery Merwin seeks, for this is the "doorway to see through / into the first thing," that "even our names are fire," as expressed in "Flight" (*CF* 94), the final poem of *The Compass Flower*. The fire figures as the phoenixlike language, always rising again, "the same fire the perpetual bird" (*CF* 94). Our names, the metaphorical trace of our being, contain this elemental fire. Unlike Wallace Stevens' "firefangled" bird, "without human meaning, / Without human feeling,"[32] Merwin desires, not the new order, but the lost plenitude of language.

Certainly the earlier poem "St Vincent's" must be seen as parallel to "Sheridan," in which the speaker questions how stories (and particularly their endings) correspond to the events the story unfolds. Through a contemplation of the general's statue, like his interrogation of the hospital, Merwin turns from a public discourse or site to a private observance. Also like "St Vincent's"— with its final, unsettling question—"Sheridan" displaces the historical moment; Sheridan has missed his time:

> The battle ended   the moment you got there
>
> oh it was over it was over   in smoke
> melted and the smoke still   washing the last away
> of the shattered ends   the roaring fray   (*OH* 53)

The past—indeed, all history, all memory—is displaced, beyond control. History is muted, turning monolithic or silent, and thus all but forgotten, like the statue in the midst of city traffic. History and the event's moment are further displaced, for the speaker interrogates the historical event through its trace or stand-in, the statue:

> there was the smoke   and someone with your head
> raised an arm toward it   someone with your mouth
> gave an order   and stepped into the century
> and is seen no more   but is said
> to have won that battle   survived that war
> died and been buried   and only you are there
> still seeing it disappear   in front of you   *(OH* 55)

The poem suggests the loneliness of memory and the difficulty of communicating its meaning and portent. Through the accretion of details, the poem discloses not only the Union general's ride but also the narrator's memory of being told the history or of having been read Read's *Sheridan's Ride*. At the same time, history is erased, for "Sheridan" is diminished to a place-name in the chaos of traffic: "everyone knows the place   by your name now / the iron fence   dry drinking fountain" (*OH* 55). "Sheridan," like "St Vincent's," mirrors New York City, but also suggests the city's potential for erasing history through the daily flux of traffic and trade.

Writing as a genealogical concern haunts *Opening the Hand* and suggests that genealogy is a primordial form of history. Stemming from genealogical anxiety, writing attempts by its very design to establish identity and kinship. Writing, like history and memory, is the conjuring of the return of apparitions. The repeated use of a particular vocabulary—doors, darkness, silence, winter, stars—expresses depletion and forms echolalic hauntings that Merwin self-reflexively comments upon in "Apparitions":

> Now it happens in these years   at unguarded intervals
> with a frequency   never to be numbered
> a motif surfacing in some scarcely known   music of my own
> each time the beginning and   then broken off   *(OH* 15)

The physical activity of writing is one of traveling across and back over the page: "those hands that were always   on the way back to something" (*OH* 16). Like genealogy, writing reveals the desire to recover the sources and all connections:

> I tell parts of a story
> that once occurred
> and I laugh with surprise at what disappeared
> though I remember it so well   (*OH* 22, "Talking")

Writing closes off the poet and us from the future, though we are always writing toward it and perhaps for it. Merwin asserts the impossibility of affirmation through the anticipation of the future when the present—let alone the past—is so provisional:

> what becomes of the house
> and the island
> and the sound of your footstep
>
> who knows it is here
> who says it will stay
> who says I will know it
> who said it would be alright   (*OH* 73, "The Truth of Departure")

Merwin also engages the strictly genealogical through his explorations of his relatives in such poems as "Birdie" and "Unknown Forbear." Central, however, is his relationship with his father, which is examined in "The Oars," "Sunset Water," "The Waving of a Hand," "Strawberries," "Yesterday," and "The Houses." Unlike Adrienne Rich in her most autobiographical poems, Merwin does not ground his poetry in a self-critical process. Merwin's diction remains distant, even nostalgic, while seeking a balance between memory, birth, death, and inspiration:

> As the shadow closed   on the face once my father's
> three times leaning forward   far off she called
> *Good night* in a whisper   from before I was born
> later through the burial   a wren went on singing
>   (*OH* 9, "Son")

While Rich pursues in her self-interrogation a critique of the culture and the language (of the father), Merwin tries to recover an atavistic poetic memory—the wren's song. Yet both poets demand to know the sources of their power. While Merwin may assign it to the natural world in general, Rich would argue that the experience of motherhood is equally significant and primal, as emblematized by the vixen in her long poem "Sources." The mother, however, is absent from Merwin's tracings—the Orphic poet has become an Oedipal poet. Like the myth of Oedipus, the collection poses the question of the poet's identity; by opening the hand, one's future or one's story is revealed, and the riddle solved. Thus, the shift from fragmented lyrics to the more discursive qualities of these more recent poems mirrors the shedding of the role of the Orphic poet. The shift is also from the hermetic to the apparent, familial, and social. Such are the concerns of Oedipus, who confronts, by solving the Sphinx's riddle, the inscription of death in the representations of the ages of man. The Sphinx imposes the conventions of order; though Oedipus may reject his future and rebuke the Sphinx, he is nevertheless stained by the law the Sphinx imposes.

The father—as an emblem of authority, law, and the word—is severed from the poet. "The Houses" describes not only the estrangement from the father—frequently described in the prose recollections in *Unframed Originals*—but the utter gap between all fathers and sons. On two occasions the son discovers houses deep in the woods, much like fairy tales in which only children cross the threshold of the forest to venture down a path to a secret and unknown house. The father cannot cross the threshold; thus, the strange remains undisclosed to him. The law of the father—the rejection of the strange—erases the sight of the houses: it is only "long after the father / is dead the son sees the two houses" (*OH* 14). Language, as the law of the father, blinds and constricts us; thus, we can only have an ambivalent relationship with language, for it is also the father—like the inspiration in "The Gift"—who carries us to the place of our own vision. The father, however, fails to see, and thus language fails to hold pres-

ent the houses waiting to be entered and inhabited. Finally, the
father and language deny presence to others; the other becomes
the imagination's domain and taboo.

Merwin's poetry is clearly one work, one vast intertext like
Whitman's enterprise or Pound's *Cantos:* "The poems reflect one
another endlessly, repeat the same messages tirelessly, clarify
one another and simultaneously complicate one another until
no image can ever be resolved."[33] Though Nelson suggests that
this intertext begins with *The Moving Target,* Merwin's first four
books must also be considered a necessary part of the whole ongoing project. They are not only the threshold but a necessary
grounding where "We turned from silence and fearfully made /
Our small language in the place of night" (*FF* 9, "Anabasis II").
The provisionality of this vision of language—a shared but depleted language and memory—haunts all of Merwin's work: "my
words are the garment of what I shall never be / Like the tucked
sleeve of a one-armed boy" (*L* 62, "When You Go Away"), or "I can
put my words into the mouths / of spirits / but they will not say
them" (*CL* 17, "Words from a Totem Animal"). The very activity
of writing falls into question:

> and I will remember the calling
> recognized at the wrong hours
> long since
> and hands a long way back
> that will have forgotten
> and a direction will have abandoned my feet
> $\qquad$ (*CL* 76, "As Though I Was Waiting for That")

Throughout Merwin's intertext we seem to be verging on the
abyss of silence, but the text, nonetheless, continues. This is not
affirmation in itself, but the demands of "the calling" and the
hard work of pilgrimage. Between silence and a depleted language we are left to "listen to both sides" (*MT* 50, "Air"). Yet between the two "there is only the sound of the cricket," the "black
jewel" that keeps watch throughout the night with its song:

> bodies of light turn listening to the cricket
> the cricket is neither alive nor dead
> the death of the cricket
> is still the cricket
> in the bare room the luck of the cricket
> echoes   (*OH* 83, "The Black Jewel")

The cricket remains in the bare room, perhaps without any choice, perhaps caged. The song is gone, but it continues to echo, "out of the wind / it has only the one sound" (*OH* 83).

"Things That Lock Our Wrists to the Past": Self-Portraiture and Autobiography in Charles Wright's Poetry

CÉZANNE: "I have my motif . . ." (He joins hands.)

GASQUET: "What?"

CÉZANNE: "Yes . . ." (He repeats his gesture, spreads his hands, the ten fingers open, brings them together slowly, slowly, then joins them, squeezes them, clenches them, inserts them together.) "There's what must be attained . . . There must not be a single link too loose, a hole through which the emotion, the light or the truth may escape . . . I bring together in the same spirit, the same faith, all that is scattered . . . I take from right,

> from left, from here, there, everywhere, tones, colors,
> shades; I fix them; I bring them together . . . My can-
> vas joins hands. It does not vacillate."
>
> ("Interview," 1979)

It's linkage I'm talking about,
      and harmonies and structures
And all the various things that lock our wrists to the past.

> ("The Other Side of the River")

Charles Wright's poetry is an autobiography of energy and transmutation, where the self's writing collaborates with the natural
world's writing. Writing extends our perception of the natural
world and, as such, writing forges interconnection through the
process of interpretation. Writing is the place of the transference
of the world's languages into our discourse; thus, writing mediates the natural world and the self. Wright's poetics share G. M.
Hopkins's emphasis on syntax, music, and the natural world
as the locus of meditation as well as instructing us in the intima-
cies of nature and mortality. Writing on Hopkins, Gerald Bruns
notes that Hopkins "figures himself in terms of a hermeneutic relation to the created world, as to a text or Book of Nature, whose
'compositions' are figures of energy that enact, as forms of language do, events of differentiation—the 'running instress,' in
Hopkins's words, that 'unmistakably distinguishes and individualises things.' To 'read' such compositions is an interpretive act, a
naming in the human language of signs of that which inscribes
itself ('distinguishes and individualises' itself) in the natural language of energy."[1] Unlike Hopkins, who privileged human speech
as the evolutionary and doxological completion of the created
world, Wright confronts a severed discourse where disclosure is
never complete and presence is always provisional and stained by
death. Nonetheless, Wright and Hopkins share a poetics in which
writing and nature are thought of as an "energetic form" of a
"continuity . . . shaped by the flow of energy, or energy made articulate in something visible and tangible."[2]

    The idea of linkage encompasses Wright's concept of language, his use of the poetic line, the structure of the poem, and the conceptual order of his collections. Language itself is generated through the energies of connection; language, while generative, embodies its own elegy or its own death: "Something infinite behind everything appears, / and then disappears" (*OS* 24, "The Other Side of the River").[3] Writing and interconnection occur through the release of motion and energy; thus, writing is relational. Connection is the betweenness of the self and the other, the place of provisional mediation of subject and object:

> When the mind is loosened and borne up,
> The body is lightened
> 　　　　and feels it too could float in the wind,
> A bell-sound between here and sleep.　　(*OS* 56, "T'ang Notebook")

Within this configuration of energy, movement, linkage, and mortality, the consideration of autobiography must be included. Autobiography, here, is not meant as a purely confessional mode: instead of dictating personal experiences (however edited) into lyrics or narratives, Wright translates and transfers those experiences into meditations on mutability, memory, and generation. Autobiography becomes the convergence of the self and language; the poem self-reflexively comments on its own making and hence mirrors the poet's regard of the self:

> It's all a matter of how
> 　　　　　　you narrow the surfaces.
> It's all a matter of how you fit in the sky.
> 　　　　　　　　(*OS* 24, "The Other Side of the River")

The craft of perception and the making of the poem reflect the making of the self. By meditating on language and situating the self within the energies and erosions of language, Wright's autobiography records the making of the poem and the irreducible energy of mortality. Thus, his speculations propose that we live in a world of language. The heterogeneous forms of discourse—

complete with tension, difference, and generation—mirror ourselves and inscribe our own mortality: to speak or write of ourselves is to speak or write about language and death.

The moment when the poet's mirrored self or imago is recognized and held in regard is an autobiographical moment analogous to a painter's composition of a self-portrait. For both painters
and poets, the creation of radical alterity through contemplation
must not become self-objectification, for that would create a death
mask instead of an interrogatory other. Self-portraiture is perhaps the most immediate and obvious form of autobiography, and
it certainly suggests the formal and thematic correspondence of
painting and poetry. In reference to his collection *Hard Freight,*
Wright has remarked that he uses "stanzas in the way a painter
will build up blocks of color, each disparate and often discrete, to
make an overall representation";[4] however, his affinity with painting extends beyond this one collection of poems and beyond an
analogous process of representation to include a similar process of
self-definition. As William Howarth has argued, not only do autobiography and self-portraiture "suggest a double entity, expressed
as a series of reciprocal transactions," but a self-portrait, unlike a
portrait or biography, demands that "the artist-model must alter-
nately pose and paint," for in "a mirror he studies reversed images, familiar to himself but not to others."[5]

Wright's explicit and self-announced "self-portraits" are
"uniquely transactional" moments,[6] in Howarth's terms, which
attempt and question re-presentation (the making present
again). In each self-portrait, the fixity of image is in tension with
the context, the transactional composition, and the duration of
the regard of the artist and reader. In the autobiographical act,
we confront the moment when the self clearly mirrors itself, but
at the same time the mirror clouds or reflects another image, so
that we never return to the original. Though all writing is what
John Ashbery calls the "leaving-out business,"[7] self-portraiture
and autobiography constitute the most radical conjunction between writing and the self expressed through the dynamic energies of repression, selection, and revelation. Whether self-

conscious or not, some detail is always included at the expense of another, and this repressed detail forms the silhouette of the original image seen in the mirror long ago. Wright attempts to recover the parts of the original imago, yet this turns to an exploration of the provisionality and fragmentation of self and narrative.

"Self-Portrait," in *The Grave of the Right Hand,* essentially quotes several of de Chirico's paintings from his metaphysical period: *Self-Portrait* (1913), *The Song of Love* (1914), *The Serenity of the Scholar* (1914), and *Portrait of Guillaume Apollinaire* (1914). Each stanza derives its imagery from de Chirico's iconography: the opening lines, "There is a street which runs / Slanting into a square" (*G* 57), fit any number of de Chirico's cityscapes, which typically play with the geometrics of perspective in Italian Renaissance paintings, generating a further interiorized quotation. Both Wright's poem and de Chirico's *Self-Portrait* (1913) contain fragments of classical statuary or the fragmentation of an idealized image; each self-portrait becomes a portrait of absence, or more precisely, the tangible memories of time's passage.

Wright's "Self-Portrait" emphasizes the distance between the self or the text and others—echoing John Ashbery's *artes poeticae* of self and text. Wright recognizes, not his own presence, but the fragments that lead toward another composition of another place, time, and hidden self. De Chirico's interest in reflexivity is easily illustrated in *Portrait of Guillaume Apollinaire,* which is alluded to in the second stanza of Wright's poem:

> There is a pair of glasses
> A statue also
> Casting a long shadow   (*G* 57)

In the painting a marble bust wears a pair of sunglasses, while in the background the silhouette of Apollonaire is glimpsed through an architectural construction in such a way that the bust and silhouette are almost back-to-back. The blinded, classical statue is isolated yet linked to the shadowy mannequinlike partial profile of Apollinaire, seen through the threshold: the past has become fixed and blinded; the present remains a mysterious shadow. The poem's final image, "Nailed to a door / There is a pair of gloves" (*G* 57), emblematizes the lack of presence: the hands that would fill the gloves are absent, and only the outer shell or lineament of that presence remains. Such images as gloves, shoes, and garments—comprising a contemporary iconography for poets like W. S. Merwin and Galway Kinnell—suggest traces of a past presence and the presence of a mysterious absence. The poem points to a nightmare of mere forms toward which language seems headed. Wright places himself into a particular poetic context in "Self-Portrait," yet his place is only provisional and can be understood only by examining what he has placed in it: the self is one of "the lost displays," Wright's apt title to this section of *The Grave of the Right Hand*.

De Chirico's use of facades and statuary creates a mysterious juxtaposition of the past and the industrialized present of locomotives and factories. Here, the signatory long shadows emerge as much from the enigma of memories as from the fragmented and scattered objects. Wright's self-portrait portrays not so much the self's presence as the presence of others. The poems of *The Grave of the Right Hand* appear to be fragments of a larger, fictive work, and thus self-reflexively point to themselves as texts that, like de Chirico's paintings, evoke an anticipated but disrupted order. The enigmatic unease of de Chirico's paintings are seized upon both to reinforce the anxiety of provisionality and to provide an anchor or iconic analogue offering stability, authority, and reference.

Wright's self-portrait in *China Trace* is again a version of himself absented. "Self-Portrait in 2035" depicts Wright in his hundredth year, buried and decomposing in the landscape:

> The root becomes him, the road ruts
> That are sift and grain in the powderlight
> Recast him. . . .   (*CT* 15)

As in the earlier self-portrait, assemblages and associative objects form the means of self-portraiture. The body sinks into the earth to be "recast" and thrown back into being in a new form. The transformative powers of such alliterations as "worm-waste," "dust-dangled," or "past pause" mirror and ground the force of organic decay; these mirrored sounds reveal the primacy of language as experience and mortality, rather than as an extracted significance.

The final couplet, "Darkness, erase these lines, forget these words. / Spider recite his one sin" (*CT* 15), points back at the poem, and in particular at the language of the poem. Like the body of the poet, which has disintegrated, the poem is about to disappear into darkness or the de-compositional monody of silence. The spider, left to recite the poet's one unnamed sin, maintains discourse—or metaphorically and allusively reopens with Arachne's challenge to weave more beautifully than Athena, to cast words as idealizations rather than as the segments of gossamer that they are. Whitman's noiseless spider, which casts its filaments into space to link with the other, also mirrors the challenge Wright seeks. Nevertheless, the speaker realizes that the other can be found only in the "sift and grain" or in the chaff and fruit. The spider of "Self-Portrait in 2035" recites the sin in the natural language of the web: a language from which the poet has fallen, becoming "Unlinked and laceless"; a language to which the poet can only return by being "recast"—thrown, molded, and given a new role—in the natural order.

Although the desire for the melding of the human into the natural world is apparent in the poem "Signature," its title points to the consideration of the paradox of presence and repetition. The poem becomes an ideogram of "Charles Wright," albeit transliterated into a linear form. As the most minimal of self-portraits, it is the signature that creates the presence of the self-portrait and not the painted and framed image. By it, we ascertain the "veracity" of a particular self-portrait, whether it be by "name" or by distinctive brushstrokes that makes the signature a seal that authenticates and authorizes what it seals. The signature, and "Signature" itself, refers to the desire for presence:

> Live like a huge rock covered with moss,
> Rooted half under the earth
> and anxious for no one.   (*CT* 52)

This Zen-like meditation demands a complete integration with the surroundings, where the self is a huge rock settled into the earth. In this state of presence in the landscape, there can be no change. To expect change as a condition for presence denies the corresponding immanence of self and spirit. The title, which suggests repetition, points to itself as writing and presents the impossibility of attaining presence anywhere outside the articulate and material energy of writing.

The self-portraits in *The Southern Cross* work equally as a group and as individual poems. The five self-portraits are contained in a single section of the collection; four longer poems punctuate the sequence. The self-portraits' symmetrical fifteen line form—also used in the "Tattoos" sequence in *Bloodlines*—maintains a concise balance and interplay without the traditional rhetorical and argumentative demands of a sonnet. The self-portraits weave other poems into their fabric and formally mirror each other. Within the poems' common frame, the force of language discloses the imposed limitation of intentional form. The long lines quite literally explore the edge, the frame, and the boundary of self, language, and page; this active form tests and pushes against the margins of the page and against form itself:

> The wind will edit him soon enough,
> And squander his broken chords
> in tiny striations above the air,
> No slatch in the undertow.   (*SC* 15)

The pressure of language against the containing walls of form describes an elemental tension in poetry. On the one hand, Wright has developed an almost ecstatic and spiritual power for poetry

through the contemplation of mortality and the desired rein-
tegration with nature. The poem points to and belongs to a transcendental process in which nature unrelentingly repossesses the
poet's corpus. The poet's place in a material and organic world informs his spiritual understanding and strength. However, there
is the contrary tradition of self-reflexivity at work. The assertion
that the wind will "edit" the poet forms a complex trope; it not
only suggests the wind riffling the dust of the poet's bones and
papers, but the dispersion of his words, even on the page, the ironically failed voice, his "broken chords."

The emblem of the poet's words dispersed into the air echoes
W. S. Merwin's poem "Sibyl."[8] Both Merwin and Wright recognize
the extreme dilemma of the lost efficacy of language when hollow
words mirror hollow men. Merwin, however, grounds his vision in
the mythological trace that, in turn, points to a different and lost
consciousness. Wright's vision always turns back to the intimacy
of the self, the poet, and the mirroring of the self in language. The
turning inward foregrounds the poem's condition as a verbal construction in continual mnemonic movement: a "night bridge / To
the crystal, infinite alphabet of his past" (*SC* 15).

The fourth "Self-Portrait" comes closest to what Wright describes as the poems' central focus: his life and where and how he
lives it. Even so, the poem suggests only a nominal autobiographical quality, for the poem consists, not of events, but of notations:

> Marostica, Val de Ser. Bassano del Grappa.
> Madonna del Ortolo. San Giorgio, arc and stone.
> The foothills above the Piave.   (*SC* 22)

The place has hardened into the minim of the name. The name
holds infinite histories and narratives, but within the lyric what
is important is the music of the names and the hermeneutic energies of remembered names. They are signposts, directions, signals
of the eye-I's travels, "Places and things that caught my eye,
Walt, / In Italy. On foot, Great Cataloguer, some 20-odd years
ago" (*SC* 22). Though Wright grounds himself in Whitman's tra-

dition of collecting and celebrating names and places, he distinguishes himself from Whitman's vision by acknowledging that these names are of public significance only in their music and that, as Calvin Bedient notes, "such naming is memory's sacrament."[9] Copious yet having limitations, lists and self-portraits are places where memory and current transactions coincide in litany.

Wright contemplates the self deferred, unaccounted for, only glimpsed through language, for any language we propose constitutes the self as another. The final line of the second "Self-Portrait," when "St. Augustine strik[es] the words out" (*SC* 15), rejects any privileging of the self. Though the autobiographer becomes a "'reader' of his own past," autobiography can be described as "'literally' the analysis of one's past discourses, of one's acts and utterances, insofar as they signify within a social and linguistic context."[10] Wright's autobiographical writings, while seeking to engage the languages of the world or St. Augustine's book of nature, always turn back upon themselves; this turning back is in itself an attempt to erase the barrier between self and other. Yet any such visionary desire is undercut by the materiality of writing, be it the poet's or the phenomenal world's. Writing, however, provides only a posthumous presence, for Wright mock-elegiacally writes, "Someday they'll find me out, and my lavish hands, / . . . / My features are sketched with black ink in a slow drag through the sky, / Waiting to be filled in" (*SC* 13). Though self-portraiture and autobiography can be described as the "process of collaboration between an individual conscious and that Other which permeates it,"[11] in Wright's poetics self and other link without synthesis or transcendent unity in discourse's "process of collaboration" or in the space of language.

At the end of the first "Self-Portrait" in *The Southern Cross,* the poet offers a psalmlike prayer to save himself from the limitations and stasis imposed on and by language:

> Hand that lifted me once, lift me again,
> Sort me and flesh me out, fix my eyes.

From the mulch and the undergrowth, protect me and pass me on.
From my own words and my certainties,
From the rose and the easy cheek, deliver me, pass me on.   (*SC* 13)

Movement, synonymous with transformation, rescues the poet from stasis and death. The hand—that of inspiration that lifts the poet towards authentic language, of the poet himself casting with words towards some hoped for permanence, of critics who will sift Wright's poetry, and of the celestial that offers salvation—will rescue the poet from complete dispersion and apocalypse in order to remake him, while "ashes and bits of char . . . will clear [his] name" (*SC* 13) of his primal sin. Language consists of the remains of a continent and its culture, debris and anonymous counters, all of which judge us. And what is the poet's "name" besides his "one sin" of "Self-Portrait in 2035"? Implied in these self-portraits is Michel Foucault's question, "What is an author?"[12] An author can only be a repository for influences and is subject to erosion. To be an author, Wright argues, is to seek some form of deliverance from the undergrowth of signs, while committing the "one sin" of desiring an unnatural or hierarchic name. This is the hubris of writing that attempts to master and authorize the world.

The imposed form of the self-portraits in *The Southern Cross* creates an assurance of presence and memory in spite of the fragmentation and dispersal of the idea of the author. The repeated forms, furthermore, provide a counterpoint to the discontinuous and associative movement of language within the form's constraints:

I see myself in a tight dissolve, and answer to no one.
Self-traitor, I smuggle in
The spider love, undoer and rearranger of all things.
Angel of Mercy, strip me down.   (*SC* 24, "Self-Portrait")

Not only is the poet "in tight dissolve" (a vortex or a photograph still in the emulsion), but he betrays himself, for the writing immortalizes and deadens. Withal, the poet is reenvisioned as a producer of texts, an "undoer and rearranger of all things"; and as such, the poet's work parallels the spider's work and reflects the spider's weaving of the poet's "one sin." Nevertheless, Wright implicitly hopes to recover his essential self: in spite of language's ability to overrun, there is some Angel of Mercy—a mysterious intervention of a Rilkean imaginative force—willing to "strip me down," or so the poet hopes, to essentiality. Yet such longing can only be nostalgic, recalling Blake's world of innocence—small, secure, distant, a place of tentative community:

> This world is a little place,
> Just red in the sky before the sun rises.
> Hold hands, hold hands
> That when the birds start, none of us is missing.
> Hold hands, hold hands.   (*SC* 24)

Here, interconnection recalls childhood, community prayers, and the gathering of the souls in the early cantos of Dante's *Purgatorio*.

Self-portraiture describes the confrontation with mortality and immanence; salvation defers to the desire for presence:

> I've been writing this poem for weeks now
> With a pencil made of rain, smudging my face
> And my friend's face, making a language where nothing stays.
> The sunlight has no such desire.
> In the small pools of our words, its business is radiance.   (*SC* 38)

The poem doubles back upon itself to comment reflexively upon what is written; thus, the writer's presence is known only through the presence of other texts. The ironic title, "Portrait of the Artist with Hart Crane," indicates the poem's textual playfulness. In "Portrait of the Artist with Li Po," Wright questions the possibility of defining presence only by continuity and not also by difference:

> Everyone knows the true story of how he would write his verses
>   and float them,

Like paper boats, downstream
                    just to watch them drift away.
Death never entered his poems, but rowed, with its hair down, far
    out on the lake,
Laughing and looking up at the sky.   (*SC* 39)

For Wright, the confrontation with death—the knowledge of difference—is central; these two poems are homages to Crane and Li
Po as well as Wright's calling forth of their apparitions. Though
Wright knows "The distance between the dead and the living / is
more than a heart beat and a breath" (*SC* 39), he longs for continuity and interconnection. The reinscription, again another form
of signature and re-presentation, of Li Po's line "*The peach blos-
som follows the moving water*" suggests that the text, whatever
its status, has the efficacy to persist and to connect, regardless of
the dissolution of the self or the author. Writing itself transcends
the anxiety of the provisionality of presence.
    While maintaining a formal sensibility throughout, the spare
early poems of his first collection give way to the exploratory
sequences of poems in the triptych comprised of *Hard Freight,
Bloodlines,* and *China Trace.* While the self-portraits are experiments in the autobiographical moment, the triptych collections,
defined by their formal organization, move diachronically and
emphasize the autobiographical in geographical, historical, familial, and generational terms. Wright's serially linked poems
are balanced and symmetrical groupings that elude closure by
spatially and temporally unfolding and infolding. The symmetry
of each collection reflects less the vision of an underlying whole
than the architecture of textuality. The poet, as architect, designs
an artifice that inquires into the order or repetitions within the
natural world, and parallels the activity of naming or the physical composition, brushstroke by brushstroke, of a painting. Paradoxically, the intimation of completeness, implicit in symmetry,
and the incomplete and undisclosed are held in tension. Wright's
use of symmetry is less intended to be "meaningful" than it is to
be the place of energized transactions. Resolution is elided; the
architecture itself turns numinous.

Hard Freight is arranged to reveal the art of the book and to point to itself, the book, as an object. The opening and closing sections, appropriately titled "Homages" and "End-papers" respectively, bracket the title section, "Hard Freight." *Bloodlines* creates a concentric and balanced grouping of poems. The progress or pilgrimage of the reader moves from the outer group of three poems, through the serial poem "Tattoos," to reach the central group of two poems. The reader then moves outward, from the serial poem "Skins" to the outer group of three poems. Such symmetry demands that the collection be viewed as a whole and not as a linear movement of diverse texts. Inside-outside, heart-body, or center-frame are evoked, yet any separation of these seeming opposites is impossible, for one is defined by the other. The book itself illustrates interconnection and movement. The book, too, atavistically mirrors the world and inscribes a provisional order— evoking the Augustinian idea of nature as book.

Each section of *China Trace* opens with the same quotation from Italo Calvino's *Invisible Cities.* The quotations, like Calvino's book as a whole, emphasize mirroring and the problematics of representation. *Invisible Cities* consists of a dialogue between Marco Polo and the Kublai Khan, in which Marco Polo recounts the cities he has seen; each city is an imaginary signifier, something desired yet always distant. Possession of the representations of the other is impossible, for, as Calvino states, the Khan would then be "an emblem among emblems."[13] Calvino, like Wright, examines the production of signs as the desire for the other that is always alienated as well as being both telos and origin. *China Trace,* the final collection of the triptych, moves away from the vision of the organic world of *Hard Freight* and *Bloodlines* to view the universe as the movement of signs puncturing silence and white space.

In *Hard Freight,* as the title makes clear, the poems travel back to past places and events. The poems meditate on the ways in which our bodies contain time and decay while our names inscribe the past, thus the poems' thematic and structural expressions of the dissolution of our connections focus on mortality and a desire to forestall time. "Primogeniture" ends with images of biological resurrection: "Rose of the afterlife, black mulch we breathe, / Devolve and restore / . . . Rechannel these tissues, hold these hands" (*HF* 54). By definition, primogeniture is the passing on of land or an inheritance to the firstborn son; yet it also indicates the bonds between generations represented through the land. The poem, an elegy for a primogenitor, a father, is also a poem about the passing on of life to another; thus, it is a companion poem to "Firstborn" and "Congenital." In the latter poem, Wright recognizes his ancestry in his own body:

> —These hands are my father's hands these eyes
> Excessively veined his eyes
> Unstill ever-turning
> The water the same song and the touch   (*HF* 58)

In the poem's first stanza, Wright locates his origins not only in his "father's hands" (one text) but also in the landscape where distinctions between things are diminished. The phenomenal world is suffused with presence, which is only recognized in the conjunction—the "hawk-light"—of being and language:

> Here is where it begins here
> In the hawk-light in the quiet
> The blue of the shag spruce
> Lumescent
>   night-rinsed and grand   (*HF* 58)

Like Elizabeth Bishop's "The Moose," the natural world is "grand" and otherworldly in its mysteriousness. For Bishop, such a moment occurs inadvertently; for Wright, the natural world translates into a spiritual moment that is potentially always near at hand. The poem's final word, "touch," hangs suspended, immanent, and immediate—"lumescent."

"Firstborn," a series of six symmetrical sections celebrating the birth of Wright's son, further develops the theme of genealogical interconnections: "We bring what we have to bring; / We give what we have to give" to "Welcome, Sweet Luke, to your life" (*HF* 27). The past will be transmitted to the child, whose identity intermeshes with the world and mirrors the interconnectedness of the landscape:

> The bougainvillaea's redress
> Pulses throughout the hillside, its slow
> Network of vines
>
> Holding the earth together, giving it breath,
> Outside your window, hibiscus and columbine
> Tend to their various needs;
>
> The summer enlarges.   (*HF* 28)

The bougainvillaea's "network" of flowering vines, the "hibiscus and columbine" that "Tend to their various needs"—indeed, the whole fertile summer—parallels Luke's growth, "the new skin / Blossoming pink and clear." The metaphoric language of growth celebrates the possibility of life and connects the son to the flower-world outside his window. Furthermore, the father links himself with his son through the self-reflexivity of metaphoric language.

Language, however, has its own limitations: the mystery of the other overwhelms discourse and almost silences it:

> You lie here beside me now,
> Ineffable, elsewhere still.
> What should one say to a son?   (*HF* 29)

There is so much to say to one's son, yet neither "Emotions and points of view," nor the "Abstractions we like to think / We live by," nor "something immediate, / Descriptive" can serve as the means of address. The father realizes not only the "ineffable" quality of his son but the abyss between what he desires to say and what he is able to say. One can only "say" what one desires by stating its impossibility when confronted with the otherworldliness of the baby. Like W. S. Merwin, Wright finds that language can only be provisional; one may look for "those few felicitous vowels / Which expiate everything," but they are not to be found. Instead, they "remain in the dark, and will / Continue to glitter there . . . No strategies, can now extract them" (*HF* 30).

Wright admits a certain exasperation with wrestling the angel of language and concedes, "What I am trying to say / Is this / . . . Indenture yourself to the land" (*HF* 31). Wright places himself in the mainstream of the tradition of American artists and thinkers concerned with the landscape and our places within it. He seldom refers to an urban setting; instead, the rural landscape retains mystery and interconnectedness that the urban landscape, for Wright, implicitly does not. Such distancing from the urban underscores his general disinclination to confront outright the political concerns constituted in language. Wright seems too accepting of male tradition, and even insists, particularly in this poem, on privileging male connections through genealogy. Wright essentially seeks to praise the natural world and our capacity for remembering it; however, he does not move to question his language in other than intimate terms. This is not to say that Wright's poetry slides into a pastoral mode or the solipsism of scenic poetry. Wright's poetry approaches being a phenomenological (a reverie of the world as writing) and theological poetry in the tradition of Hopkins. The natural world is the place of the other's language and energy that transform his perceptions into the poem's vectoring and traveling lines.

The fifth section of "Firstborn" ends with echoes of devotional hymns: "Surrender yourself, and be glad; / This is the law that endures" (*HF* 31). Wright anchors himself in the various traditions of Whitman, Faulkner, the Hudson River School of painters, American Transcendentalists, and Native American teaching with this statement that affirms the primacy of the land. And through this statement he also enacts the continuation of this particular tradition's life and authority, for he passes it on—as it was passed to him—to his son and to his readers. To invoke and pass on the law of the father is to assure one, within discourse, of certain identity. Unlike Adrienne Rich and W. S. Merwin, who offer various critiques of the father (symbolic and autobiographical), Wright essentially celebrates the father as a symbol of generation, connection, and salvation. Language, for Wright, is less a subject for criticism than it is for Rich or Merwin, who emphasize the political and cultural corruption by and of language. In contrast, Wright envisions language, not as an arena of authority, but as the closest reach of the other. In the sixth and final section of "Firstborn," Wright names the sources of his vision of connection: "Nantahala, / Unaka and Unicoi," the Indian tribal names that "Brindle and sing in your blood; / Their sounds are the sounds you hear" (*HF* 32). Each name is a palimpsestic trace, hence a memory of previous traces. Luke's name is "like a new scar," something corporeal and, like a signature, identifiable and repeatable. The name or scar is the place where two edges fuse together, always marked and always re-membered.

Though "Firstborn" occupies a central place in Wright's work, the longer, meditative, and autobiographical poems of *Hard Freight* that describe the landscape of his youth are the most stunning in their richness of language and point to the direction taken up in *Bloodlines*. The opening lines of "Dog Creek Mainline" reveal words stripped to their energies of presence (nouns) and transformation (verbs):

> Dog Creek: cat track and bird splay,
> Spindrift and windfall; woodrot;
> Odor of muscadine, the blue creep
> Of kingsnake and copperhead;
> Nightweed; frog spit and floating heart,
> Backwash and snag pool: Dog Creek
>
> Starts in the leaf reach and shoal run of the blood;
> Starts in the falling light just back
> Of the fingertips; starts
> Forever in the black throat
> You ask redemption of, in wants
> You waken to, the odd door:

Its sky, old empty valise,
Stands open, departure in mind; its three streets,
Y-shaped and brown,
Go up the hills like a fever;
Its houses link and deploy
—This ointment, false flesh in another color.   (*HF* 43)

The landscape incorporates the poet's body; sounds generate new
sounds; the colon opens new stanzas and creates a movement of
growth and dehiscence.

Wright travels back into the past landscape of Hiwassee, North
Carolina, and into his own childhood of 1941 and the outbreak of
the Second World War. It is here that he confronts the body and
the "black throat"—the always-present death within our bodies
that gives us definition. "Cross-tie by cross-tie" of "indigent spur"
carrying "hard freight" takes Wright back to his beginnings,
where he discovers loss:

Dog Creek is on this line,
Indigent spur; cross-tie by cross-tie it takes
You back, the red wind
Caught at your neck like a prize:

(The heart is a hieroglyph;
The fingers, like praying mantises, poise
Over what they have once loved;

The ear, cold cave, is an absence,
Tapping its own thin wires;
The eye turns in on itself.

The tongue is a white water.
In its slick ceremonies the light
Gathers, and is refracted, and moves
Outward, over the lips,
Over the dry skin of the world.
The tongue is a white water.).   (*HF* 44)

The eye or I "turns in on itself" to retrieve and renew memories of what was once loved. The parenthetically enclosed inward turn suggests the alienation of heart, fingers, ears, and eyes. Only the tongue, the metonym for the poet, remains undistanced and moving. From the tongue, like a river's source, language flows (ostensibly the poem above or beside the stanzas marked [off] by the parentheses) "over the dry skin of the world" and replenishes and reconnects the world with memories and names.

Landscape, like language, is, however, a topography created by rifts and abysses: "Half-bridge over nothingness, / White sky of the palette knife; blot orange, / Vertical blacks" (*HF* 51, "Northanger Bridge"). And like the landscape, language can be "stripped of its meaning" (*HF* 51) and of its capacity for interconnection. These abysses signal the difficulty of autobiography and of re-presentation. Wright writes over nothing—the blank page and death. Writing becomes a form of grace, and memory a spiritual activity.[14] The vocabulary consisting of "signatures," "emblems," "sentences," "nouns," "blue idiom," "pale semaphore," "inked-in valley," and "language of numerals" suggest that discourse penetrates everything so far as to be the medium of interconnection:

> The past, wrecked accordion, plays on, its one tune
> My song, its one breath my breath,
> The square root, the indivisible cipher . . .
> > (*HF* 47, "Sky Valley Rider")

Walking along "the evening water," where he had once hunted unsuccessfully with his father, the writer in "Blackwater Mountain" startles a duck into a flight that

> shows me the way to you;
> He shows me the way to a different fire
> Where you, black moon, warm your hands.
> > (*HF* 49, "Blackwater Mountain")

The dark, absent moon—the absent father—is retrieved and conserved by the return to the place of previous union. Language is mysterious and material—its mysteriousness lies in its materiality.

The theme of linkage is further explored in Wright's third volume, *Bloodlines;* the collection's title itself emphasizes this pervasive theme. Though the birth of writing was "often linked to genealogical anxiety,"[15] bloodlines are genealogical exfoliations and the body's circulatory system, as well as the very lines of the poems in the book. The transposition of genealogy into poetic lines retains personal and familial voices while also decentering a vast cycle of flux, change, and reemergence:

> As we slide slide to the music, humming
> An old tune, knee touching knee,
> Step-two-three, step-two-three
> Under a hard hatful of leaves,
> The grass with its one good limb holding
> The beat, a hint of impending form.
> It gathers, it reaches back, it is caught up.   (*B* 75, "Link Chain")

Wright dances not only with his past childhood but with the cycle of life that "gathers," "reaches back," and "is caught up" in some intuited "impending form." The autumnal dance of life recollects past events: big sister's hair is "heaped like a fresh grave" and her "fingers [are] cool tubers" (*B* 74–75, "Link Chain"). In the midst of this harvest dance arises an awareness of mortality, but mortality must include life, for the dance never stops; nothing remains fixed in a particular form, but always metamorphoses into another, new form. The music of the poem transforms the autobiographical moment into one of the steps of the dance of metaphors, "where all is a true turning, and all is growth" (*B* 69, "Skins").

The two most important poems of this collection are the paired and mirrored series "Tattoos" and "Skins." As their titles suggest, the tattoos inscribe events upon the skin, the body, and the poet without the possibility of erasure. The events, not to be celebrated in and of themselves, make up the partial alphabet of the poet. Tattoo, defined also as a rhythmic drumming, describes a form of signaling various events. Each poem of the series "Tattoos" is dated and carries a footnote identifying the place and the core autobiographical event alluded to, so that the notes further inscribe or tattoo the event. Each poem or tattoo is the inscription of an event on the poet's memory; the poem is a resurrection and "palm print, / The map that will take me there" (*B* 27). Memory and renewal work dialetically, for presence is stained by its other, death: "You stand in your shoes, two shiny graves / Dogging your footsteps" (*B* 38).

In the first poem of the sequence "Tattoos," the sight of camelias prompts Wright to propose the fusion of inspiration and redemption, while also questioning his memory and his song:

> So light the light that fires you
> —Petals of horn, scales of blood—,
> Where would you have me return?
> What songs would I sing,
> And the hymns . . . What garden of wax statues . . .   (*B* 19)

The provisional initiation of light and song opens the sequence. What follows are the songs he sings—about his parents' deaths, his sexual initiations, Italy, his childhood religious experiences. The poet enacts his Orphic role and sings the world into a provisional, mnemonic revival: "The dead grass whistles a tune, strangely familiar" (*B* 36). Nonetheless, Orphic dismemberment haunts these poems, in that the poems arise out of a severed past that must be readdressed and reinscribed:

> The hemlocks wedge in the wind.
> Their webs are forming something—questions:
> *Which shoe is the alter ego?*
> *Which glove inures the fallible hand?*
> *Why are the apple trees draped in black?*

And I answer them. In words
They will understand, I answer them:
The left shoe.
The left glove.
Someone is dead; someone who loved them is dead.   (*B* 37)

In each of these sections, the poet emphasizes the salvational role of language. As a house of accumulated memories, language connects the poet with the discourses and actions of the natural world. The origin and inspiration—literally, the breathing in of life—remains unnamed, mysterious, and other. Inspiration, however, is made manifest in language, in the poet's fire-burnished syllables:

Nameless, invisible, what spins out
From this wall comes breath by breath,
And pulls the vine, and the ringing tide,
The scorched syllable from the moon's mouth.
And what pulls them pulls me.   (*B* 25)

Describing the effect of the rhetoric of composition in Piero della Francesca's "Resurrection," this poem transfers visual energy into linguistic energy, which is the movement of change and transformation resulting in the resurrection of language. Though Wright's conjunction of the personal vision and a larger, connective energy recalls romantic impulses, he continually displaces the self so that any romantic visionary union of the self and the other in language is vastly distant. Furthermore, language does not mirror or provide the vehicle to the other, but becomes the other, which can be known only as a provisional, ghostly trace.

In "Skins," Wright compresses long, chantlike lines, rich in assonance, alliteration, and imagery, into fourteen-line blocks. No stanza breaks or dropped half lines crack the tabletlike effect of these poems on the page. Each tabula rasa is fully impressed with the history of the self's intellectual past.[16] Like a pilgrim in an allegory structured as a dream, the speaker ascends and descends a ladder of knowledge that is symmetrically ordered and divided between fire, air, earth, and water. Like the skins, or "impermanent clothes" (*B* 51), we cover ourselves with interpretations—recalling Blake's bound and tattooed Albion, illuminated in plate 25 of *Jerusalem*. The compression of each poem demands language's release from abstraction. Energy, or the inherent potential of transformation and of transmutation, cannot remain in thrall. As a form of energy, language overruns and releases us from a single interpretation, intellectual design, and autobiographical moment. Wright distinguishes between the poem and the page's white space, which is "what the line lives in and breathes in, if it is to breathe at all."[17] The line, like Blake's line etched by burin and acid, is energy and presence—Blake's "eternal delight." The "white sound" of the page "pulls the lines through the poem, gauging their weights and durations, even their distances," and it "is the larger sound out of which the more measured and interruptable sounds of the line are cut."[18] Language opens up a place where one recognizes, participates in, and is attentive to movement and transformation. To the writer's and reader's attention, writing draws forth interpretations and forms the liminal moment and place for continuing and participating in a dehiscent and semiotic world.

Particular concerns of each section of "Skins" form inside the music of the line; nonetheless, the music or energy is so strong that the words themselves gain a sonoral presence that overruns meaning, since language foregrounds movement and accumulation. Though interpretation does not cease to be meaningful, meaning loses its privileged status. Autobiography becomes an imago for the release, continuation, and conservation of poetic energies:

> Under the rock, in the sand and the gravel run;
> In muck bank and weed, at the heart of the river's edge:
> Instar; and again, instar,
> The wing cases visible. Then
> Emergence: leaf drift and detritus; skin split,
> The image forced from the self.

And rests, wings drying, eyes compressed,
Legs compressed, constricted
Beneath the dun and the watershine—
Incipient spinner, set for the take-off . . .   (B 56)

The eye-I moves inward to "the heart of the river's edge" and is simultaneously emergent. "The image forced from the self" describes both the poem's emergence from memory and the mayfly or "imago rising out of herself." The poem, while casting back to Hopkins and Yeats, is not simply an epistemological meditation on poiesis; instead, the poem makes visible the dynamics of transformation found in the permeation of natural language and the poet's observation and recording of nature's signatures.

Wright yearns for a spiritual and transcendent engagement. With this desire, the poet becomes a solitary, a pilgrim, "one meandering man / . . . who looks for the willow's change" (B 69), knowing "There is a shine you move towards, the shine / Of water. . . . The river, rope of remembering, unbroken shoe, / The flushed and unwaivering mirror" (B 68). As Wright proclaimed in "Firstborn," the natural world holds us and is the one law to which we are responsible. In "Skins," this theme evolves from a father's didactic narrative to an embrace, in the poetic line and image, of a landscape and a field of sensations.

By ambitiously seeking the possibility of presence in language, Wright recalls Pound's interest in the energies housed in a Chinese ideogram, where, according to Fenollosa, "in all poetry a word is like a sun, with its corona and chromosphere; words crowd upon words, and enwrap each other in their luminous envelopes until sentences become clear continuous light bands." [19] Unlike Pound's and Fenollosa's enthusiasms for the potential of an archaeology of knowledge in a single sign, Wright understands that his language has limits and margins:

And what does it come to, Pilgrim,
This walking to and fro on the earth, knowing
That nothing changes, or everything;

> And only, to tell it, these sad marks,
> Phrases half-parsed, ellipses and scratches across the dirt?
> It comes to a point. It comes and it goes.   (*B* 70)

In these concluding lines to "Skins," Wright emerges in the role of the pilgrim-writer, who turns his back upon his journey and realizes that its value can only be found in the dynamics and energies of the process, not in the completion or the expectation of completion. "Skins" thus asks us to turn back to what transpired, to look again at the signatures of language and its reinvention.

"Rural Route," the final poem of *Bloodlines,* addresses the issue of image and self found in the sixth section of "Skins," where the imago rises out of herself. Here, however, no transcendental and iridescent imago rises. Instead, the past persists:

> I back off, and the face stays.
> I leave the back yard, and the front yard, and the face stays.
> I am back on the West Coast, in my studio,
> My wife and my son asleep, and the face stays.   (*B* 78)

The mirror image of himself—doubly reflected as a twelve-year-old boy seeing his face (a self-portrait) framed in a dark windowpane and that reflection haunting Wright twenty-six years later—describes the impossibility of escaping one's past, the persistence and repression of the trace, and the failures of the past. The face "still looks in, still unaware of the willow, the boxwood / Or any light on any leaf. Or me" (*B* 77). This passage describes the pilgrim's progress: now he can see the light on the leaves; therefore, he can name the willow and boxwood and provide their scripts with signatures. The persistence of the face reminds Wright the Pilgrim of who he is and, like the final section of "Skins," of his limitations—thus comes his recognition of his own provisional self.

In *China Trace,* the final panel and stage of his triptych, Wright moves away from his past autobiography toward his future one. Wright attempts to free himself from the reflection of the face at the window; in fact, the opening poem of *China Trace,* "Childhood," answers the final poem of *Bloodlines:*

You've followed me like a dog
I see through at last, a window into Away-From-Here, a place
I'm headed for, my tongue loosened, tracks
Apparent, your beggar's-lice
Bleaching to crystal along my britches leg:

I'm going away now, good-bye.   (*CT* 13)

The poet joins his past to look at the vision of his future. There is
a complete shedding of the past, its "names / Falling into the
darkness, face / After face, like beads from a broken rosary" (*CT*
13). *China Trace* explores "one man's relationship to the endlessness, the ongoingness, the everlastingness of what's around
him, and his relationship to it as he stands in the natural world"[20]:
it is a book recording his yearning for salvation and recongrega-
tion in nature. Wright even considered "The Book of Yearning" as
its title—and it suggests the difficulty of those yearnings: "the
nitty-gritty of my wishes . . . would be to be saved, but there is no
such thing."[21] To return to the congregation of dust and to issue
again from that dust, forms Wright's vision of the only salvation
one has to look forward to:

If we, as we are, are dust, and dust, as it will, rises,
Then we will rise, and recongregate
In the wind, in the cloud, and be their issue . . .   (*CT* 14, "Snow")

The future tense and the repetition push language into greater
motion to create the inexorable movement of time as it erodes
presence. His is a pessimistic evolutionary vision coupled with
the ideas of the conservation and ongoingness of poetic energy.

Wright states that writing is "the closest I got to 'salvation,'
since salvation doesn't exist except through the natural world."[22]
In "Reunion," which echoes W. S. Merwin's "For the Anniversary
of My Death," Wright writes against death and toward death:
"I write poems to untie myself, to do penance and disappear /
Through the upper right-hand corner of things, to say grace" (*CT*
49). In this self-reflexive statement lies the paradox of the self as-

serting its presence with the pronoun "I," while desiring to relinquish his self-consciousness.

Wright intends to create a tracery of the self: "I wanted these [poems] to have a journal-like, everyday quality."[23] The collection must be read as a whole rather than as a collection of separate poems, for it works as a dynamic group of brushstrokes that are defined by each other's movements. The *poem* thus emphasizes that writing is a place of transference and translation of perceptions. Like a journal, the poems of *China Trace* mediate between the world-as-language and our later devisive interpretations: "The river stays shut, and writes my biography" (*CT* 21, "Quotidiana"). These poems are also mediations between a past and an elegiac present: "In some other language, / I walk by this same river, these same vowels in my throat" (*CT* 20, "Wishes").

The poems of *China Trace,* Wright comments, are like Chinese ideograms in that they are traces of Chinese poems without imitating them yet share the aesthetic of compression and transference between words.[24] In that each poem is an emblem, glance, or stroke, they constitute one larger emblem—the book as ideogram. This ideogram, though meaningful and the place of hermeneusis, nonetheless, is the site of the energies of movement, relation, and transformation: "I mimic the tongues of green flame in the grass" (*CT* 50, "Where Moth and Rust Doth Corrupt"). The desire for the self-contained ideogram, emblem, or symmetrically balanced and thus designed collection indicates a desire for an ideal form and a hope for a salvational closure. The ideal design would, in fact, de-sign itself by arresting the dynamic movements of language and hermeneusis. The self-reflexive, interlinking quality of language, however, subverts the attainment of this ideal. Through this subversion, the word and the self rejoin the world of things as things themselves:

> The wind harps its same song
> Through the steel tines of the trees.
>
> The river lies still, the jeweled drill in its teeth.

> I am glint on its fingernails.
> I am ground grains on its wheel.   (*CT* 22, "At Zero")

In "At Zero," the self disappears into the frigid winter landscape, into the zero as origin and absence. The pilgrim, as a speck in time, is placed or inscribed on the "wheel" of fortune or a Tantric wheel of destiny. Appropriately, Fenollosa remarks that Chinese notation is "much more than arbitrary symbols" and "is based upon a vivid shorthand picture of the operations of nature" and that "in this process of compounding, two things added together do not produce a third thing but suggest some fundamental relation between them." [25]

Although Wright desires linkage and the fullness of emblems, he finds himself, like the sign, always already departing:

> I'm going away now, goodbye.
> Goodbye to the locust husk and the chairs;
> Goodbye to the genuflections. Goodbye to the clothes
> That circle beneath the earth, the names
> Falling into the darkness, face
> After face, like beads from a broken rosary . . . (*CT* 13, "Childhood")

China Trace commences with this litany of the relinquishment of childhood and one's past, and thus of the autobiographical. The cloak of childhood and belief is exchanged for one of spiritual loss: "And I turn in the wind, / Not knowing what sign to make, or where I should kneel" (*CT* 27, "1975"). Whatever we might expect or yearn for to save us ultimately rejects us and severs each link: "Like a bead of clear oil the Healer revolves through the night wind, / Part eye, part tear, unwilling to recognize us" (*CT* 47, "Stone Canyon Nocturne"). Throughout, the final isolation of the self resounds, as does the desire to return to a condition of belief where the poet "wait[s] for something immense and unspeakable to uncover its face" (*CT* 56, "Cloud River").

By the end of *China Trace,* presence and possibility of a sustained belief have shrunk. In "Sitting at Night on the Front Porch," Wright discovers "Everyone's gone / And I'm here, sizing the dark" (*CT* 63). In "Saturday 6 A.M.," he loses motion and speech:

> There's something I want to say,
>
> But not here, stepped out and at large on the blurred hillside.
> Over my shoulder, the great pane of the sunlight tilts toward
>   the sea.
> I don't move. I let the wind speak.   (*CT* 64)

The wind, rustling through all these poems, intimates the everlastingness and interconnectedness of all things to which Wright accords salvation. What could be salvational lies beyond Wright's language and metaphor; because it escapes belief, Wright tries to listen or watch for its immanent traces. In the final poem, addressed to a transcendent other, the "I" vanishes and leaves the poem to instruct us to

> Look for him high in the flat black of the northern Pacific sky,
> Released in his suit of lights,
>   lifted and laid clear.   (*CT* 65, "Him")

Wright's poetry, like so much of American autobiographical writing, is concerned with place and his relationship to a particular place. Through one geography he maps another, interior landscape. In *Southern Cross* and *The Other Side of the River* Wright pursues a much more intimate and gestural poetry than in the earlier triptych and self-portraits. "The Southern Cross," "Lonesome Pine Special," "The Other Side of the River," "Italian Days," and "T'ang Notebook" form long notations and accretions of memories, geographies, sensations, and discrete harmonies. Suggestive of narratives—in that stories and anecdotes are offered but not pursued—each poem describes an intersection of pathways rather than one single highway. Radically supplanting and healing the division of signifier and signified, intersection and linking constitute Wright's vision of language.

In Wright's most recent collections, each poem becomes a "silvery alphabet" (*OS* 25, "The Other Side of the River"). In turn, the poems of *Southern Cross* and those of *The Other Side of the River* construct jeweled nets, as in the Zenist Hua-yen doctrine, for the collection is formed of intertwined poems, each reflecting the others: "The ten thousand star-fish caught in the net of heaven / Flash at the sky's end" (*OS* 55, "Tiang Notebook"). The structure of each poem in *The Other Side of the River* consists of interwoven sections typographically set apart from each other, yet each forms a knot that ties together the entire fabric of the poem. Each section and each poem weave into one larger text, and thus into a larger shared memory. The texture of the overlay of lines and images corresponds to the overlay of recollected durations. One moment or one memory eclipses and calls forth, associatively, another. The extended lines, furthermore, suggest an inexorable movement: "There is no stopping the comings and goings in this world, / No stopping them, to and fro" (*OS* 36, "Italian Days").

In "The Southern Cross," Wright states that "No trace of a story line" (*SC* 49) exists; though stories arise, they are impossible to trace to their source or to complete. We find that memories, like stories, are compositions of places and scenes built upon an originary but unrecoverable moment:

> It's 1936, in Tennessee. I'm one
> And spraying the dead grass with a hose.
> The curtains blow in and out.
>
> And then it's not. And I'm not and they're not
>
> Or it's 1941 in a brown suit, or '53 in its white shoes,
> Overlay after overlay tumbled and brought back,
> As meaningless as the sea would be
>   if the sea could remember its waves . . . (*SC* 49)

These poems form palimpsestic "overlay after overlay," where brushstrokes and memory fuse together:

The dead are a cadmium blue.
We spread them with palette knives in broad blocks and planes.

We layer them stroke by stroke
In steps and ascending mass, in verticals raised from the earth.

We choose, and layer them in,
Blue and a blue and a breath,

Circle and smudge, cross-beak and buttonhook,
We layer them in. We squint hard and terrace them line by line.

And so we are come between, and cry out,
And stare up at the sky and its cloudy panes,

And finger the cypress twists.   (*SC* 6)

"Homage to Paul Cézanne" illustrates Wright's *ars poetica:* writing is seen as building textures of images and memory.[26] The painters Cézanne and Giorgio Morandi are Wright's closest visual analogues, and Cézanne's method of the accumulation of moments (and perspectives) parallels Wright's poetic craft. Yet the poetic line—not as structure, but as an ontological expression— parallels Morandi's line, which, Wright states, "is always on the point of disappearing, of not *seeming* to be there," traveling beyond the sense or notion of containment. Morandi's art is one of transference. Like a map, it offers, not discovery, but "affirmation: the voyage of discovery is ours now." Like his commentary on Morandi, Wright's own observations within his poems, "flicked off in a phrase," take on the weight of an entire life—"they are lifelines to the unseen."[27] Thus, what is lost or past converges with what is mysterious, primitive, and unseen.

Unlike the triptych, where language mediates the autobiographical narratives in such a way that the self is erased, "The Southern Cross" suggests that what is left of the self are myriad memories that mirror the otherness of ourselves. The litany of "I remember" creates an elegiac self-portrait and reveals the core of loss: the autobiographical impulse is an elegy for the self. All that Wright records reaffirms this elegiac chant:

> Ebb and flow of the sunset past Sirmio,
> flat voice of the waters
> Retelling their story, again and again, as though to unburden
> itself
>
> Of an unforgotten guilt,
> and not relieved
> Under the soothing hand of the dark,
>
> The clouds over Bardolino dragging the sky for the dead
> Bodies of those who refuse to rise,
> Their orange robes and flaming bodices trolling across the hills,
>
> Nightwind by now in the olive trees,
> No sound but the wind from anything
> under the tired, Italian stars . . .
>
> And the voice of the waters, starting its ghostly litany.   (*SC* 51)

Within these lines come the recovery and homage to Sirmio on Lake Garda, which is Pound's as well as Wright's magical place. Here Pound's Taoist vision fuses with Pound's "unforgotten guilt" and our "one sin" the spider recites in "Self-Portrait in 2035." Pound's influence is found throughout Wright's work, but it is certainly Pound's energy that is recalled in Wright's use of vectored lines; nonetheless, Wright seems to look toward the early, more elegiac Pound intent on what Hugh Kenner describes a "poiesis of loss."[28] Wright works from the aesthetic of seized glimpses that harden into worded moments—the ideogram of energy Pound developed throughout his writing.[29] Sirmio also mirrors the levels assigned to sinners in Dante's *Inferno,* who must be forever at their punishments; thereby their sins are metaphorically revealed and the interpretation of each sin forever remembered and reinscribed. Whoever gazes at Lake Garda must recognize and thus link with Pound, Dante, and the ebb and flow of daily life:

> Everything has its work,
> everything written down
> In a second-hand grace of solitude and tall trees . . .   (*SC* 64)

As time's landscape is language, all writing traces an autobiography of what has been lost and accumulated.

Our search for our lost self, always and already an other is finally limited, like language and time:

> There is an otherness inside us
> We never touch,
> no matter how far down our hands reach.
> It is the past,
> with its good looks and *Anytime, Anywhere* . . .
> Our prayers go out to it, our arms go out to it
> Year after year,
> But who can ever remember enough?   (*SC* 57)

The interminable process of remembering—forestalling silence and the last word—is paradoxically the unfulfilled reconstitution of the lost self. Thus, absence and a provisional presence coexist. The recovery of the imago or mirrored self occurs only at the last word—death—where we enter our "old outline as though for the 1st time, / And lie down, and tell no one" (*SC* 65). The full knowledge of the self occurs only at such thresholds; otherwise it remains unrecoverable:

> It's what we forget that defines us, and stays in the same place.
> And waits to be rediscovered.
> Somewhere in all that network of rivers and roads and silt hills,
> A city I'll never remember,
> its walls the color of pure light,
> Lies in the August heat of 1935,
> In Tennessee, the bottom land slowly becoming a lake.
> It lies in a landscape that keeps my imprint
> Forever,
> and stays unchanged, and waits to be filled back in.
> (*SC* 65)

With overlay after overlay of memory, influence, and imagery, the hand that was dealt "blank, blank, blank, blank, blank" (*SC* 53) fills with luminous details and light. The palimpsestic overlay of autobiographical elements fills in the self's outline and links layer with layer: the "network of rivers and roads and silt hills" is a "language that keeps my imprint."

Wright's more recent poems could be said to resemble Theodore Roethke's "North American Sequence," for both poets explore the long, traveling lines that contain an organic and mnemonic world within them. Wright and Roethke search out communions with a natural landscape. Roethke, however, assumes the attainment of transcendence:

> Silence of water above a sunken tree:
> The pure serene of memory in one man—
> A ripple widening from a single stone
> Winding around the waters of the world.[30]

These final lines of "The Far Field" embrace a Zen conception of centeredness and focused contemplation that winds outward into the world, though always belonging to the world, and further into reflective nothingness. The "Silence of water" and "pure serene" celebrate Zen contemplation. Roethke, furthermore, sees the possibility of embracing the world, whereas Wright cannot assume such a stance spiritually because each link forged—transcendent as each link may be—remains provisional and at best only a suggestion of a larger harmony.

Wright also lacks the raw, open, raucous language that distinguishes Roethke's poetry. Instead, his poetry appears polished, refined, almost alchemically transmuted. A disturbing distance, however, checks our intimacy with Wright's language, though his poetry is in part the intimate process of remembering. The image—and self-reflexively the portrait and hence the self—always retreats deeper into an untranslated music. The intent is to plunge, not into silence, but into folds of music or layers of brushwork. Roethke moves us always to the concrete and discrete: the touchstone of Zen meditation and Zen poetry. Wright, distinctively, takes us away from the particular to the mnemonically mediated and to the abstraction of the particular image. The inherent distance found in abstraction evokes the difficulty of hermeneusis, self, and the very proposal of interconnection.

Wright's recent collection, *The Other Side of the River,* more persuasively proposes the provisional assemblages of the self than do his previous collections. To remember is to inform the self and is an act of self-portraiture:

> The poem is a self-portrait
>   always, no matter what mask
> You take off and put back on.
> As this one is, color of cream and a mouthful of air.
> Rome is like that, and we are,
>   taken off and put back on.   (*OS* 46, "Roma II")

To remember is to revise and thus to craft one's own portrait. Remembering is also a means of survival, both in terms of the self and of history: "To speak of the dead is to make them live again: / We invent what we need" (*OS* 61). Memory is thus the force of invention, rising out of a deep need to pull ourselves from isolation into a world where "the frog-shrill and the insect-shrill" are "as palpable as a heartstring, / Whatever that was back then, always in memory" (*OS* 61, "Arkansas Traveller"). Memory holds the possibility of writing; in turn, writing retraces connections between the self and the world, defining the very craft of the poem:

> It's linkage I'm talking about,
>   and harmonies and structures
> And all the various things that lock our wrists to the past.
> And something infinite behind everything appears
>   and then disappears.
>
> It's all a matter of how
>   you narrow the surfaces.
> It's all a matter of how you fit in the sky.
>   (*OS* 24, "The Other Side of the River")

To write is to mirror the world's writing, "To summon the spirits up and set the body to music" (*OS* 7, "Lost Souls"). Throughout *The Other Side of the River,* Wright maps the connections between Tennessee and Italy, the self and nature: "all the various things that lock our wrists to the past" (*OS* 24) or "the residue / Of all our illuminations and unnamed lives" (*OS* 9, "Lost Souls"). Names of places and friends rise out of bare narratives and anecdotes to claim some provisional presence. Wright, even in the brevity of a name and slight context, creates an intimate poetry: "you're part of my parts of speech. / Think of me now and then. I'll think of you" (*OS* 67, "To Giacomo Leopardi in the Sky"). The poetry is a process of self-definition and self-composition; yet, the possibility of composition or intimacy always has the shadow of time and loss passing over, which ultimately distances us from the other, be it text or human experience. Writing, by traveling to the pages' margins, attempts to recover presence, but in this act writing reinscribes loss:

> I have nothing to say about the way the sky tilts
> Toward the absolute,
>   or why I live at the edge
> Of the black boundary,
>   a continent where the waves
> Counsel my coming in and my going out.
>   (*OS* 41, "Three Poems for the New Year")

Nonetheless, language remains luminous, fecund, transformative—and implicitly subject to decay. We yearn, Wright suggests, for some form of transcendence that comes from the possibility of the fullness of words and discourse:

>   What language does light speak?
>   Vowels hang down from the pepper tree
>   in their green and their gold.
>   (*OS* 51, "Cryopexy")

The possibility of a full language is always and already on the other side of the river. Rather than seeking something outside the self and language, as in the modernism of Eliot, Wright seeks to define the self with whatever bits and pieces of the world and the world-as-language can be found. He understands that the language of light—literal and metaphorical—is closed and divided from us. These poems thus mark our distance from our histories and landscapes; in this way, the language is transformational and alchemical: "Everything comes from fire" (*OS* 51, "Cryopexy"). Wright's quest, if we wish to call it that, is a search for presence—both of self and of world. Fire, then, is passion and transformation, as well as "The form inside the form inside" (*OS* 44, "Roma I"). Amidst time and the flux of self and world, Wright looks for some essential presence within himself and within what he sees:

> Weightlessness underwrites everything
> In the deep space of the eye,
>   the wash and drift of oblivion
>
> Sifting the color out,
>   polishing, still polishing
> Long after translucence comes.   (*OS* 52, "Cryopexy")

We are recipients of the regard of others, which with light penetrates our consciousness "Into the endlessness behind the eye" (*OS* 52):

> Radiance comes through the eye
>   and lodges like cut glass in the mind,
> Never vice versa,
> Somatic and self-contained.   (*OS* 51, "Cryopexy")

Wright envisions the world as a book of signs, where each thing is an inscription we must interpret, and where such interpretation becomes increasingly difficult:

> These nights are like that,
> The silvery alphabet of the sea
>   increasingly difficult to transcribe,

And larger each year, everything farther away, and less clear,
Than I want it to be,
                    not enough time to do the job,
And faint thunks in the earth,
As though somewhere nearby a horse was nervously pawing the
        ground.   (*OS* 25, "The Other Side of the River")

Indeed, there is some radiant utterance behind each thing, which
can turn the sea into a "silvery alphabet"; each thing is, in fact, a
figuration of "that luminous, nameless body whose flesh takes
on / The mottoes we say we live by" (*OS* 5, "Lost Bodies"). Language—our Augustinian reading of the world as a book—
describes both intimacy and difficulty, for any approach toward
understanding is shadowed by a constant sliding away of what is
desired.

In *The Other Side of the River,* the world is full of departures
and mortalities. Indeed, Wright's central thematic concern
throughout his poetry is the meditation on mortality:

What other anagoge in this life but the self?
What other ladder to Paradise
                    but the smooth handholds of the rib cage?
High in the palm tree the orioles twitter and grieve.
We twitter and grieve, the spider twirls the honey bee,
Who twitters and grieves, around in her net,
                    then draws it by one leg
Up to the fishbone fern leaves inside the pepper tree
                    swaddled in silk
And turns it again and again until it is shining.
                    (*OS* 71, "California Dreaming")

Refuting the opposition of life and death (while undercutting the
high seriousness of the concern with the repeated phrase "twitter
and grieve"), Wright confronts their interwoven immanence,
which is apprehended only through the mediating energies of language. Each moment and object, in itself, marks the

> point when everything starts to dust away
> More quickly than it appears,
> when what we have to comfort the dark
> Is just that dust, and just its going away.
>
> (*OS* 25, "The Other Side of the River")

"It's not age," Wright states, but "It's discontinuity / . . . That sends us apart and keeps us there in a dread" (*OS* 21, "Two Stories"). The lines between silence and language or separation and connection blur; to write necessitates the venturing close to what Rilke in his sonnets called "the breath around nothing."[31]

The further Wright considers mortality, the more insistent is the place of language:

> Surely, as has been said, emptiness is the beginning of all things.
> Thus wind over water,
> thus tide-pull and sand-sheen
> When the sea turns its lips back . . .   (*OS* 46, "Roma II")

The meditation on silence and emptiness becomes reinscribed through anecdotes and rhetoric. Nonetheless, language is as elusive as the making palpable of emptiness. The question of silence or the end, however, persists: "At the end of the last word, / When night comes walking across the lake on its hands, / and nothing appears in the mirror" (*OS* 38, "Italian Days"). What happens on the other side of the river when our self-portraits disappear? The loss of language will mean the loss of self-definition and interconnection. We "ask again if our first day in the dark / Is our comfort or signature" (*OS* 39, "Italian Days"). Do we write toward our death and away from our presence—where words are elegies of themselves and ourselves? Or does our signature, as at the end of a letter, insure our presence despite all distances?

Writing is our trace and afterlife: "What if inside the body another shape is waiting to come out" (*OS* 71, "California Dreaming"). The poems travel and build layer upon layer, so that there is always something that shines through a given pigment, informing the surface with depth, the past, and the measure of distance. Wright's meditations celebrate, for "What gifts there are are all here in this world" (*OS* 40, "Italian Days"). Wright eloquently confronts our ends so as to turn back to this world, having discovered

> That all beauty depends upon disappearance,
> The bitten edges of things,
> > > the gradual sliding away
> Into tissue and memory,
> > > the uncertainty
> And dazzling impermanence of days we beg our meanings from,
> And their frayed loveliness.   (*OS* 15, "Lonesome Pine Special")

NOTES

INDEX

NOTES

Introduction

1. Charles Newman, *The Post-Modern Aura: The Act of Fiction in an Age of Inflation* (Evanston: Northwestern University Press, 1985), 10.

2. See Charles Altieri's *Self and Sensibility in Contemporary American Poetry* (Cambridge: Cambridge University Press, 1984). Also see *Salmagundi* 65 (1984): 63–96 for Mary Kinzie's essay "The Rhapsodic Fallacy" and responses to Kinzie's essay in the same issue by Terrence Diggory and Charles Molesworth. See *Salmagundi* 67 (1985): 135–62 for further responses to Kinzie's essay by Paul Breslin, Alan Shapiro, Stephen Yenser, Marjorie Perloff, Julia Randall, and Bonnie Costello as well as Kinzie's response "Learning to Speak."

3. See Gregory Ulmer, *Applied Grammatology: Post(e)-Pedagogy from Jacques Derrida to Joseph Beuys* (Baltimore: Johns Hopkins University Press, 1985), 11.

4. M. M. Bakhtin, *The Dialogic Imagination: Four Essays,* ed. Michael Holquist, trans. Caryl Emerson and Michael Holquist (Austin: University of Texas Press, 1982), 293.

5. See W. R. Johnson, *The Idea of the Lyric: Lyric Modes in Ancient and Modern Poetry* (Berkeley: University of California Press, 1982), 3–23.

6. See David Kalstone's *Five Temperaments* (New York: Oxford University Press, 1977), which considers autobiographic resources in recent American poetry; Robert Pinsky's *The Situation of Poetry: Contemporary Poetry and Its Traditions* (Princeton: Princeton University Press, 1976),

which describes several dominant forms of poetry and their place within an ongoing but increasingly failed romantic tradition; and Cary Nelson's *Our Last First Poets: Vision and History in Contemporary American Poetry* (Urbana: University of Illinois Press, 1981), which argues that external and historical pressures have made verbal union and harmony impossible to sustain in contemporary American poetry. Marjorie Perloff's *The Dance of the Intellect: Studies in the Poetry of the Pound Tradition* (Cambridge: Cambridge University Press, 1985) points to a different arena of poetics than those of Altieri, Kalstone, Nelson, or Pinsky. Perloff argues that the Pound tradition is a set of poetics that questions narrative and romantic lyricism while asserting a phenomenology of the present.

7. In reviewing Charles Altieri's *Self and Sensibility in Contemporary American Poetry,* Daniel T. O'Hara (in "The Poverty of Theory: On Society and the Sublime," *Contemporary Literature* 26 [1985]: 339–42) argues that Altieri fails to examine the historical, social, and political pressures in what Altieri sees as a compromised, if not a failed, poetry. One further outcome of this project is that the critic has become arbitrator or judge. The poet David Young, in his review "Out Beyond Rhetoric: Four Poets and One Critic" (*Field* 30 [1984]: 83–102), writes "Once we have taken up the question of technique, we're in Altieri's fallen world, where rhetoric and artifice rule in matters of art, critics are just smarter versions of artists, comparative judgments are reflections of cultural stimuli, and a relativity reigns whereby now some rhetorics are fashionable, now others."

8. Altieri, *Self and Sensibility,* 20.

9. In describing what he views as the dominant mode of poetry, the "scenic," Altieri sees two models. One is an "intense moment of psychological conflict" and the other extends an "evocative metaphor by a more discursive and tonally complex reflective summary," but in both models poems lack "any sustained act of formal, dialectical thinking or an elaborate, artificial construction that cannot be imagined as taking place in, or at least extending from, settings in naturalistically conceived scenes" (*Self and Sensibility,* 10–11). Altieri, however, sees John Ashbery and Adrienne Rich as offering the most significant directions away from the shortcomings of the scenic mode through their self-reflective poetics.

Chapter 1. Concordances and Travels: the Poetry of Elizabeth Bishop

1. Elizabeth Bishop, *The Complete Poems: 1927–1979* (New York: Farrar, Straus, and Giroux, 1983), 25. All quotations will be from this edition and will be documented in the text.

2. For a sample of poets' admiration of Bishop's work see "Elizabeth Bishop: A Symposium," *Field* 31 (1984): 7–45.

3. Hans-Georg Gadamer, *Truth and Method* (New York: Crossroad, 1982), 377.

4. Svetlana Alpers, *The Art of Describing: Dutch Art in the Seventeenth Century* (Chicago: University of Chicago Press, 1983), 98.

5. See Wendy Steiner, *The Colors of Rhetoric: Problems in the Relation Between Modern Literature and Painting* (Chicago: University of Chicago Press, 1982), 41–42.

6. Ibid., 45.

7. Jerome Mazzaro, *Postmodern American Poetry* (Urbana: University of Illinois Press, 1980), 183.

8. Louis L. Martz, *The Poetry of Meditation: A Study in English Religious Literature* (New Haven: Yale University Press, 1954), 27.

9. Robert Lowell, *Life Studies* and *For the Union Dead* (New York: Farrar, Straus, and Giroux, 1980), 7, 13.

10. Mazzaro, *Postmodern American Poetry*, 173.

11. Ibid.

12. Lee T. Lemon and Marion J. Reis, eds., *Russian Formalist Criticism: Four Essays* (Lincoln: University of Nebraska Press, 1965), 12, 18.

13. Helen Vendler, *Part of Nature, Part of Us* (Cambridge: Harvard University Press, 1980), 97.

14. Mutlu Konuk Blasing, "'Mont D'Espoir or Mount Despair': The Re-Verses of Elizabeth Bishop," *Contemporary Literature* 25 (1984): 353.

15. Vendler, *Part of Nature, Part of Us*, 108.

16. Larry Levis, "Some Notes on the Gazer Within," *A Field Guide to Contemporary Poetry and Poetics*, ed. Stuart Friebert and David Young (New York: Longman, 1980), 110.

17. Galway Kinnell, *Body Rags* (Boston: Houghton Mifflin, 1968), 63.

18. Lee Edelman, "The Geography of Gender: Elizabeth Bishop's 'In the Waiting Room,'" *Contemporary Literature* 26 (1985): 188, 192, 196.

19. This moment parallels Jacques Lacan's mirror stage, where the self discovers its own existence by seeing a mirroring of itself, that is seeing and identifying itself as another. What must be stressed is the aspect of difference and supplementarity. The mirror image, furthermore, holds for Lacan the Ideal-I and the name of the father, which the child interminably seeks. This phallocentric description—one of usurpation of place and language, and of the perpetuation of patriarchy—is not one Bishop's poem describes. But Lacan's basic premise, that of the self mirrored as the self-as-other, does illuminate the situation and is in fact vital for any discussion of *looking* in Bishop's work. See Jacques Lacan, "The Mirror Stage," in *Ecrits: A Selection,* trans. Alan Sheridan (New York: Norton, 1977).

20. David Kalstone, *Five Temperaments* (New York: Oxford University Press, 1977), 35. See Vendler, *Part of Nature, Part of Us,* pp. 105–7.

21. Mazzaro, *Postmodern American Poetry*, 179.

22. Edelman, "The Geography of Gender," 194. Writing on "In the Waiting Room," Edelman argues that in an earlier version of the poem the narrator's shyness when confronted with the breasts of the naked women "surely corresponds to the fearful embarrassment that expresses desire in the very act of trying to veil it." Edelman also argues that

Bishop "covertly discredits" what Adrienne Rich has called "the false universal of heterosexuality" (Adrienne Rich, "The Eye of the Outsider: The Poetry of Elizabeth Bishop," *Boston Review* 8 [1983]: 16, cited by Edelman in "The Geography of Gender," p. 194).

23. John Golding, *Cubism: A History and Analysis, 1907–1914* (New York: Icon Editions, 1968), 81–82.

24. Maurice Merleau-Ponty, "Eye and Mind," in *The Essential Writings of Merleau-Ponty,* ed. Alden L. Fisher (New York: Harcourt, Brace and World, 1969), 260.

25. Cathrael Kazin pointed this out to me, noting how flower, eye, and rainbow are linked in *iris,* a pun on *iri*descent. Like discoursing, looking in Bishop's poetry expresses constant speculation; a traveling into place, voice, and word. Within the process of looking is a cornucopia: the iris of the eye-I opens to others—flower and rainbow—to evoke the world as iridescent when we choose to look closely.

26. Merleau-Ponty, "Primacy of Perception: Philosophical Consequences," in *Essential Writings,* 62.

Chapter 2. John Ashbery's *Artes Poeticae* of Self and Text

1. John Ashbery, "Self-Portrait in a Convex Mirror," *Self-Portrait in a Convex Mirror* (New York: Penguin, 1976), 69. The following titles by John Ashbery are abbreviated, and citations for quotations from these works are provided in the text: *AW—As We Know* (New York: Penguin, 1979); *DD—The Double Dream of Spring* (New York: Ecco Press, 1976); *HD—The Houseboat Days* (New York: Penguin, 1977); *RM—Rivers and Mountains* (New York: Ecco Press, 1977); *S—Shadow Train* (New York: Penguin, 1981); *SP—Self-Portrait in a Convex Mirror; ST—Some Trees* (New York: Ecco Press, 1978); *TC—The Tennis Court Oath* (Middletown, Conn.: Wesleyan University Press, 1962); *TP—Three Poems* (New York: Penguin, 1977); *W—A Wave* (New York: Viking Press, 1984).

2. George Steiner, in his *On Difficulty* (London: Oxford University Press, 1972), writes that difficulty "implicates the function of language and of the poem as a communicative performance, because it puts in question the existential suppositions that lie behind poetry as we have known it"; furthermore, "Ontological difficulties confront us with blank questions about the nature of human speech, about the status of significance, about the necessity and purpose of the construct which we have, with more or less rough and ready consensus, come to perceive as a poem" (41).

3. Elizabeth Bishop, *The Complete Poems: 1927–1979* (New York: Farrar, Straus, and Giroux, 1983), 23–25.

4. David Shapiro, *John Ashbery* (New York: Columbia University Press, 1979), 20.

5. Dallas Museum of Fine Arts, *Kurt Schwitters: A Retrospective Exhibition* (Dallas: Dallas Museum of Fine Arts, 1965).

6. Ihab Hassan, *The Dismemberment of Orpheus* (Madison: University of Wisconsin Press, 1982), 13–18.

7. Fred Moramarco, "The Lonesomeness of Words," in *Beyond Amazement: New Essays on John Ashbery*, ed. David Lehman (Ithaca, N.Y.: Cornell University Press, 1980), 158.

8. Maurice Blanchot, *The Writing of the Disaster*, trans. Ann Smock (Lincoln: University of Nebraska Press, 1986), 106.

9. The rearticulation of the beginning of the poem parallels Jacques Derrida's description of the process of invagination in his "Living On: Border Lines," trans. James Hulbert, in Harold Bloom et al., *Deconstruction and Criticism* (New York: Continuum, 1979), 97–100.

10. Elizabeth Sewell, *The Orphic Voice: Poetry and Natural History* (New Haven: Yale University Press, 1960), 403.

11. Shapiro dismisses *The Double Dream of Spring* as "quiet Wordsworthian ruralism" (*John Ashbery*, 130). Charles Berger, in his "Vision in the Form of a Task" demonstrates that Ashbery is "the poet of high imagination, the visionary" (*Beyond Amazement*, 164).

12. John Koethe, "The Metaphysical Subject of John Ashbery's Poetry," in *Beyond Amazement*, 91–92.

13. Ibid., 99.

14. Charles Altieri, *Self and Sensibility in Contemporary American Poetry* (Cambridge: Cambridge University Press, 1984), 147.

15. Ashbery's insistent "always," which denotes persistence of presence, parallels Derrida's phrase "always already" in *Of Grammatology* (trans. Gayatri Chakravorty Spivak [Baltimore: Johns Hopkins University Press, 1976]). Derrida's arguments shadow Ashbery's own explorations of the usurpation of one trace by another as well as a temporal dislocation: an ebbing pastness is combined with the sense of the present moment. For both Ashbery and Derrida, usurpation describes the process of institutions and metaphysics as well as the dynamic between writing and speech.

16. David Kalstone uses "Self-Portrait in a Convex Mirror" as the primary means of entering into the autobiographical sensibility of Ashbery's poetry. In reviewing *Self-Portrait in a Convex Mirror*, Richard Howard states that though one may like or loathe Ashbery, "There is no choice, however, about the title poem and half a dozen others, which are, as everyone seems to be saying, among the finest things American poetry has yet to show, and certainly the finest things Ashbery has yet shown" (*Alone in America*, 2d ed. [New York: Atheneum, 1980], 50).

17. Ashbery explicitly invokes Derrida's notion of parergon in the poem "Parergon": "Yet each knew he saw only aspects, / That the continuity was fierce beyond all dream of enduring" (*DD* 56). The parergon, or ornamentation and framing, is supplementary and effacing. It disappears yet provides us with an object's content or form: the marginal can no longer be marginalized. As Ashbery notes again and again, his concern is the movement of the poem and the desire to include everything. For Derrida's discussion of *parergon*, see "The Parergon," trans. Craig Owens, *October* 9 (1979): 3–40.

18. Jacques Derrida, "Limited Inc.," trans. Samuel Weber, *Glyph* 2 (1977): 236.

19. David Bromwich, "John Ashbery: The Self against Its Image," *Raritan* 5, no. 4 (1986): 54.

20. Bromwich discusses "City Afternoons" (*SP* 61) as a critique of the "counterfeit immortality" a photograph seems to offer, because "it is the medium in which most people recognize themselves as the heroes of their own lives"; thus the photograph, for Ashbery, is "another name for death, against which poetic reflection may appear as an act of recovery" ("John Ashbery," 49).

Chapter 3. "Fiery Iconography": Language and Interconnection in the Poetry of Adrienne Rich

1. Adrienne Rich, "When We Dead Awaken: Writing as Re-Vision" (1971), in *On Lies, Secrets, and Silence: Selected Prose, 1966–1978* (New York: Norton, 1979), 44.

2. The following titles by Adrienne Rich are abbreviated, and citations for quotations from these works are provided in the text: *DCL—The Dream of a Common Language: Poems, 1974–1977* (New York: Norton, 1978); *DW—Diving into the Wreck: Poems, 1971–1972* (New York: Norton, 1973); *FD—The Fact of a Doorframe: Poems Selected and New, 1950–1984* (New York: Norton, 1984); *L—Leaflets: Poems, 1965–1968* (New York: Norton, 1969); *NL—Your Native Land, Your Life* (New York: Norton, 1986); *PSN—Poems Selected and New, 1950–1974* (New York: Norton, 1975); *SDL—Snapshots of a Daughter-in-Law: Poems, 1954–1962* (New York: Norton, 1967); *WP—A Wild Patience Has Taken Me This Far: Poems, 1978–1981* (New York: Norton, 1981); *WTC—The Will to Change: Poems, 1968–1970* (New York: Norton, 1971).

3. See Rich's discussion of the "lesbian continuum" in her essay "Compulsory Heterosexuality and Lesbian Existence," *Signs* 5 (1980): 631–60. Rich seeks to connect women historically, culturally, politically, and sexually within a continuum and describes this connectedness or intensity between women as lesbian. See also "It Is the Lesbian in Us . . ." (1976), in *On Lies, Secrets, and Silence*. Also see Ann Ferguson, Jacquelyn N. Zita, and Kathryn Pyne Addelson, "On 'Compulsory Heterosexuality and Lesbian Existence': Defining the Issues," *Feminist Theory: A Critique of Ideology*, ed. Nannerl O. Keohane, Michelle Z. Rosaldo, and Barbara C. Gelpi (Chicago: University of Chicago Press, 1982), 147–88.

4. In *Part of Nature, Part of Us* (Cambridge: Harvard University Press, 1980), Helen Vendler questions Rich's poetry when it exerts its feminist grounding. In *Our Last First Poets: Vision and History in Contemporary American Poetry* (Urbana: University of Illinois Press, 1984), Cary Nelson questions many of Rich's political and historically referential poems on the basis of effective style. In *Self and Sensibility in Contemporary American Poetry* (Cambridge: Cambridge University Press, 1984), Charles Altieri argues that the best of Rich's poetry assumes the

responsibility of creating a self-critical ethos; however, he also faults Rich on style and, on the whole, elides mention of her politics. Jane Roberta Cooper's collection *Reading Adrienne Rich: Reviews and Revisions, 1951–81* (Ann Arbor: University of Michigan Press, 1984) contains—in addition to essays that tend to focus on *The Dream of a Common Language*—reviews that range from the laudatory to outright rejection. The essays by various critics collected in Cooper's volume tend to trace Rich's development as a poet or to focus on a particular poem. The collection is a useful companion to *Adrienne Rich's Poetry*, edited by Barbara C. Gelpi and Albert Gelpi (New York: Norton, 1975). Also important is Sandra Gilbert's redefinition of confessionalism in "'My Name is Darkness': The Poetry of Self-Definition," *Contemporary Literature* 18 (1977): 443–57. Two extensive studies of the autobiographic in relation to Rich's poetry are Wendy Martin's *An American Triptych: Anne Bradstreet, Emily Dickinson, and Adrienne Rich* (Chapel Hill: University of North Carolina Press, 1984) and David Kalstone's *Five Temperaments* (New York: Oxford University Press, 1977).

5. In "Power and Danger: Works of a Common Woman" (1977), Rich writes "Poetry is above all a concentration of the power of language, which is the power of our ultimate relationship to everything in the universe. It is as if forces we can only lay claim to in no other way become present to us in sensuous form. The knowledge and use of this magic goes back very far: the rune; the chant; the incantation; the spell; kenning; sacred words; forbidden words; the naming of the child, the plant, the insect; the ocean, the configuration of stars, the snow, the sensation in the body. The ritual telling of the dream" (in *On Lies, Secrets, and Silence,* 248).

6. Some examples of her occasional poems include "To Franz Fanon" (*Leaflets*), "The Burning of Paper instead of Children" (*The Will to Change*), "Rape" (*Diving into the Wreck*), "Tear Gas" (*Poems Selected and New*), "A Woman Dead in Her Forties" (*The Dream of a Common Language*), "Turning the Wheel" (*A Wild Patience Has Taken Me This Far*), and "Contradictions: Tracking Poems" (*Your Native Land, Your Life*). These poems range from a memorial to a voicing of anger and protest to journallike sequences; each emphasizes the immediate.

7. Rosemond Tuve (*Elizabethan and Metaphysical Imagery* [Chicago: University of Chicago Press, 1947], 192–247) locates the decorous in the image and in its suitability to the discourse and subject at hand. Angus Fletcher (*Allegory: The Theory of a Symbolic Mode* [Ithaca, N.Y.: Cornell University Press, 1970], 110–12) suggests that decorum, etymologically aligned with ornament, is microcosmic and metonymic—it reveals the law of society and cosmos. Though Tuve suggests decorum has shifted in application since the Symbolists because there are no essential subjects outside the self, her application still holds true in terms of a prescribed discourse that should not be broken—the force of the prescribed discourse underwrites what is fashionable as well as the notion that poets must, by definition, break forms to be new. Tuve's location of decorum

with image fits with Fletcher's idea that an ornament, marginal as it may seem, reflects the law or the symbolic structures of the dominant culture. By dismissing many aspects of Rich's style as not poetically fulfilling, critics align themselves with the decorum or law of a particular social discourse and ideology that Rich critiques.

8. Rachel Blau DuPlessis, *Writing Beyond the Ending: Narrative Strategies of Twentieth-Century Women Writers* (Bloomington: Indiana University Press, 1985), 139.

9. Altieri, *Self and Sensibility*, 186–87.

10. Martin, *American Triptych*, 174.

11. Rich, *On Lies, Secrets, and Silence*, 40.

12. In "When We Dead Awaken: Writing as Re-Vision," Rich defines *re-vision* as "the act of looking back, of seeing with fresh eyes, of entering an old text from a new critical direction—[re-vision] is for women more than a chapter in cultural history: it is an act of survival" (*On Lies, Secrets, and Silence*, 35).

13. Rich describes her changing definition of herself as a poet in "When We Dead Awaken: Writing as Re-Vision": "I despaired of doing any continuous work at this time. Yet I began to feel that my fragments and scraps had a common consciousness and a common theme, one which I would have been very unwilling to put on paper at an earlier time because I had been taught that poetry should be 'universal,' which meant, of course, nonfemale. Until then I had tried very much *not* to identify myself as a female poet" (*On Lies, Secrets, and Silence*, 44).

14. Kalstone, *Five Temperaments*, 131–37.

15. Nelson, *Our Last First Poets*, 171.

16. DuPlessis, *Writing Beyond the Ending*, 125.

17. Rich looks to the sky and implicitly invokes the Great Goddess. In *Of Woman Born: Motherhood as Experience and Institution* (New York: Bantam, 1977), Rich writes that "gynocentric pantheism imagined the sky itself to be female, with the sun and moon her sons. 'The female sky is the fixed and enduring element,' in a number of cultures and myths cited by Neumann: Egyptian, Aztec, Vedic, Babylonian. The Great Mother, the female principle, was originally personified both in darkness and in light, in the depths of the water and the heights of the sky. Only with the development of a patriarchial cosmogony do we find her restricted to a purely 'chthonic' or tellurian presence, represented by darkness, unconsciousness, and sleep" (97).

18. Claire Keyes, "'The Angels Chiding': *Snapshots of a Daughter-in-Law*," in Cooper's collection, *Reading Adrienne Rich*, 49.

19. See P. V. Glob, *The Bog People: Iron Age Man Preserved* (London: Faber and Faber, 1977), and Lucy R. Lippard, *Overlay: Contemporary Art and the Art of Prehistory* (New York: Pantheon, 1983).

20. For a full discussion of the "glance" and the "gaze," see Norman Bryson, *Vision and Painting: The Logic of the Gaze* (New Haven: Yale University Press, 1983), 87–131. Also see Jacques Lacan on the gaze in

The Four Fundamental Concepts of Psycho-Analysis, trans. Alan Sheridan (New York: Norton, 1978), 67–69, 82–89, 100–119.

21. Altieri, *Self and Sensibility,* 174.

22. See Annette Kuhn, *Women's Pictures: Feminism and Cinema* (London: Routledge and Kegan Paul, 1982), 158. Also see Zoë Sophia, "Exterminating Fetuses: Abortion, Disarmament, and the Sexo-Semiotics of Extraterrestrialism," *Diacritics* 14, no. 2 (1984): 47–59.

23. Susan R. Van Dyne, "The Mirrored Vision of Adrienne Rich," *Modern Poetry Studies* 8, no. 2 (1977): 145.

24. DuPlessis, *Writing Beyond the Ending,* 133.

25. In *Adrienne Rich's Poetry,* Rich states that "we have a history of centuries of women in depression: really angry women, who could have been using their anger creatively. . . . And therefore it's not only that there are unwritten books, but that many of the books that were written are subdued, they're like banked fires . . . I think anger can be a kind of genius if it's acted on" ("Three Conversations," 111).

26. See M. M. Bakhtin, *The Dialogic Imagination: Four Essays,* ed. Michael Holquist, trans. Caryl Emerson and Michael Holquist (Austin: University of Texas Press, 1982), 263.

27. Elizabeth Bishop, *The Complete Poems: 1927–1979* (New York: Farrar, Straus, and Giroux, 1983), 159–61.

28. Gelpi and Gelpi, *Adrienne Rich's Poetry,* "Three Conversations," 119.

Chapter 4. W. S. Merwin's Poetics of Memory

1. W. S. Merwin, *The Lice* (New York: Atheneum, 1970), 50. The following titles by W. S. Merwin are abbreviated, and citations for quotations from these works are provided in the text: *CF—The Compass Flower* (New York: Atheneum, 1977); *CL—The Carrier of Ladders* (New York: Atheneum, 1970); *FF—The First Four Books* (New York: Atheneum, 1975); *FI—Finding the Islands* (San Francisco: North Point Press, 1982); *L—The Lice; MT—The Moving Target* (New York: Atheneum, 1963); *OH—Opening the Hand* (New York: Atheneum, 1983); *W—Writings to an Unfinished Accompaniment* (New York: Atheneum, 1973).

2. Charles Altieri, *Enlarging the Temple: New Directions in American Poetry During the 1960's* (Lewisburg, Pa.: Bucknell University Press, 1979), 196.

3. Gerald Bruns, *Inventions: Writing, Textuality, and Understanding in Literary History* (New Haven: Yale University Press, 1982), 18.

4. Altieri, *Enlarging the Temple,* 199.

5. Adrienne Rich, *The Will to Change: Poems, 1968–1970* (New York: Norton, 1971); see her poem "The Burning of Paper Instead of Children."

6. Altieri, *Enlarging the Temple,* 209.

7. Geoffrey H. Hartman, *Saving the Text: Literature / Derrida / Philosophy* (Baltimore: Johns Hopkins University Press, 1981), 148.

8. Bruns, *Inventions,* 17, 31.

9. Ibid., 20.

10. Elizabeth Sewell, *The Orphic Voice: Poetry and Natural History* (New Haven: Yale University Press, 1960), 47.

11. In his *Dismemberment of Orpheus* (Madison: University of Wisconsin Press, 1982), Ihab Hassan, while discussing Maurice Blanchot's interpretations of Orpheus, writes, "Eurydice, for instance, represents the obscure 'point' toward which art, desire, death, and night seem to tend; she represents the silence that Orpheus must and can not attain" (19).

12. Robert Graves, *The White Goddess: A Historical Grammar of Poetic Myth* (New York: Farrar, Straus, and Giroux, 1976), 180, 196, 260.

13. Ihab Hassan, *Paracriticisms: Seven Speculations of the Times* (Urbana: University of Illinois Press, 1975), 53.

14. Cary Nelson, *Our Last First Poets: Vision and History in Contemporary American Poetry* (Urbana: University of Illinois Press, 1981), 196–97.

15. Altieri, *Enlarging the Temple,* 198.

16. Ibid., 202.

17. Hartman, *Saving the Text,* 123.

18. Bruns, *Inventions,* 43.

19. W. S. Merwin, "W. S. Merwin: An Interview," *Black Warrior Review* 8, no. 2 (1982): 15.

20. Richard Howard, *Alone in America,* 2d ed. (New York: Atheneum, 1980), 449.

21. Roland Barthes, *Empire of Signs,* trans. Richard Howard (New York: Hill and Wang, 1982), 78.

22. See Gaston Bachelard's *The Poetics of Space,* translated by Maria Jolas (Boston: Beacon Press, 1969), 3–37.

23. Maurice Blanchot, *The Gaze of Orpheus,* trans. Lydia Davis (Barrytown, N.Y.: Station Hill Press, 1981), 102.

24. Ibid., 95, 95–96.

25. Barthes, *Empire of Signs,* 78.

26. Ibid., 83.

27. Ibid., 76.

28. Ibid., 75.

29. Ibid., 78. Also see Alan Watts, *The Way of Zen* (New York: Pantheon, 1964), 77, 121.

30. John Ashbery, *Some Trees* (New York: Ecco Press, 1978), 51.

31. See Michel Foucault's *Discipline and Punish: The Birth of the Prison,* translated by Alan Sheridan (New York: Vintage, 1979), 137–41 and 195–228.

32. Wallace Stevens, *Opus Posthumous* (New York: Knopf, 1957), 117–18.

33. Nelson, *Our Last First Poets,* 189.

Chapter 5. "Things That Lock Our Wrists to the Past": Self-Portraiture and Autobiography in Charles Wright's Poetry

1. Gerald Bruns, *Inventions: Writing, Textuality, and Understanding in Literary History* (New Haven: Yale University Press, 1982), 132–33.

2. Ibid., 136.

3. Charles Wright, *The Other Side of the River* (New York: Random House, 1984), 24. The following titles by Charles Wright are abbreviated, and citations for quotations from these works are provided in the text: *B—Bloodlines* (Middletown, Conn.: Wesleyan University Press, 1975); *CT—China Trace* (Middletown, Conn.: Wesleyan University Press, 1977); *G—The Grave of the Right Hand* (Middletown, Conn.: Wesleyan University Press, 1970); *HF—Hard Freight* (Middletown, Conn.: Wesleyan University Press, 1974); *OS—The Other Side of the River;* and *SC—The Southern Cross* (New York: Random House, 1981).

4. Charles Wright, "Charles Wright at Oberlin," in *A Field Guide to Contemporary Poetry and Poetics*, ed. Stuart Friebert and David Young (New York: Longman, 1980), 268.

5. William Howarth, "Some Principles of Autobiography," in *Autobiography: Essays Theoretical and Critical*, ed. James Olney (Princeton: Princeton University Press, 1980), 85.

6. Ibid., 85.

7. John Ashbery, *Rivers and Mountains* (New York: Ecco Press, 1977), 39.

8. W. S. Merwin, *Writings to an Unfinished Accompaniment* (New York: Atheneum, 1976), 53.

9. Calvin Bedient, "Tracing Charles Wright," *Parnassus* 10, no. 2 (1982): 69.

10. Candace Lang, "Autobiography in the Aftermath of Romanticism," *Diacritics* 12, no. 4 (1982): 11.

11. Ibid., 16.

12. Michel Foucault's essay "What Is an Author?" in *Language, Counter-Memory, Practice* (trans. Donald F. Bouchard [Ithaca, N.Y.: Cornell University Press, 1977]), raises the question of authorship. Foucault substitutes "author-function" for "author" and suggests we look at a work in terms of its interactions, functions, and production, all of which could be subsumed into Wright's intertext and the idea of interconnection and linking.

13. Italo Calvino, *Invisible Cities,* trans. William Weaver (New York: Harcourt, Brace Jovanovich, 1974), 22–23.

14. Bedient, "Tracing Charles Wright," 61.

15. Jacques Derrida, *Of Grammatology,* trans. Gayatri Chakravorty Spivak (Baltimore: Johns Hopkins University Press, 1976), 124–25.

16. Wright, "Charles Wright at Oberlin," in *A Field Guide,* (251), describes the movement of "Skins" as a ladder; later (257–59), he provides

thematic labels for each of the poem's sections: 1—Situation, Point A; 2—Beauty; 3—Truth; 4—Destruction of the Universe; 5—Organized Religion; 6—Metamorphosis; 7—Water; 8—Water / Earth; 9—Earth / Fire; 10—Aether; 11—Primative magic; 12—Necromancy; 13—Black magic; 14—Alchemy; 15—Allegory; 16—Fire; 17—Air; 18—Water; 19—Earth; 20—Situation, Point A.

17. Wright, *A Field Guide*, 268.

18. Wright, "Interviews" in *Wright: A Profile*, 38.

19. Ernest Fenollosa, *The Chinese Written Character as a Medium for Poetry*, ed. Ezra Pound (San Francisco: City Lights, n.d.), 32.

20. Wright, "Charles Wright at Oberlin," in *A Field Guide*, 260.

21. Ibid., 262.

22. Ibid., 266.

23. Ibid.

24. Ibid., 262.

25. Fenollosa, *The Chinese Written Character*, 8–10.

26. Wright comments that in "Homage to Paul Cézanne," the "sections aren't haphazard or substitutable, however, any more than certain layers or brushstrokes or colors are. They go in the order they have, which is I hope, an accumulative order, but they are not numbered, hence they are not sections as we usually understand them in poems" (*Wright: A Profile*, 41).

27. Charles Wright, "Giorgio Morandi," *Antaeus* 54 (1985): 186–87.

28. Hugh Kenner, *The Pound Era* (Berkeley: University of California Press, 1973), 56.

29. Ibid., 71.

30. Theodore Roethke, "North American Sequence," in his *The Collected Poems* (Garden City, N.Y.: Doubleday, 1975), 195.

31. See Rainer Maria Rilke's Sonnet III in his *Sonnets to Orpheus;* the final stanza is "lerne / vergessen, dass du aufsangst. Das verrinnt. / In Wahrheit singen, ist ein andrer Hauch. / Ein Hauch um nichts. Ein Wehn im Gott. Ein Wind." *Ausgewählte Werke*, Vol. I (Leipzig: Insel-Verlag, 1938), p. 270. The English version: "learn / to forget that sudden music. It will end. / True singing is a different breath. / The breath around nothing. A gust inside the God. A wind."

INDEX

"After Dark" (Rich), 98, 118
Alpers, Svetlana, 9
Altieri, Charles, 2, 5, 72, 90, 106,
    132–33, 135, 144, 146, 216n, 220n
"Anabasis II" (Merwin), 133–34, 154,
    169
"Animals, The" (Merwin), 136, 143
"Annunciation, The" (Merwin), 135
"Apparitions" (Merwin), 166
"Arkansas Traveller" (Wright), 206
"Armadillo, The" (Bishop), 26, 36
Arnold, Matthew, 123
"Arrival at Santos" (Bishop), 24
Art of Painting, The (Vermeer), 10
"Ascent" (Merwin), 150
Ashbery, John, poetry of, 1, 46–86, 88,
    89, 99, 151, 163, 175; "As One Put
    Drunk into the Packet-Boat," 75;
    "Clouds," 65–66, 68, 82; collagiste
    method in, 47–48, 81; "Definition
    of Blue," 64; "Drunken Ameri-
    cans," 85; elegiac, 61–68; explora-
    tion of surface, 47, 51, 55, 56, 57,
    64, 73, 75; expressions of affirma-
    tion, 60, 69; "Fragment," 66–68;
    "Frontispiece," 84–85; gram-
    matological, 50, irony in, 49, lan-
    guage in, 5, 6, 51–53, 59–60; "A
    Last World," 53–54; "leaving-out
    business," 72, 174; letter as em-
    blem of interconnection, 58–59;
    meditations on mortality, 47,
    57–58, 60, 65–66, 72; mirror of
    reader, 46, 55, 60, 69–70, 73–74,
    84, 85–86; myth of Orpheus,
    54–55, 81–82; myth of Semele,
    65–66, 68, 82; "The New Spirit,"
    68–71; "Pantoum," 49–50; "Para-
    doxes and Oxymorons," 84; parody
    in, 51; "The Picture of Little J. A.
    in a Prospect of Flowers," 51;
    "Rain," 54; "The Recital," 73–75;
    self-criticism in, 52, 86; self-
    definition in, 48, 59, 63–64, 69,
    75, 84–85; self-portrait in, 75–81;

"Self-Portrait in a Convex Mirror,
    46–47, 59, 75–81; self-reflexivity
    in, 3, 49, 53; "The Skaters," 55–60;
    "Some Trees," 50–51; "Spring
    Day," 63–64; "Street Musicians,"
    81; "Summer," 62–63; "Sunrise in
    Suburbia," 65; "Syringa," 81–82;
    "The System," 71–73; "The Task,"
    63; use of stars, 61; view of art,
    74, 78, 82, 83–84; view of criti-
    cism, 46–47, 83, 84; "A Wave,"
    86; as writing of the disaster, 53–
    54, 60
"As One Put Drunk into the Packet-
    Boat" (Ashbery), 75
"As Though I Was Waiting for That"
    (Merwin), 150, 169
"As We Know" (Ashbery), 1, 83–84
"At a Bach Concert" (Rich), 91
"At the Fishhouses" (Bishop), 43–45
"At Zero" (Wright), 198–99
Auden, W. H., 48, 90
"Aunt Jennifer's Tigers" (Rich), 90
"Autumn Equinox" (Rich), 93

Bakhtin, M. M., 4
Barthes, Roland, 154, 161
"Bear, The" (Kinnell), 31
Bedient, Calvin, 180
Bishop, Elizabeth, poetry of, 7–45, 92,
    120; animals in, 31, 36; "Arrival
    at Santos," 24; "At the Fish-
    houses," 41–43; beauty and pain
    in, 11; "Brazil, January 1, 1502,"
    24–26, 36; "Crusoe in England,"
    26–27, 36–41; drive into the inte-
    rior, 27, 33, 41–42, 150; ekphras-
    tic, 9, 25; expression of knowledge,
    44–45; "The Fish," 9, 11, 12–17,
    26; historical landscape in, 24–26;
    idea of place in, 8, 9–10, 17–18,
    19, 32–33; "The Imaginary Ice-
    berg," 12, 40; importance of obser-
    vation in, 7, 9, 28, 30, 31–32, 45,
    164; "In the Waiting Room," 26,

Bishop, Elizabeth (*continued*)
32–36, 120; language in, 5, 6, 8,
14–15, 19–20; loss of childhood
in, 11, 16, 19, 35, 36; "The Map,"
18–20; memory in, 38, 41, 42;
"The Monument," 15, 20, 47; "The
Moose," 27–32, 185; natural
world in, 12, 25–26; personal
voice in, 8, 10, 19, 27, 34; "Poem,"
41–43; "Questions of Travel," 8,
20–24; relationship to Dutch
painting, 8, 9–10, 42, 45; role of
human relations, 40–41; self-definition in, 19, 20, 34–36; self-
reflexivity in, 3–4, 8, 10, 12, 14,
34; travel as metaphor in, 8–9,
11, 12–14, 21, 27–29, 47, 131,
150; view of art, 38–40, 41–43;
view of women, 26, 33–34
"Black Jewel, The" (Merwin), 170
"Blackwater Mountain" (Wright),
190–91
Blake, William, 132, 194
Blanchot, Maurice, 53, 158–59
Bloodlines (Wright), 184, 191–96
Braque, Georges, 42
"Brazil, January 1, 1502" (Bishop),
24–26, 36
Bromwich, David, 82
Bruns, Gerald, 137, 172
"Burgler of Babylon, The" (Bishop), 26
"Burial of the Dead" (Eliot), 145
"Burning of Paper Instead of Children,
The" (Rich), 105, 135

"California Dreaming" (Wright), 209,
210
Calvino, Italo, 184
"Canso" (Merwin), 138–40
Carrier of Ladders, The (Merwin), 148,
149, 150–53
Cézanne, Paul, 202
Change of World, A (Rich), 90–92
"Child, The" (Merwin), 149–50
"Childhood" (Wright), 196–97, 199
China Trace (Wright), 176–78, 184,
196–200
"Civilization and Its Discontents"
(Ashbery), 47
"Cloud River" (Wright), 199
"Clouds" (Ashbery), 65–66, 68, 82

Cocteau, Jean, 111
"Collective Dawns" (Ashbery), 83
Compass Flowers, The (Merwin),
158–61, 165
"Congenital" (Wright), 185
"Corpse-Plant, The" (Rich), 97
"Crusoe in England" (Bishop), 26–27,
36–41
"Cryopexy" (Wright), 207, 208
"Culture and Anarchy" (Rich),
123–24, 127

Dante's *Inferno*, 203
David, Louis, 62
"Daybreak" (Merwin), 146
"December among the Vanished"
(Merwin), 143–44
De Chirico, 61–62, 175–76
"Definition of Blue" (Ashbery), 64
"Demon Lover, The" (Rich), 102
"Denaturalization of the Planet and
the End of Man" (Merwin), 143
Derrida, Jacques, 3, 219n
Diamond Cutters, The (Rich), 92–97
Dickinson, Emily, 95, 125
"Diving into the Wreck" (Rich), 93,
109–11
Diving into the Wreck (Rich), 109–11,
112–16
"Dog" (Merwin), 142
"Dog Creek Mainline" (Wright),
188–90
Double Dream of Spring, The (Ash-
bery), 61–68
"Double Monologue" (Rich), 97
Dream of a Common Language, The
(Rich), 116–22
"Drunken Americans" (Ashbery), 85
DuPlessis, Rachel Blau, 89, 95
"Dwingelo" (Rich), 102–3

Edelman, Lee, 33, 34
Eliot, T. S., 68, 90, 95, 96, 140, 143,
145, 208
"Europe" (Ashbery), 54

"Fantasia on 'The Nut-Brown Maid'"
(Ashbery), 82
"Far Field, The" (Roethke), 205–6
Fenollosa, Ernest, 195, 199
Finding the Islands (Merwin), 161–63

"Firstborn" (Wright), 185–88
"Fish, The" (Bishop), 9, 11, 12–17, 26, 32
Fletcher, Angus, 221n, 222n
"Flight" (Merwin), 165
"Florida" (Bishop), 7, 9
"Footprints on the Glacier" (Merwin), 150
"For Julie in Nebraska" (Rich), 122–23, 124
"For the Anniversary of My Death" (Merwin), 151, 197
"For the Conjunction of Two Planets" (Rich), 87, 92, 103
Foucault, Michel, 164, 181
"Fragment" (Ashbery), 66–68
Francesca, Piero della, 193
"French Poems" (Ashbery), 64
"Frontispiece" (Ashbery), 84–85

Gadamer, Hans-Georg, 7–8
Geography III (Bishop), 8, 32, 40, 41
"Ghazals: Homage to Ghalib" (Rich), 101, 102, 103
"Gift" (Merwin), 157–58
Gilbert, Sandra, 221n
"Glass" (Merwin), 138
"Grand Galop" (Ashbery), 75, 76
Grave of the Right Hand, The (Wright), 175–76
Green with Beasts (Merwin), 140–43

"Halfway" (Rich), 98–99
Hard Freight (Wright), 174, 184–91
Hartman, Geoffrey, 136
Hassan, Ihab, 48, 143
Herschel, Caroline, 105
"Homage to Paul Cézanne" (Wright), 202
"Homage to Winter" (Rich), 128
Hopkins, G. M., 172, 195
Houseboat Days (Ashbery), 81–83
"Houses, The" (Merwin), 168–69
Howard, Richard, 154, 219n
Howarth, William, 174
"'How Much Longer Will I Be Able to Inhabit the Divine Sepulcher . . .'" (Ashbery), 52
Hua-yen, 162, 201

"Ideal Landscape" (Rich), 92

"I Dream I'm the Death of Orpheus" (Rich), 111–12
"Images for Godard" (Rich), 106
"Imaginary Iceberg, The" (Bishop), 12, 40
"Implosions" (Rich), 102
"Inauguration Day: January 1953" (Lowell), 17
"Interview" (Wright), 172
"In the Time of Blossoms" (Merwin), 152
"In the Waiting Room" (Bishop), 26, 32–36
Invisible Cities (Calvino), 184
"Invocation" (Merwin), 145
"Italian Days" (Wright), 201, 210, 211

Jerusalem (Blake), 194

Kalstone, David, 36, 94
Kazin, Cathrael, 218n
Keats, John, 9
Kenner, Hugh, 203
Keyes, Claire, 97
Kinnell, Galway, 31
Kinzie, Mary, 2
Koethe, John, 64, 71
"Kore" (Merwin), 152, 158–61

Lacan, Jacques, 217n
Language: erosion of, 1–2; self-reflexive, 3
Las Meniñas (painting), 78, 80
"Last People" (Merwin), 135
"Last World, A" (Ashbery), 53–54
Leaflets (Rich), 87–88, 101
"Learning a Dead Language" (Merwin), 137
"Letter" (Merwin), 152
"Letter from the Land of Sinners" (Rich), 92
Levis, Larry, 31
Lice, The (Merwin), 147–48
Life Studies (Lowell), 8
"Link Chain" (Wright), 191
"Litany" (Ashbery), 83, 86
"Living Together" (Merwin), 162
"Lonesome Pine Special" (Wright), 211
"Looking for Mushrooms at Sunrise" (Merwin), 147
"Lost Bodies" (Wright), 209

"Lost Souls" (Wright), 207
Lowell, Robert, 8, 17, 90, 94

"Map, The" (Bishop), 18–20
Martin, Wendy, 90
Mazzaro, Jerome, 16, 19, 39
"Meditations for a Savage Child"
    (Rich), 115–16
"Memory of Spring" (Merwin), 150
"Merced" (Rich), 113–14
Merleau-Ponty, Maurice, 43, 45
Merwin, W. S., poetry of, 76, 88,
    130–70, 179, 186, 187–88, 197;
    affirmation and, 139, 148, 160,
    167, 169; "Anabasis II," 133–34,
    154, 169; "The Animals," 136;
    "Canso," 138–40; "The Child,"
    149–50; confrontation with death,
    150–51, 153, 155; "December
    among the Vanished," 143–44; de-
    pleted language and memory,
    145–46, 152–53, 169–70; dis-
    placement of history, 165–66;
    Finding the Islands, 161–63; ge-
    nealogical concern in, 166–67;
    "Gift," 157–58; "The Houses,"
    168–69; interpretation and lan-
    guage, 136; ironic presence in,
    132; "Kore," 152, 158–61; "Learn-
    ing a Dead Language," 137;
    "Letter," 152; Liminal in, 145,
    157, 158; "Living Together," 162;
    materiality of signs, 145; memory
    and language, 134, 136–38, 142,
    144, 146, 147, 155, 169; mythic
    imagery in, 143, 149–50, 158–59;
    Oedipal, 168–69; *Opening the
    Hand,* 163–68; Orphic memory in,
    132, 137; Orphic moment in, 148;
    poetic inspiration and, 153, 154,
    157–58; reiteration of memory,
    152; rejection of sentimental past,
    159–60; renewal of language,
    146–47, 152, 156–57; "Rime of the
    Palmers," 131–32; "St. Vincent's,"
    164–65; self-reflexivity in, 3,
    139–40, 154, 155, 162; "Sheri-
    dan," 165–66; "Sibyl," 154–56; si-
    lence from discourse, 130–31,
    134–35, 145–46, 162; silence of
    closure and death, 130, 135–36,
    140, 155–56, 162; "Snowfall,"
    150–51; theme of impending ex-
    tinction, 130, 148, 152–53, 156;
    theme of pilgrimage/journey,
    131–32, 149–51; "Third Psalm:
    The September Vision," 151;
    "Turning to You," 162; use of
    memory, 132–34; vision of lan-
    guage, 5, 135, 152, 163, 169; "The
    Well," 148–49, 150; "White Goat,
    White Ram," 141, 142; "Winter
    Storm," 161
"Mirror in Which Two Are Seen as
    One, The" (Rich), 109
"Monument, The" (Bishop), 7, 15,
    20, 47
"Moose, The" (Bishop), 27–32, 185
Moramarco, Fred, 53
Morandi, Giorgio, 202
"Moth Hour" (Rich), 99–100
Moving Target, The (Merwin), 147, 169

"Natural Resources" (Rich), 120–21, 122
Necessities of Life (Rich), 97–98
Nelson, Cary, 95, 144, 216n, 220n
"New Spirit, The" (Ashbery), 68–71
"92 Revere Street" (Lowell), 17
"North American Sequence"
    (Roethke), 205–6
"North American Time" (Rich), 127
North and South (Bishop), 8, 18
"Northhanger Bridge" (Wright), 190

"Ode on a Grecian Urn" (Keats), 9
O'Hara, Daniel T., 216n
"Old Boast" (Merwin), 156
"One Art" (Bishop), 38, 39
"One Time" (Merwin), 153
"Origins and History of Conscious-
    ness" (Rich), 116–17
"Other Side of the River, The"
    (Wright), 172, 173, 200, 201, 206,
    208–9, 210
Other Side of the River, The (Wright),
    172, 173, 200, 201, 206–11
"Over 2,000 Illustrations and a Com-
    plete Concordance" (Bishop), 9–10

"Pantoum" (Ashbery), 49–50
"Paradoxes and Oxymorons" (Ash-
    bery), 84

"Parergon" (Ashbery), 219n
Parmigianino, 59, 75, 77, 78, 79
"Path to the White Moon, The" (Ashbery), 86
"Paula Becker to Clara Westhoff" (Rich), 117, 122
"Pens, The" (Merwin), 152–53
Perloff, Marjorie, 216n
"Phantasia for Elvira Shatayev" (Rich), 117, 119, 121
"Phenomenology of Anger, The" (Rich), 114–15
"Photograph of the Unmade Bed, The" (Rich), 105–6
"Picture of Little J. A. in a Prospect of Flowers, The" (Ashbery), 51
"Pierrot Le Fou" (Rich), 106, 108, 109
"Pink Dog, The" (Bishop), 36
Pinsky, Robert, 215n
"Planetarium" (Rich), 103, 104–5
Plath, Sylvia, 98
"Poem" (Bishop), 41–43
"Poem, The" (Merwin), 144
Poetry: cultural role of, 2, 3, 5; ekphrastic, 9; in expressive mode, 2; grammatological, 3; interconnection in, 2–3, 4–5; of modernism, 3; personal voice in, 5; postmodern, 6; self-reflexive, 3–4; task of, 2
"Poetry III" (Rich), 128
Portrait of Guillaume Apollinaire (painting), 175–76
"Portrait of the Artist with Hart Crane" (Wright), 182–83
"Portrait of the Artist with Li Po" (Wright), 182–83
"Postcard" (Rich), 100
Pound, Ezra, 95, 169, 195, 203, 216n
"Primogeniture" (Wright), 185
"Prodigal, The" (Bishop), 26
"Prodigal Son, The" (Merwin), 134

"Questions of Travel" (Bishop), 8, 20–24
"Quotidiana" (Wright), 198

"Rain" (Ashbery), 54
"Rain Moving In" (Ashbery), 86
"Recital, The" (Ashbery), 73–75
"Resurrection" (Francesca), 193

"Reunion" (Wright), 197–98
Rich, Adrienne, poetry of, 1, 26, 74, 84, 87–129, 153, 187–88, 218n; "After Dark," 98; anger of poet, 114–15; "Aunt Jennifer's Tigers," 90; autobiographical, 93, 98–99, 125–26, 167, 168, 221n; "Autumn Equinox," 93; break with poetic decorum, 89–90, 94; charge of propaganda, 89; chronicle of personal change, 88, 91, 99–100; "Culture and Anarchy," 123–24; "Diving into the Wreck," 93, 109–11, 112–16; "Dwingelo," 102–3; "Ghazals: Homage to Ghalib," 101, 102, 103; "Halfway," 98–99; "I Dream I'm the Death of Orpheus," 111–12; "Images for Godard," 106; influences on, 90; interconnection among women, 88, 90, 91, 101, 102–3, 115, 118, 122, 128–29; lesbianism in, 88, 119–20, 220n; "Meditations for a Savage Child," 115–16; meditations on language, 88, 100–102, 105–9, 115–16, 120–21; "Merced," 113–14; "Moth Hour," 99–100; mythic structure in, 110–13, 116, 118–19, 125; "Natural Resources," 120–21, 122; occupations of women, 121; and oppressor's language, 95–96, 105–6, 115–16, 120, 135; "Origins and History of Consciousness," 116–17; "Paula Becker to Clara Westhoff," 117, 122; "The Phenomenology of Anger," 114–15; "The Photograph of the Unmade Bed," 105–6; "Planetarium," 103, 104–5; as public voice, 89, 121, 123; self-definition in, 87, 91, 93–94, 101, 108, 113, 117, 118, 120, 121; self-reflexivity in, 3–4, 106, 116; "Shooting Script," 107, 109, 112, 116; "Sibling Mysteries," 118–19; "Snapshots of a Daughter-in-Law," 94–97, 99; "Sources," 125–29, 168; "Stepping Backward," 90–91, 109; transformational, 102, 103–4, 107, 110; "Turning the Wheel,"

Rich, Adrienne (*continued*)
125; "Twenty-One Love Poems,"
118, 119–20, 124, 125; view of
androgyny, 112, 113; "Villa
Adriana," 93–94, 109; voices of
women in, 116–24; weaving his-
torical and personal, 94–95, 122–
24, 126–27, 129; woman's con-
sciousness in, 88, 94
Rilke, Rainer Maria, 61, 210, 226n
"Rime of the Palmers" (Merwin),
131–32
Rivers and Mountains (Ashbery),
55–60
Roethke, Theodore, 205–6
"Roma I" (Wright), 208
"Roma II" (Wright), 206, 210
"Room, The" (Merwin), 144
"Roosters, The" (Bishop), 9, 26, 36
"Rural Route" (Wright), 196

"St. Vincent's" (Merwin), 164–65
"Santarém" (Bishop), 40
"Scale in May, A" (Merwin), 130
Schwitters, Kurt, 47–48
"Search, The" (Merwin), 156–57
*Self and Sensibility in Contemporary
American Poetry* (Altieri), 5
"Self-Portrait" (Wright), 175, 179–82
Self-Portrait (painting), 175
"Self-Portrait in a Convex Mirror"
(Ashbery), 46–47, 59, 75–80, 86
"Self-Portrait in 2035" (Wright),
176–77, 181, 203
Serenity of the Scholar, The (painting),
Sewell, Elizabeth, 61
Shadow Train (Ashbery), 84–85
"Sheridan" (Merwin), 165–66
Shklovsky, Viktor, 22
"Shooting Script" (Rich), 107, 109, 112
"Sibling Mysteries" (Rich), 118–19
"Sibyl" (Merwin), 154–56, 179
"Signature" (Wright), 177–78
"Signs" (Merwin), 131
"Sitting at Night on the Front Porch"
(Wright), 199–200
"Skaters, The" (Ashbery), 55–60
"Skins" (Wright), 184, 191–92,
193–96
"Sky Valley Rider" (Wright), 190
"Snapshots of a Daughter-in-Law"
(Rich), 94–97, 99

"Snowfall" (Merwin), 150–51
"Some Trees" (Ashbery), 50–51
Some Trees (Ashbery), 49–51
"Son" (Merwin), 167
Song of Love, The (painting), 175
"Sources" (Rich), 125–29, 168
"Southern Cross, The" (Wright), 201,
202–5
Southern Cross, The (Wright),
178–83, 200, 201–5
"Spring Day" (Ashbery), 63–64
Steiner, George, 218n
"Stepping Backward" (Rich), 90–91,
109
Stevens, Wallace, 165
"Stone Canyon Nocturne" (Wright),
199
"Storm Warnings" (Rich), 91
"Street Musicians" (Ashbery), 81
"Summer" (Ashbery), 62–63
"Sunrise in Suburbia" (Ashbery), 65
"Syringa" (Ashbery), 81–82
"System, The" (Ashbery), 71–73

"Talking" (Merwin), 167
"Task, The" (Ashbery), 63
"Tattoos" (Wright), 191–93
Tennis Court Oath, The (Ashbery),
51–55, 58
Tennis Court Oath, The (painting), 62
"Third Psalm: The September Vision"
(Merwin), 151
Three Poems (Ashbery), 68–75
"Three Poems for the New Year"
(Wright), 207
"Tiang Notebook" (Wright), 173, 201
"To Be Sung while Still Looking"
(Merwin), 153
"To Giacomo Leopardi in the Sky"
(Wright), 207
"Tourist and the Town, The" (Rich),
92, 93
"Transcendental Etude" (Rich), 122
"Truth of Departure, The" (Merwin),
167
"Turning the Wheel" (Rich), 125, 127
Tuve, Rosemund, 221–22n
"Turning to You" (Merwin), 162
"Twenty-One Love Poems" (Rich), 1,
118, 119–20, 124, 125
"Two Stories" (Wright), 210

Van Dyne, Susan, 109
"Vegetarians, The" (Ashbery), 84
Valazquez, 78
Vendler, Helen, 25, 26, 30, 36, 220n
Vermeer, Jan, 10
"Villa Adriana" (Rich), 93–94, 109

"Wave, A" (Ashbery), 86
Wave, A (Ashbery), 86
"Weed, The" (Bishop), 26
"Well, The" (Merwin), 148–49, 150
"When We Dead Awaken" (Rich), 109
"When You Go Away" (Merwin), 169
"Where Moth and Rust Doth Corrupt"
   (Wright), 198
"White Goat, White Ram" (Merwin),
   141, 142
"White Roses" (Ashbery), 55
Whitman, Walt, 169, 179–80
Wild Patience Has Taken Me This Far,
   A (Rich), 122 25
Will to Change, The (Rich), 104–9, 111
"Winter Storm" (Merwin), 161
"Wishes" (Wright), 198
"Woman Dead in Her Forties, A"
   (Rich), 119
"Words from a Totem Animal" (Mer-
   win), 169
Wright, Charles, poetry of, 171–211;
   "Blackwater Mountain," 190–91;
   Bloodlines, 184, 191–96; "Child-
   hood," 196–97, 199; China Trace,
   176–78, 184, 196–200; concept of
   language, 5-6, 172–73, 186–87,
   188, 200; "Congenital," 185; con-
   vergence of self and language,
   173–74, 207–8; "Dog Creek
   Mainline," 188–90; elegy for the
   self, 202–3; "Firstborn," 185–88;
   The Grave of the Right Hand,
   175–76; Hard Freight, 174,
   184–91; "Homage to Paul
   Cézanne," 202; ideograms in,

198–99; image and self, 196; imagery from de Chirico, 175–76; interconnection with natural world,
   172, 185, 187; landscape of youth,
   188–91; meditation on mortality,
   183, 209–11; Orphic role in,
   192–93; "The Other Side of the
   River," 172, 173, 200, 201, 206,
   208–9, 210; The Other Side of the
   River, 172, 173, 200, 201, 206–11;
   overlay of memory, 201; presence
   in language, 193–96; relationship
   to Hopkins, 172; relationship to
   Roethke, 205–6; "Reunion,"
   197–98; "Rural Route," 196; salvational, 193, 200; search for lost
   self, 203–5; "Self-Portrait,"
   175–76, 179–82; "Self-Portrait in
   2035," 176–77, 181, 203; self-
   portraiture and autobiography in,
   174–84, 206; self-reflexivity in,
   3–4, 179; serially linked, 183–84;
   "Signature," 177–78; "Skins,"
   184, 191–92, 193–96; "The Southern Cross," 201, 202–5; The
   Southern Cross, 178–83, 200,
   201–5; "Tattoos," 191–93; theme
   of genealogical interconnections,
   185–86, 187–88, 191; use of symmetry, 183; vision of future, 197;
   visual analogues in, 202
Writings to an Unfinished Accompaniment (Merwin), 153–58
"Wrong Kind of Insurance, The" (Ashbery), 83

Yeats, W. B., 95, 96, 132, 195
Young, David, 216n
Your Native Land, Your Life (Rich),
   125–29

Xenophon, 133